ACCLAIM FOR
HOW TO LOVE A BLACK WOMAN

"Enlightening and introspective advice. . . . An inspiring book for any seeker of a successful relationship."
—Kenny Lattimore, R&B recording artist

❖

"Well-organized . . . humorous . . . straightforward. . . . Elmore translates the needs and desires of black women into a language men will understand. . . . Highly recommended."
—Library Journal

❖

"This is a wake-up call for men who want to 'hook it up' at home. Dr. Ronn Elmore has sounded a trumpet in the African-American community that we cannot ignore. You must read it."
—Bishop T. D. Jakes, bestselling author of
Woman Thou Art Loosed

❖

"Informative. . . . Gives men a new lens to view black women and cues to meeting their needs."
—*Ebony*

❖

"Elmore beautifully tempers his challenging 'in-your-face' approach with affirming 'got-your-back' encouragement. His readers will be elevated and enriched by both."
—Teresa E. Hairston, publisher, *Gospel Today*

❖

more . . .

"Amazing . . . Ronn has done it again! . . .This tome shows [black men] how to realize their dream, and dream woman, [and] covers virtually every situation that could perplex or frustrate a man. . . . Let me be the first to thank Dr. Elmore for black men everywhere!"

—Darryl L. Mobley, *Family Digest*

"I'm recommending to any potential gentleman callers to read this book before they come a knockin'."

—Terrie Williams, author of *The Personal Touch*

"Empowers and invites African-American men to seek and achieve satisfying intimacy. . . .Dr. Elmore shows men how to find deeper satisfaction through balanced and deliberate commitment—demonstrated by action to the women they love."

—*Tennessee Tribune*

"Ronn Elmore has done it again. He has balanced the gender love scale between men and women. With his new emphasis upon loving black women, surely women will get the best romantic care and sensitivity there is."

—Audrey B. Chapman, author of *Getting Good Loving: How Black Men and Women Can Make Love Work*

"Ronn Elmore has once again provided nuggets of wisdom on this entrancing subject of male-female relationships."

—Jawanza Kunjufu, Ph.D., author of *Good Brothers Looking for Good Sisters*

"Rejoice! . . .Dr. Elmore not only reaffirms his comprehensive wisdom in the area of interpersonal relationships, but also substantiates his commitment to truth and justice."

—Mae L. Blake, West Angeles Church of God, Los Angeles, California

How to Love a Black Woman

Also by Ronn Elmore

How to Love a Black Man

How to Love a Black Woman

GIVE—AND GET—THE VERY BEST
IN YOUR RELATIONSHIP

Dr. Ronn Elmore

WARNER BOOKS

A Time Warner Company

Copyright © 1998 by Ronn Elmore
All rights reserved.

Warner Books, Inc. 1271 Avenue of the Americas, New York, NY 10020
Visit our Web site at www.warnerbooks.com

 A Time Warner Company

Printed in the United States of America

First Trade Printing: August 1999

10 9 8 7 6 5 4 3 2 1

The Library of Congress has cataloged the hardcover edition as follows:

Elmore, Ronn.
    How to love a Black woman : give and get the very best in your
relationship / Ronn Elmore.
        p. cm.
    ISBN 0-446-52281-3
    1. Man-woman relationships—United States. 2. Afro-American
women—Psychology. 3. Afro-American men—Psychology. 4. Intimacy
(Psychology) I. Title.
HQ801.E43   1998   97-31311
158.2—dc21   CIP
ISBN: 0-446-67510-5 (pbk.)

Cover design by Rachel McClain
Cover illustration by Rob Blackard
Book design by H. Roberts Design

ATTENTION: SCHOOLS AND CORPORATIONS
WARNER books are available at quantity discounts with bulk purchase for educational, business, or sales promotional use. For information, please write to: SPECIAL SALES DEPARTMENT, WARNER BOOKS, 1271 AVENUE OF THE AMERICAS, NEW YORK, N.Y. 10020

To the Lord Jesus Christ,
who daily tutors me in the lessons of love.
And to Aladrian, the best homework
a man could ever hope for.

Table of Contents

Introduction   1

PART I   *The Straight Facts*   9
Your Phenomenal Woman: Who She Really Is and Isn't   *11*
Like AM and FM   *21*
This Is How We Do It   *29*
The Five Most Common Love Substitutes   *37*
 Charmers   *37*
 Improvers   *44*
 Blamers   *50*
 Givers   *57*
 Rulers   *65*
Slow Down . . . Men at Work!   *73*
The Policies and Procedures and You   *77*

PART II   *How to Love a Black Woman*   79
 1. *Reality-Check Your Expectations of Her*   *81*
 2. *Give Her Your Love in Her Language*   *83*
 3. *Expect to Have to Earn Her Trust*   *86*
 4. *Be Responsive to Her Without Taking Responsibility*
  for Her   *88*
 5. *Don't Start What You Won't Continue*   *91*
 6. *Accept Her for Who She Is Now (Not Who You Think You*
  Can Make Her Into)   *93*

7. *Study Other Men 95*

8. *Don't Require That Your Every Move Be Applauded 98*

9. *Tell Her Exactly What Your Commitment Means 100*

10. *Listen to Her Problems Without Rushing to Solve Them 102*

11. *Refer to All Black Women with Respect 104*

12. *Take the Blame (But Only When It's Yours) 106*

13. *Never Compare Her 109*

14. *Show Her Off 111*

15. *Give Her the Space to Disappoint You 113*

16. *Invest in the Things That Nourish Her 115*

17. *Lighten Up 118*

18. *Get Serious 120*

19. *Say "I Don't Know" When You Don't 122*

20. *Tell Her What You Assume She Already Knows 125*

21. *Read Between the Lines 127*

22. *Avoid Analyzing Her to Her 130*

23. *Call Her by Name 132*

24. *Touch Her 134*

25. *Do Your Best, Then Be Yourself 136*

26. *Own Up to and Express Your Fears 139*

27. *Let Her Know When You're Headed Underground 142*

28. *Tolerate Her Rambling 144*

29. *Never Run from Her Tears 146*

30. *Remind Her Daily of Why You Love Her 148*

31. *Be Willing to Sacrifice Your Schedule for Her 151*

32. *Follow Her Lead Sometimes 153*

33. *Initiate Physical Affection That Doesn't Always Lead to Sex 156*

34. *Share Your Insides with Her 158*

35. *Expect to Love Her Out of Both Desire and Duty 160*

36. *Protect Her 163*

37. *Be Conservative in the Promises You Make 165*

38. *Never Beg 167*

39. *Rock the Boat When Necessary*   *169*

40. *Monitor Your Complaint Output*   *171*

41. *Adjust Your Tone of Voice*   *173*

42. *Share Her Load*   *175*

43. *Let Her Help You*   *177*

44. *Resist Procrastination*   *180*

45. *Be Patient*   *182*

46. *Keep Your Fascination with Passing Women to Yourself*   *185*

47. *Hold Her Even When You Don't Have To*   *187*

48. *Surprise Her*   *189*

49. *Let Her Romance You*   *191*

50. *Tell the Truth*   *193*

51. *Explain*   *196*

52. *Keep Her Secrets*   *198*

53. *Resist the Urge to Punish Her*   *201*

54. *Season Your Criticism with Praise*   *203*

55. *Don't Cheat on Her*   *205*

56. *Show Your Love by How You Handle Your Money*   *208*

57. *Become and Remain Clean and Sober*   *211*

58. *Change Your Running Crowd*   *213*

59. *Apologize with Words*   *215*

60. *Resist the Sugar Daddy in You*   *217*

61. *Never Play with the Word "Marriage"*   *219*

62. *Stop Comparing Paychecks*   *222*

63. *Take Good Care of Your Kids*   *224*

64. *Remember the Big Events*   *226*

65. *Become Her Best Mirror*   *228*

66. *Don't Let Pride Rob You of the Help You Need*   *230*

67. *Love Her in Ways You Want Your Son to Imitate*   *233*

68. *Don't Let Your Love Life Become Your Whole Life*   *235*

69. *Stay*   *238*

70. *Keep on Loving Her Even if You Don't Always "Get It"*   *241*

Introduction

No, this is *not* "one of *those* books." Contrary to what images a quick glance at the title may stir, THE BOOK YOU ARE NOW HOLDING IS DEFINITELY *NOT* ABOUT:

- How to pick up Black women, anywhere, anytime, *or*
- How to satisfy Black women in bed, and keep them coming back for more, *or*
- How to keep the Black woman in your life from ever getting mad at you, *or*
- How to "score points" and get anything you want from a Black woman.

Loving Black women with wisdom, sensitivity, and skillfulness is what this book is all about. It's focused on the near limitless power you have to give and get the very best—spiritually, physically, mentally, and emotionally—in your relationship with her.

Make no mistake. Loving another person, any other person, is a job. It's a profoundly appealing job and one that many of us take quite seriously. But it is a job. And as is the case with any job you are working to excel at, discovering ways to do it even more capably, and to get even greater results, is the goal. The quality of your love, and your effectiveness at expressing it to the Black woman in your life (or the one on her way), is one of the key measures of our manhood.

The fact that you are reading this book suggests to me that you have much in common with countless men I have met through my counseling practice, seminars, and on radio and television talk shows, in addition to the men who have written me since the release of my earlier book, *How to Love a Black Man*.

I find them to be, like me, men who already love Black women and who have every intention of continuing to. They are both married and single men, brash but sincere young upstarts, and brothers who have been on the job for much longer than a hot minute. What they have in common is that they have become tired of all the drama that surrounds Black male-female relationships—the finger-pointing back and forth, the mistrust and hostility that divides us along gender lines, and, of course, the statistics that are constantly trotted out to dramatize the hopeless state of affairs that supposedly exists between Black men and women.

In spite of it all, they are men who are captivated by the best of Black women's strength and dignity, and the infinite ways in which their beauty is manifest. They continue to feel honored by the admiration, respect, and support that their women have lavished upon them. And they are men who are still wholly committed to contributing powerfully and meaningfully to her life as well.

Men do that best when they are sure they know the answer to this fundamental question: "What exactly does she want and need from me?" The pages ahead provide the answers to that question. And when you are armed with clear answers, deeper satisfaction in love is available to both of you.

When I say "love," I'm talking about a balanced and deliberate commitment to another person, one that is demonstrated by action. Action that benefits your mate without discounting yourself. Action that is caring, creative, and consistent, without being self-devaluing, manipulative, or self-centered.

And when I say "satisfaction," I mean the abiding contentment and confidence that result from committing to love someone, being loved in return, and knowing and doing the actions that most effectively demonstrate that love. That's *the job,* and for men, deep satisfaction comes from doing it extremely well.

This book will tell you what women say they need and want from us—but it will also explain it, and, most importantly, apply it in the "language of men," which is:

- Logical and concrete rather than abstract and inconclusive.
- Constructive and compelling rather than critical and condemning.
- Practical and goal-oriented rather than theoretical and unattainable.
- Simple and concise rather than complicated and repetitive.

Women have not always known exactly how to get their points across to their men, with the kind of directness and clarity that helps unlock our highest intentions and our most determined efforts. We *hear* them, but we can't swear we always *understand* what they want, why they want it, and what they want us to do about it. And if you don't understand that, even when you're willing to give it, you're very likely to miss the mark anyway.

Men *need* answers. We need them so we can draw conclusions, so we can feel confident that we understand, and, ultimately, so that we can perform effectively. Since you were a little boy, you wanted answers. When something was broken, you wanted to know how to fix it. If something was working just fine, you wanted to know why it was, and what you could do to make it work even better. Men don't ever want to be left in the dark, without answers about anything that we've got to deal with. That's especially true when it comes to our love lives.

Men are inherently possessors of the characteristics and inclinations of a conqueror-adventurer. You are not the sort to rise to a challenge or set sail on a course without first observing, analyzing, and assessing what you are trying to do and what obstacles stand in the way of getting it done—excellently. Having solid facts—in advance—is what men want, and probably always will.

Straight facts are the basis of your confidence. When you are confident, you get all kinds of good things done. Men treasure the sense of empowerment that comes from confidence. Having the facts helps us to get it.

Think about it. When you are engaged in any endeavor in which your confidence level is high, your commitment level tends to be high as well. Conversely, when you aren't confident that you know enough, or have enough of what you need to excel, your commitment can easily wane. That's because for you, commitment is a direct by-product of confidence.

If you're a man who ever did, does now, or ever will love a Black woman, you have probably already heard more than you wanted to hear about what they expect of the men in their lives, how hard a time they've had getting it, and how angry they are about it. Black women, no longer willing to settle for vague hopes of love's "payday, someday," are challenging the men in their lives to offer a more sensitive, demonstrative, consistent love that delivers as promised. After hearing women's requests, demands, complaints, and criticisms, some men have begun to believe that Black women are *never* satisfied, and never will be. But if you believe that, before long you could get the idea that it's not even worth it to try. And if it's not worth it to try—or to try again and again—then attempting to apply the advice you'll find here will be an exercise in futility. All pain and no gain.

But we men must also take responsibility for the ways we have indeed flunked. All of us, at one time or another, have been guilty of giving less than love's best to some Black woman, or several. For a multitude of reasons, some simple, others very complex, we have displayed everything from self-seeking, self-protecting, and self-justifying to short attention spans, poor discipline, broken promises, and the tendency to drift. Of course you know men who are more guilty of these offenses than are you. But all of us have, at some time or another, compromised ourselves and blown it. And too often, rather than acknowledge it, and repent of our offense against her, we have responded with defensiveness, blame, or utter silence. All of these have wounded our women and misrepresented our highest intentions.

But *How to Love a Black Woman* is not merely a critique of what's wrong with us in love. It is a celebration of what's right with us, and how to make it better than ever.

Nothing you'll read here is meant to imply that Black men and women are plagued with certain unconquerable psychological, behavioral, or relational dysfunctions that are only found in our race and culture. I have not written with that erroneous belief in mind, and I caution you not to read it with that in mind either. The fact is, getting and keeping a meaningful and mutually satisfying love relationship is no easier or harder for Black folk than anybody else.

But even our best skills can stand to be sharpened. Though they may seem to have stood the test of time, our most brilliant insights about the opposite sex can always be polished to a yet higher gleam. This book will further sharpen your skills in reading the heart of your woman—not just hearing her words, or observing her behavior and reacting to it. I suspect that often, when we don't have the fullest understanding of what's in their hearts, we miss our women's deepest needs of us, and respond only to what we *think* they mean, which may be far different from what they actually meant. Everything you'll find ahead is designed to help you *know,* not think, assume, hope, or guess, but *know.*

For too long, too many of us have secretly held the belief that women are the more qualified experts on loving. If we are honest, we'll admit that we often tend to take our cues from them, assuming that, when it comes to matters of the heart, women are always the ones who know the "right" way.

That belief is responsible for our style of loving becoming reduced to finding out what they think we ought to be doing and doing it just that way (or at least something that we think will look like it to them). Even when it "works" (meaning our women liked it, and they let us know they did), we have eventually come away strangely dissatisfied. We are haunted by the uneasy suspicion that, if we're just dancing to her music, then she's got our noses wide open!

Maybe it was woven into our masculine souls at creation. Or perhaps it's the legacy handed down to us from our tribesmen forefathers. But the fact is, men rise to their highest levels of excellence in any endeavor—especially love—based on definitions, standards, and models of functioning that have been established by other men. Men empower men. Literally or symbolically, we have each stood as one man amongst a million men, and have been challenged to recommit to a standard of integrity and excellence that includes how we love our women.

How to Love a Black Woman is written by a man, for men. It is, of course, appreciative of what our women are asking of us and needing from us. But it is no less appreciative of what you need and how you feel, think, and function, and what it takes for you to remain true to yourself.

Simply put, if you act on the no-nonsense, practical advice found here, not only will your understanding of Black women and your love for them grow, but you will grow personally, as well.

I promise no magic formula or "one-size-fits-all" solutions here, but you should expect these practical principles to work, and to work well.

I'm sure they will, if you will.

PART I

The Straight Facts

Your Phenomenal Woman: Who She Really Is and Isn't

The Straight Facts

Whatever your own personal images and perceptions about the nature of Black women are, they will stare you straight in the face as you read this book. You will find that some of those images of her will be confirmed here and you will take pleasure in knowing that, in that specific area, you have been working with solid, reliable facts that have helped you to relate effectively to the Black woman in your life.

However, there are likely to be other images and perceptions about them that you may hold which, as you read this book, will be challenged for their accuracy and their usefulness in your efforts to love her in a way that benefits you both. These faulty, albeit perhaps well-meaning, misperceptions can be seen for what they are, and some more accurate and thus more useful ones will replace them.

Remember: How you perceive Black women has everything to do with how you will relate to them (and of course, how they will relate back to you).

For the next few pages, you will have the opportunity to fine-tune your own image of Black women.

If you are honest and open-minded, and willing to boldly examine your own thinking, this section will benefit you greatly. Here you'll take inventory of the facts you have and how well they have served you in the adventure of loving a Black woman.

As I share with you some of men's most commonly held images of Black women, ask yourself constantly:

Is this image truthful?
Is this image fair?
Is this image respectful?
Is this image useful?
Is this image mine?

The Fits on Me Black Woman

From somewhere beyond a sincere brother's hopes, high standards, and way beyond reality, comes the phenomenal female of myth and legend, the Fits on Me Black Woman. In spite of the fact that she really doesn't exist, she's perceived as perfection personified and many a man either thought he had seen one locked on to some other brother's arm, or that he had one himself, only to eventually discover that he had been (once again) sadly mistaken. The Fits on Me Black Woman possesses every impressive quality you'd ever want, and not a thing you don't. She fits our fantasies like a glove, and holds the promise of being worth the very long wait for her glorious arrival. Their superior good taste and limitless patience is what keeps some men eternally searching for her, while repeatedly dismissing the real-life women all around them. If a man believes in the existence of the Fits on Me Black Woman, then his woman has to fit all his idealized "got to's."

- She's *"gotta"* be incredibly, completely, eternally fine, with no visible flaws, thus perfectly fitting his lofty daydreams about himself.
- She's *"gotta"* be an absolute genius, with the kind of brilliance and extraordinary ability that elevates his status. She fits him, because her brilliance can be turned on and off—and he controls the switch.
- She's *"gotta"* be extroverted enough to prove he's snagged a winner, but introverted enough to keep others from thinking he picked a tramp. She fits him because she's willing to become what he dreams up.
- She's *"gotta"* be interested in what he's interested in, to the same degree that he is. She fits him because she doesn't place a high value on things he doesn't care about.
- She's *"gotta"* be highly spiritual, but she fits him by not letting pleasing her God become more important than pleasing her man.
- She's *"gotta"* be honest and outspoken, but she fits him by only saying what he loves to hear.
- She's *"gotta"* be ambitious and self-reliant, but she fits him because she's willing to trash her ambitions and goals if they inconvenience or intimidate him.
- She's *"gotta"* be passionate and sexually proficient, but she fits him because she's willing to let him decide the when and how of it all.
- She's *"gotta"* intuitively know his values, desires, and expectations, but she fits him because she doesn't need him to tell her what they are.
- She's *"gotta"* have all the nurturing qualities of his mother, but she fits him because she never treats him like he's her son.

Obviously this image of Black women is the figment of a highly creative, but completely self-absorbed, imagination. It's a naive and unrealistic stereotype of Black women that characterizes them as their men's perfect trophies, and the ultimate badge of his status and significance. But the Fits on Me image of Black women is way over the top. The facts are way off, and to use them will keep you endlessly waiting for the "right" Black woman to come along and constantly dissatisfied with the real-life one you already have.

THIS IS NOT WHO BLACK WOMEN REALLY ARE

The Steps on Me Black Woman

Far out at the opposite extreme from the previous fantasized portrait of Black women is the Steps on Me Black Woman. She is that hopelessly negative woman that embodies men's worst perceptions. It's an overgeneralized misrepresentation of all Black women, based on the most glaring faults of some of them. This distorted image of them has helped make Black male-female relations increasingly become a hotbed of mistrust, hostility, and alienation.

- She competes with men, trying hard to outdo them in nearly every area, including love, career, finances, morality, and self-sufficiency. And she feels justified in pointing out how men come up short in them all.
- She's never satisfied, and constantly demands more and more sensitivity and emotional expression from her man, then criticizes him for being "weak" and coming up short when he gives it.
- She's critical, comparing her man unfavorably to men of other races and cultures, and delights in showing him how he comes up short.
- She's suspicious, convinced that her man means her no

good and either just lied to, cheated on, or disrespected her, or is about to somehow come up short integrity-wise.

- She's unfaithful and either has had, or is secretly fantasizing about having, some other man, against whom her man comes up short.
- She's bitchy, all neck-swiveling, hip-holding, eye-rolling, and acid-tongued when he fails. She believes when he comes up short, he deserves it.

Are there any Black women who possess these harsh, judgmental qualities? Absolutely. But does this image accurately reflect the way most Black women relate to their men? Of course not. Your disgust with them and perhaps some exhausted unwillingness to take a closer look at Black women and the nature, intent, and meaning of their style of relating may threaten to lock this scathing generalization into your mind. In fact, few women deserve to be placed in this category. It is as extreme and unrealistic as the previous one.

THIS IS NOT WHO BLACK WOMEN REALLY ARE

The Leans on Me Black Woman

The Leans on Me Black Woman is yet another worthless misrepresentation of the facts. It's sure to steer you down a dead-end street rather than reliably guide you through the adventure of mutually gratifying love with a Black woman. This distortion of Black women's image is based on the suspicion that some men hold, which suggests that:

- She *needs* me to make her life work.
- She *needs* me to take away all her hurts.

- She *needs* me to fulfill her romantic fantasies.
- She *needs* me to finance her existence.
- She *needs* me to give her a reason to live.
- She *needs* a minimum of 200 percent of me for her to feel loved and secure.

"Emotionally dependent," "smothering," and "insecure" are words that describe this image of Black women that many men hold. Reading all Black women this way can cause you to view them as an energy-depleting burden who need way too much from you. She overwhelms you with responsibility for her needs. Or, equally bad, she's exactly what you desire, because when she leans on you, you feel like Superman! But what you may interpret as "terminal neediness" in her could be the manifestation of a woman's natural pursuit of a vital sense of stability and security in her relationship with you. To a man, her determined pursuit of a mutual and interdependent connection with you can easily be mislabeled as "emotional disability."

THIS IS NOT WHO BLACK WOMEN REALLY ARE

The Works on Me Black Woman

Maybe you're a man whose internal video image and personal dictionary definition of Black women is closer to the Works on Me Black Woman, with all her ridiculously high standards, precise tastes, and unceasing preoccupation with making improvements upon the man in her life:

- She's determined to make her man suit her ideals, her fantasies, and her agenda.
- She's full to overflowing, with unsolicited advice and

subtle or overt attempts to instruct the man who loves her.

- She's chronically controlling, a walking book of rules and regulations that she expects her man to follow explicitly, if his love is sincere.
- She can't seem to "connect" romantically when her man's pace or performance does not match her preferences.
- She thinks his job is to find out what she wants him to do or be, and immediately get in step with it.
- She talks too much and listens too little.
- She's pushy, manipulative, bossy, and vengeful.
- She expects her man's love to be demonstrated by bowing to her standards, values, and expectations.
- She's a combination schoolteacher, mother, and foreman.

The Works on Me Black Woman image could be firmly embedded in your psyche due to even a single previous experience with a "compulsive controller." But beware, it can also come from inside you, if you tend to have a hard time accepting Black women who really aren't compulsive improvers, but are assertive, self-assured women who do not fail to voice their desires, expectations, and opinions. And if they sound to you like demands or instructions, it can feel as if your competence to achieve results on your own is inadequate.

THIS IS NOT WHO BLACK WOMEN REALLY ARE

Left with only the four previous perceptions of Black women, you may find the idea of developing and maintaining intimate relationships with them a not so appetizing proposition. With those stereotyped generalizations, loving a Black woman will be a start-again, stop-again, can't-wait-to-get-in, then can't-wait-to-get-out nightmare. The four images of Black women outlined above are actually distortions. Though it's not hard to see how these images have come to persuade us of their accuracy, they are untrue. They steer us away from mutually satisfying love, rather than toward it.

Take a closer look. Something is definitely wrong with these pictures.

I want to offer you a more balanced, comprehensive, and realistic view of real-life Black women than any of the previous ones. It comes closest to the straight facts, and not those rare, one-time-only experiences that aren't even close to the norm. And straight facts are what men rely upon in love, as in everything else.

The Counts on Me Black Woman

- She treasures spiritual, physical, emotional, and psychological intimacy with her man, which may sometimes appear to him as "clingy neediness." Mutuality and demonstrative affection are key. She treasures balance and therefore keeps close tabs on the score.
- She is at her best in relationships when she is confident of her man's devotion, faithfulness, and consistency—as demonstrated, not merely declared.
- She often speaks first from her subjective world of feelings, then from her precise, objective awareness.
- She has a love style that relies heavily on verbal expression.
- She has high expectations of her man and of loving relationships, which may appear too much like "demands to perform" to him.
- She can give almost limitless love, encouragement, and affection to her man when she is secure in her man's love for her.

- She can feel the need to withdraw, defend, or retaliate if she experiences fatigue, frustration, and the fear of being rejected, ignored, or taken advantage of.
- She has become increasingly more cautious and less trusting about showing vulnerability to the men in her life.

Contrary to appearances, and some of men's most fiercely held beliefs, the Counts on Me Black Woman is who really exists in the heart and soul of the woman in your life. More than likely, that's who the Black woman you have loved in the past, the one you love now, or will love in the future really is. Admittedly, it is not always easy to detect her presence inside your mate. The Counts on Me Black Woman comes in all shapes and sizes and hues, with every possible personality type and behavioral trait. To truly see her, you will sometimes need to look beyond a woman's tone and attitude, or hear the words she *didn't* speak, or respond to the feelings she failed to express. It can completely transform your picture of her.

She wants, above all, to be able to depend on you for the steady, willing supply of your very best treasures—your sincere and demonstrated devotion and commitment.

She doesn't *need* you, in the "can't make it without you" sense, any more than you need her. She deeply *desires* you, and the love you are able to bring into her life.

To attempt to give her that love while holding on to the distorted images and stereotypes means you'd be working in the dark, without the real facts. You'd labor in vain trying to give and get real love without the good understanding that matters so much to men.

You have, there inside you, abundant power that, when properly harnessed and creatively applied, can make incredibly fulfilling love possible for both of you.

Believing that will make all the difference in the world, as you navigate your way through this book. Because now the straight facts are in:

THIS IS WHO BLACK WOMEN REALLY ARE

Like AM and FM

Men have repeatedly told me that when it comes to loving Black women they feel as if we speak two different languages, come from different planets, or are on different wavelengths. They are right. And it's perfectly okay that we are. You see, with men and women, aside from the fact that both are of the human species, nearly everything else about them is as different as night is from day.

In terms of quality of character, neither gender is inherently better or worse than the other. When I say *different,* I'm not talking about what's good or bad, normal or abnormal. I'm talking about somebody else's perfectly valid way of being that doesn't always match your own.

But even if you say you accept that fact, yet you fail to understand *how* these differences play out in your relationship, it'll be next to impossible to create a relationship that's fulfilling to you both.

In the course of loving a Black woman, a lightbulb may have come on and you've gotten the revelation that the things that mean the most to her in the realm of romance are often far different from the things that mean the most to you. Therefore, how she expects you to demonstrate your love and commitment to her is vastly different from what you expect from her. You've seen this principle in operation when something that truly thrills or saddens her honestly has nothing like that effect on you. Or that what she does when stressed out or in conflict with you usually doesn't match your style at all.

Much of this is not because of the *kind* of woman she is, or the kind of man you are. It's because she's a woman and you are a man—and the two of you are "wired" quite differently.

Whether you've noticed it previously or are considering it for the first time now, you have made an all-important discovery: that Black women and the men who love them are just like AM and FM radio. Though we have our similarities, you'll never hear exactly the same programming on one that you do on the other.

By saying we're on different frequencies, I mean that you and your woman have two distinctly different internal driving forces as primary motivators (i.e., the thing that matters most to you, and how you are naturally inclined to go after it). Your driving force is the thing that propels you and what explains, in a broad sense, why you relate in life and in love the way you do.

For women in love relationships, the internal driving force is the high-priority pursuit of an overall sense of *security* (i.e., stability, harmony, and intimacy). She is at her best in life, and particularly in relationships, when she feels secure that "everything is going to be okay"; and that your desire for her, commitment to her, and intimate bond with her cannot be easily broken. To her, satisfaction is spelled: s-e-c-u-r-i-t-y. Think of women as being on the FM frequency.

Men, on the other hand, have a different, but no less significant, internal driving force. Our primary motivation is the high-priority pursuit of an overall sense of *significance* (i.e., competency, admiration, approval, and self-confidence).

To you, real satisfaction comes from significance. Think of men as being on the AM frequency.

The Black woman you love is happiest, most content, and most fulfilled when you've (perhaps without even knowing it) scratched her itch for security. She's been at her worst when you've ignored, insensitively treated, and looked down on her for having that need. She flourishes when you consistently prove that you treasure her and are thoroughly devoted to her emotional, physical, psychological, and spiritual well-being. When she senses that you care about what's in her best interest as much as your own, and, above all, when she's confident that you are not going to kick her to the curb, she relaxes. She is secure. She exhales.

You, on the other hand, find that kind of deep satisfaction when you feel assured that you have her respect, admiration, and appreciation.

We hate to fail. We're instinctively prone to avoid it, at almost any cost, because we shun anything that we perceive as a threat to our sense of significance. On the AM frequency, blame, disapproval, ridicule, and self-doubt are our relentless adversaries.

One effective way to get a clearer picture of a Black woman's internal driving force is to contrast the key components of her frequency with those of your own.

Now here's where it gets tricky. How can she get from you the kind of love that fits her FM frequency when you're on an altogether different one? And, if you do manage to give what she needs, how can you be sure you'll get from her what fits your AM frequency?

The fact to remember is, you are much more likely to get the kind of approving, affirming, admiring love your frequency is tuned to if you give the kind of sensitive, supportive, stable kind of love your woman needs. Real-life love has a mathematical law of reciprocity that's constantly at work. Give

Men Are on AM **The Key Features of** **His *Significance* Agenda**	**Women Are on FM** **The Key Features of** **Her *Security* Agenda**
Consistent applause for what he does	Constant affection for who she is
The ability to control his emotions	The freedom to express her emotions
Nonverbal demonstration	Verbal communication
Being effective at improving how things look	Being effective at improving how things feel
Mastery of applied logic	Master of applied intuition
Well-developed high-quality achievements	Well-developed high-quality relationships
Attentive to the possibilities of the future	Attentive to the realities of the past
Feeling that he's needed	Feeling that she's wanted
Focused on where we're trying to go (the goal/destination)	Focused on how we're trying to go (the process/means)

her more of her kind, get back more of your kind. It doesn't even matter which of you starts first, the results tend to be the same.

Even a superficial examination of the respective features of the two frequencies helps you understand how it is that Black women and their men have been reaching out for each other, yet too often sadly missing each other, failing to sustain an intimate connection. In fact, my years of clinical work with couples indicate that a large percentage of the confusion, anger, and disillusionment that sometimes keeps Black women from trusting your love, and sometimes keeps you from wanting to offer it, is because both men and women have not known about, allowed for, or adequately responded to each other's very different frequencies.

Sensitively and skillfully responding to her security agenda doesn't mean disposing of your significance agenda. (It's impossible for a man to do that anyway!) It does mean loving her will challenge you to give, do, and be with her in ways that strengthen and enhance her sense of security in you, in the relationship, and in herself.

In my previous book, *How to Love a Black Man,* I took Black women on a guided tour of the characteristics of your frequency, and how they should expect it to show up in relationships with you. I also explained to them the practical and mutually beneficial ways they should relate to you that could help you both get the satisfaction you desire and deserve.

Now it's your turn.

The bottom line is, you can't serve her from the same menu of delicacies that feeds your masculine hunger for significance and expect it to nourish and satisfy her hunger for security. It's a major mistake to assume that what you love to get from love is what you should dole out to her. Even if you give her the very best of what you freely give to other men, and they give to you, you will not have met the "dietary requirements" of a security-seeking woman by doing so.

FM Puts Up a Fight and AM Takes Flight

You can huff, puff, and sweat with the utmost sincerity to offer the Black woman in your life your preferred kind of love, but if you're only giving out the kind you like to take in, it's nearly the same to her as saying, "You don't matter to me!"

The hurt and rejection that result from that sincere but misdirected approach to love can easily and automatically switch on her "fight impulse"—the urge to blame, bash, and berate you as a self-defense against attacks on her sense of security, as well as a way to launch an offensive assault on you.

Since the closeness and connection of intimacy feeds her security hunger, if she can't achieve that feeling with you in

What Men Offer to Other Men They Care About	How Women Might Perceive It When It's Offered to Them	What Women Want from Men Instead
PRIVACY AND INDEPENDENCE *"Let me leave you alone to figure out that problem of yours. I'll know you need me when you call for me."*	**ABANDONED IN A CRISIS** *"You pulled away, leaving me alone when I most needed you."*	**ON-SITE SUPPORT** *"I want you to want to be intimately attached to me in this problem/ experience."*
COLLABORATION THROUGH COMPETITION *"We're both doing it. We'll both do it better if we try to do it better than each other."*	**SELFISH RIVALRY** *"It can't be us together when it's you against me. You'd rather win alone than with me."*	**COLLABORATION THROUGH INTERDEPENDENCE** *"I want to be a part of an 'Us,' not just a 'Me.'"*
HIGH RESPECT FOR VISIBLE ABILITIES AND ACCOMPLISHMENTS *"Bravo! Man, you worked it, won it, and whipped it. You are so good at that."*	**MISPLACED PRIORITIES** *"Wait a minute. Don't feelings, dreams, and intentions matter to you? Am I only important based on what I do or have?"*	**PASSION FOR HER AS A PERSON REGARDLESS OF HER PERFORMANCE** *"I long for you to love me, not just approve of me."*
GOAL-ORIENTED ADVICE AND CRITICISM *"Brother, you shouldn't do it like that. Your way won't work. Let me tell you what you should do instead. . . ."*	**BLAME AND REJECTION** *"Why must you be so critical? Can't you see I'm trying?"*	**MORE FOCUS ON HER GOOD INTENTIONS RATHER THAN ON SOLUTIONS AND OUTCOMES** *"I don't want to lose your love if I don't follow your advice."*
THE BLUNT LITERAL TRUTH *(Function over Feelings)* *"Actually I think it looks ridiculous."*	**CARELESS INSENSITIVITY** *"It's not so much what you say; I have a hard time with the way you say it."*	**GENTLY CONVEYED TRUTH** *(Feelings over Function)* *"You speak so sensitively to me, I must matter to you."*
MEANINGFUL SILENCE *(When They Are Content)* *"All is well between us, so what is there to talk about?"*	**SHUT-OUT** *"When people care about each other, they talk about themselves. You're not talking, so you must not care."*	**FREQUENT UNSOLICITED VERBAL DISCLOSURE** *"I feel like I'm so special to you when you volunteer to share more of your thoughts and feelings."*
THE RIGHT TO "RUN HOT AND COLD" *"Hey man, where have you been keeping yourself all these months? I know I haven't called or come by either, but it's sure good to see you again."*	**INSTABILITY, INATTENTIVENESS, AND LACK OF COMMITMENT** *"You're not as intense about me or our relationship as you once were. If you really cared for me, it would be impossible to become distracted."*	**STEADY, CONSISTENT EMOTIONAL INTENSITY** *"Your love really is here to stay. I feel secure."*

love, she's apt to try it in war. At least in war, her pained insides tell her, we are fully engaged together and focused on each other. It's a negative form of intimacy.

So when she is in fight mode, she'll tend to relate to you in a way that sends the message that "you are a no-good man." Now your sense of significance is assaulted. You feel the dreaded loss of esteem, and your sense of goodness and competence are in jeopardy. Feelings of failure seep in. Your automatic response? Flight. Finding a way out, by withdrawing, unplugging, and disconnecting, is what feels right, safe, and necessary. Physically, mentally, or emotionally you are likely to "check out" when your flight impulse is triggered.

When you take flight, her sense of security is profoundly injured—which can trigger her fight impulse. In turn, she'll be inclined to cease from offering you any more of the approval, applause, or admiration you thrive on, and you'll fly away even further, bringing less and less of yourself to the relationship. As her hurt feelings, and your mutual disdain for each other, intensify, she may also employ, in "fight mode," scolding, punishments, and dismissal. All of which sends the message that there is something wrong with you. Thus she effectively frustrates your sense of significance and triggers your "flight" response. And back and forth it goes.

In a self-perpetuating, circular, yet sometimes completely undetectable pattern, the fighting and the fleeing—both subtle and overt—can go on and on forever. Like AM and FM, on two different frequencies we can go right on missing each other's love in whole or in part.

It is essential that you take a closer look at what's uniquely important to the Black woman you love or one day will, and the dynamic interplay between her primary motivation and yours. I suspect your mind has already begun to do what men's minds do once they spot a problem: (a) We try to break the problem down into smaller, more manageable pieces, and (b) We systematically develop strategies targeted to those various pieces, one by one, until we conquer the whole. It's your natural and very powerful way to analyze problems, rise to challenges, and effect change in your life.

This Is How We Do It

Before we rush headlong into the security-building how to's for loving a Black woman, you'd do well to take an honest look at yourself and your approach to love. How effective is your characteristic style of relating to Black women? How well has it worked to foster a genuine sense of security in her and genuine significance in you? Have you seen the same dead-end patterns played out repeatedly in your relationship, where only the names have been changed—the stories are only reruns of your last relationship and the one before that and the one before that. . . . Or are you married or in an established long-term relationship where nobody's packing up to go anywhere, but neither of you are giving or getting much fulfillment or have any sense that your love is climbing to ever higher levels?

When we take a closer look at our own approaches to love, we often discover how easy it is to unknowingly sabotage the very satisfaction we desire in our relationships. You can get in your own way and set yourself up for disappointment. It's easy to do, hard to recognize, and harder still to admit.

The big drawback with love is that to do it right means you consume lots of time, and expend lots of energy, all the while running the risk that you could become distracted, misunderstood, or exposed as a novice. Love makes even strong, confident men vulnerable to the possibility of criticism, fatigue, and failure, and the erosion of self-esteem that goes with it. On top of that, love offers no up-front guarantees that you will be loved in return. It's very risky business. Contrary to popular misconceptions, men do want fulfilling love and solid relationships no less than do women. But the risks can make pursuing deeper levels of love with a Black woman seem complicated, uncertain, burdensome, and thus continually unsatisfying.

Love Substitutes

In an attempt to minimize the risks, avoid the pain of failure, and conserve mental and emotional energy, many men have opted for a safer alternative to real-life love—love substitutes. Love substitutes are the well-ingrained thought and behavior patterns that you may have adopted over the years. Though they can talk, look, act, and feel like genuine love, they really aren't at all. They come from a distorted view of masculinity, of women or their expectations of you, your expectations of yourself, and often from the hidden obsession with protecting and preserving your sense of significance at all costs.

Using love substitutes instead of the real thing works well to decrease the risk level in your relationships with Black women. But love substitutes never work to build long-term mutual satisfaction. They are, however, powerfully appealing. Just ahead I will introduce you to the five most common love substitutes. Your version of one or more of them could be exactly what you have used unknowingly and repeatedly in your relationships with women.

How exactly do love substitutes work? Consider this.

Your perception of what it means to be a man is based largely on positive performance. How you see yourself and discern your significance is often linked to knowing the right thing to do, the right way to do it, and getting the right response for having done it. Deep on the inside, men have imprinted in us the idea that being a good man means doing a good job and getting a good response from those who see them do it. There is no place where a man wants more to be right, good, and thus significant, than in the eyes of his woman. How you define what it means to be a good man and how you think you live up to that standard will always affect how you choose to present yourself and relate to women.

I have found that many men have distorted perceptions— either a little or a lot—of themselves and the basis for their significance, as well as distorted perceptions of women and their expectations. These distortions arise from our experiences, upbringing, erroneous or incomplete self-definitions, as well as from our own emotional baggage. If your perception of manhood and of women's expectations is off target, what you expect and how you relate to women will be also. Which makes you susceptible to picking up one or more ineffective and ultimately self-sabotaging love substitutes.

If you think the way to win a woman's applause and avoid her displeasure with you is to only let her see your shiny parts, never your rusty ones, instead of loving them you can easily become obsessed with charming them—your love substitute.

If you're a *Charmer,* having a woman who stays utterly impressed with most everything about you is how you work to get applause and its vital by-product, significance. You shape, for her, a perfectly positive image that is sure to send her head over heels for you. But when she gets close enough to see your imperfections and her standing ovations get fewer, you tend to "get out of Dodge" and start your one-man show all over again elsewhere. Instead of satisfaction, you feel *fear of being exposed.*

If you see Black women as the raw material that you can mold into the kind of trophy companion who'll get you plenty of the sense of esteem and self-importance you yearn for, instead of loving them, you may be prone to improving them—your love substitute.

If you're an *Improver,* you will only have use for the woman who is willing to let you transform her into an impressive extension of your own identity. When others see her as special, she is acceptable according to your blueprint, and you get the applause you crave. But when she stops submitting to your suggestions, though, you have little use for her and start searching for another "fixer-upper" project. Instead of satisfaction, you feel *unappreciated.*

If you see Black women as insecure, overemotional, self-absorbed, undependable, overaggressive, or any other characteristics that men are highly allergic to, instead of loving them you may tend to blame them—your love substitute.

If you're a *Blamer,* you believe that whatever minor faults you may have are far outweighed by what you see as the major dysfunction in her. You uphold your sense of significance by casting yourself as mostly right and women as mostly wrong. Like a saintly and long-suffering martyr you endure her glaring deficiencies, or you give her a life sentence locked away from your love. Instead of satisfaction, you feel *seething resentment.*

If you see women as the "real" authorities on love and what your role should be in the relationship, and if you see yourself as responsible for living up to their demands, you will be tempted to overgive—your love substitute.

If you're a *Giver,* you're constantly working to be and do

whatever you think she requires. Your significance agenda tells you that her disappointment or dissatisfaction will shrink you to nothingness. Instead of satisfaction, you feel *responsible for everything*.

If you see Black women as unruly, immature, and inferior to you, and if you see yourself as The Man, whose job it is to direct the process and control the outcomes of everything, you are likely to lean toward ruling—your love substitute.

If you're a *Ruler,* you maintain your significance by establishing a dictatorship and requiring her unquestioning submission to it. To you, manhood means not just having power, but having power over somebody else. Instead of satisfaction, you feel *pressure to perform*.

Men who have adopted love substitutes may be very sincere in the "love" they offer. They call it love, but love that comes from Charmers, Improvers, Blamers, Givers, and Rulers is only a counterfeit version of the real thing. Love substitutes end up keeping Black women and the men who love them apart—even in the same home. They never make for lasting satisfaction for either of you. They may help you feel pride, efficiency, control, or esteem, but never abiding satisfaction. They can't. Love substitutes arise out of concern for yourself, not the other person. Your mate then responds by "loving" you in some equally self-serving way. Selfishness is the opposite of love.

This may explain why it sometimes seemed so impossible to make loving a Black woman work and last. She's looked out for her security needs, and you've looked out for your significance needs; and both of you have tried to play it safe by using an imitation form of love.

Without knowing our own self-sabotaging patterns we are completely focused on our mate's relational flaws. Loving a Black woman begins to look like too much of a bother. Other endeavors, like making money and getting famous, appear to be better uses of your time and energy. Then the devastation caused by love substitutes is complete. Another Black man's and another Black woman's souls become strangers to each other.

It is important to note that the love substitutes listed here and in the following pages are generalizations—and, in some cases, exaggerated ones at that. They won't describe your personal style word for word or quirk for quirk, but much of what you find under one or more of these five headings will probably describe you fairly closely in some area. Don't check out. Keep your focus and this could be your chance to do a total overhaul or just to work on some needed finishing touches in your approach to loving your woman. Recognizing the patterns that don't work in your relationship is the first step toward establishing patterns that do.

In the next section we will take a closer look at these five most common love substitutes (there are probably a million more!). If you are bold and honest, you will be able to identify the one or ones that apply to you. Of course, none of the love substitute categories say all there is to say about one person's relationship patterns, and virtually no man uses only one of these substitutes. Typically we are all "combination counterfeiters." But watch closely for whatever may hold even a few threads of truth about you and your style of loving up to this point in your life. These may be the very threads that, with a little tug, will make your previously unidentified love substitute(s) come completely unraveled.

Although it may be tempting to skip these pages and go directly to the action-oriented Policies and Procedures, resist. First face your own love substitutes head-on, through the descriptive profiles, the brief analysis, and the self-tests in the next chapter. That, combined with a reexamination of your perceptions of Black women, will make the Policies and Procedures much more meaningful and of more strategic benefit.

In Part II, all seventy Policies and Procedures will have one or more symbols above the title, representing each love substitute. By the time you get there, you will know well which love substitute(s) is (are) yours. Watch closely. Wherever your symbol(s) appears, it is indicating a Policy or Procedure that you should consider a high priority.

The Five Most Common Love Substitutes

Charmers

Your favorite line to her: *"Ain't I something?"*
Your favorite response from her: *"Wow! You really are something."*

Lloyd is attractive, but certainly not movie-star hand-some. He earns decent money, but is by no means living large. He's always perfectly groomed, impeccably dressed, and clearly possesses a polite, self-assured, highly charismatic manner that causes him to stand out. Lloyd comes across as refreshingly down-to-earth, a sensitive Southern gentleman who always appears to have it all together. His frat brothers all envy him and work hard to emulate his style. Women see Lloyd as a fascinating, generous, highly spiritual, and emotion-ally expressive man with no signs of the ego-driven, macho baggage that sisters often complain about in men. He lavishly performs every possible romantic detail, dazzling women with what seems to be a perfect blend of finesse and sincerity. In recent years, nearly two dozen women have phoned their mother and their closest sister-friends to rave about this "incredible brother called Lloyd, who just may be the one . . ."

But none of these women ever found out whether he was or wasn't. For in every case, in anywhere from three days to three months, Lloyd would "evaporate." He'd stop calling and returning calls, he'd stop sending those sweetly worded, handwritten notes, and he'd stop leaving those surprise single yellow roses on her windshield. As usual, charming Lloyd had appeared in an impressive flash of glory, then mysteriously ended up missing in action. And, as usual, he'd never be heard from again.

Gregory's sensitivity and extravagantly affectionate ways had swept Vanessa off her feet. It didn't take but a hot minute for him to start talking marriage. "Why not," thought Vanessa: Gregory was the most romantic and devoted man she'd ever met. Gregory really got into the whole wedding process. He was energized by making the plans and deciding the details of the grand-scale ceremony befitting royalty. Gregory felt like Prince Charming, and he knew how to make Vanessa feel like Cinderella. During the early months of their marriage, Gregory, intoxicated by passion for his awestruck bride, proved to be a generous provider, not to mention a sensational lover, with a flair for the dramatic. He took pains to make sure they had just the right house, the right car, the right clothes and vacations, all of which made them the most admired and envied couple in their circle.

Later, when the intense adrenaline rush of a new marriage with new experiences and lots of new stuff gave way to the normal, often uneventful, pace of day-to-day married life, Gregory's interest and enthusiasm began to wane. Eventually, painfully bored, restless, and claustrophobic, Prince Charming shocked Cinderella when "out of nowhere" he informed her that the ball was over and he wanted to move out of the palace.

Charmers live to impress. They believe maintaining their woman's undistracted attention and unending applause is what love is all about. Always seductive, a Charmer promises to exceed his woman's most idealistic romantic fantasies, no matter what the costs. Thrilling her is what thrills him and pumps up his sense of significance.

Underneath it all, Charmers look to women to decide their worth and value as men. They feel they must become her knight in shining armor. Only they can't afford for her to spot any cracks in that armor. He presents her a perfect picture of masculine greatness—goodness is not enough, only greatness will do. Charmers aren't at peace until their women say, "Wow!" That's why they are at their best during the early hyper-romantic stages of a relationship, when intensity is high and appearances can be carefully controlled. They repeatedly find relationships to be all quick-hot passion—yet superficial and temporary. Keeping up his perfect image and hiding his flaws from her scrutiny become increasingly difficult as a growing relationship requires more openness, substantive self-disclosure, and depth. To Charmers, that kind of intimacy soon feels too close for comfort. They work overtime to protect their sense of significance from the risks associated with her close examination of him, and the less-than-glorious estimation of him she could make. Charmers "check out," mentally, emotionally, and physically, *before* their women get a chance to see anything that could make them less than 100 percent in awe of him.

Charmers:

- Are image-obsessed and instinctively know how to construct and maintain an image that thoroughly impresses women.
- Constantly compare themselves with other men and are driven by a secret need to be more than other men (more romantic, more sensitive, more honest, more committed . . . more everything).

- Think they truly desire close, committed relationships, when in fact they are commitment-phobic.
- Don't withdraw out of a desire to hurt, exploit, or abandon women, but to protect themselves from the potential "dangers" of intimate long-term relationships.

Are You a Charmer?

True or false?

1. In the early stages of a new relationship (or at the start of a newly reconciled one), you use massive amounts of your time, your money, and your words to romance her, with the goal of "blowing her mind."
2. You brag to your male friends about how "hooked" she is on you and what you did to cause her to be.
3. You usually require a tremendous amount of prep time (for your clothes, car, hair, mood, and so forth) before you go out with her.
4. You tell little white lies, leave out facts, justify or keep secret things that don't cast you in your best light before her.
5. You feel a euphoric kind of high when your woman shows she is overwhelmed by your splendor.
6. You tend to be painfully bored in relationships after the conquest is over and you are married or otherwise officially committed to a Black woman.
7. Before you drift from a woman, you stop to figure out a justifiable reason for moving on, one that casts her in a negative light.
8. Though you tolerate it, you have to work hard to listen to her speak at length about herself. But it's no work at all to listen to her rave about you.

9. You seldom, if ever, maintain friendship on any level with a previous lover you've broken up with.

10. You have little patience with Black women who are emotionally reserved or stingy with their praise.

11. Though you work to cultivate many impressive qualities, there is one unique feature you have (your trademark) that you really love women (and even other men) to notice and admire.

12. The beginning, middle, and end of your relationships tend to have a distinct and often repeated pattern, with the way into and out of them seldom varying.

13. You are constantly trying to come up with new ways to make her more and more impressed with you.

14. You resent women's probing questions.

15. You have moved to break off a relationship even before you wanted to when you have sensed that she was about to do it first.

If you answered true to any of these, you could well have a bit of the Charmer in you. The more times you answered true, the more deeply ingrained and acceptable to you this significance-seeking love substitute has become, and the more it shows up in your style of relating to Black women.

All of the Policies and Procedures to come are for you, but especially those that have the ▲ symbol. Pay closest attention to them, because for you they are the most crucial—and the ones you are most likely to deny, resist, or ignore.

Your Dream Woman

She is the kind of flawless Black woman whom every man on the planet would love to have, but can't. She is utterly captivated by you and is extremely vocal about how much of a romancer you are. She spends her days approving, applauding, and standing in reverent awe of you. You spend your days working successfully to maintain the euphoric buzz that you get from creating new ways for her to see how fabulous you are.

Your Obstacle to Overcome

Self-obsession. You are so focused on what will make you look good, sound good, and—above all—feel good, you can't afford to care much about her for very long.

As You Read This Book

You will resent and take issue with criticism directed at you and your "charming" ways. You will work very hard to find the holes in my words and proof of how little you need to hear this. You'll think Black women are happy with your captivating style of loving. Taking constructive criticism and exerting effort to actually be (as opposed to merely appearing) more excellent seem just too tedious and uneventful. To you looking well is as good as being well. You could also be tempted to browse through the advice ahead simply to discover the "tricks" and "techniques" that could help you do even better at "wowing" women and manipulating their response to your image.

The action advice to come can be especially beneficial to Charmers, because it will provide you some concrete ways to work against your natural self-centeredness and relate to Black women with a fresh new priority on what they can get out of it. The beauty of it is when you begin to give for her sake, you'll end up on the getting end yourself. Your love could get some new discipline and therefore some new depth as well. You'll get to settle down and sample real-life, day-to-day love where two people get to accept, value, and remain committed to each other. And, most importantly, they will continue to, in spite of the fact that neither of them really is eternally extraordinary!

As you move through this book I highly recommend that you:

ADMIT that you possess Charmer tendencies. Your love substitute is one of the trickiest of them all when it comes to applying the Policies and Procedures. If you aren't honest with yourself you'll apply this advice with the same old tired motives—to create drama, to impress and to get standing ovations from the Black women in your life. If you continue that way you are sure to keep impressing them. And you are just as sure to keep experiencing quickie romances or an extremely hollow marriage.

RESIST the urge to decide the quality of the advice here and your response to it solely based on your feelings. Your feelings have not always led you to what is honorable, excellent, and important, but only to what boosts your ego and elevates your adrenaline.

EXPECT that by throwing off your performing ways and following the advice ahead you'll feel naked and less in control of the flow of the relationship, or of her perceptions of your greatness. Stay on the job anyway. It will eventually prove liberating for you to be able to stick around and not give in to fakeness or flight, or sacrifice another Black woman's hopes and emotions on the altar of your self-image.

COMMIT to allowing yourself some trial-and-error time as you apply the Policies and Procedures. Remember, you are working to gain more excellence in love—and not just to avoid the exposure of your imperfections. Reclaim from women the power you give them to define your worth based on their approval. Start from the belief that your worth and value are already established because of who you are, not because of the impressive things you do.

Improvers

Your favorite line to her: *"Why don't you just try my suggestion? I'm only trying to help."*
Your favorite response from her: *"Thanks. That's exactly what I'll do."*

There's only one thing that frustrates Phillip about Anita. It's that she has so much potential but sometimes won't let him show her how to develop it. Phillip feels that, among other things, her style of dress, the way she expresses herself, her career choices, and even her hairstyle (*especially* her hairstyle) are all things that he could dramatically improve if she would just listen. After all, he swears, he's only trying to help the woman he loves become all that she can be.

When he ended nearly thirty years of a rocky marriage to Doris, Melvin swore he'd never get involved with another Black woman. His experience was that they were way too stubborn and arrogant to deal with. It always irked Melvin that when he offered Doris his opinion or advice on a decision she had to make, she'd listen, thank him politely, then choose a completely different course of action than the one he had "suggested." Melvin couldn't bear Doris's ingratitude any longer.

Following a very brief courtship, Melvin married his secretary, Shanel, who was over twenty years his junior. Now here was a good woman who was willing to learn from her man, thought Melvin. Shanel was like a mound of clay ready and willing for him to mold into something exceptional. He knew he'd be good for her and, when he was finished making his improvements on her, she'd be good for him as well.

Both Phillip and Melvin are Improvers. They have very definite ideas as to what kind of woman they want and need. She is, of course, the kind who perfectly fits the image of himself he wants to project. She enhances his self-portrait by adding all her impressive glory to his. Improvers look for women who hold the promise of becoming an extension of his own identity. All in the name of love, he attempts to refurbish that woman into a perfect accessory to himself. Improvers don't know anymore where he ends and she begins. To them there is no you or me; there is only us.

Improvers "need" their women to listen up and willingly follow the blueprint they have designed for her. Love, to him, means caring enough about her to show her how he'd like her to be. He feels she should care enough about him to become it. An Improver has very exacting specifications and countless tools and techniques to rearrange, refurbish, or completely rebuild his woman into the image that he believes will get him applause and thus inflate his sense of significance.

Improvers mean their women no harm; they truly believe that they have their highest good in mind. They just know how rotten they can feel if the way their women come across is anything less than glorious perfection.

Improvers:

- Derive much of their sense of identity and significance from the external, observable things they do, possess, or are closely identified with, for example, their appearance, jobs, cars, homes, and especially their women.
- Are motivated by how others perceive them.
- Are creative, hardworking, and constantly on guard to protect, reframe, or enhance their image.
- Expect their women's love to be evidenced by their willingness to express his tastes and expectations, preferably without him having to ask them to.
- Use subtle forms of punishment (like silence, withdrawal, or guilt) to influence their women's willing participation in their improvement efforts.

- Try to convince their women and themselves that the opinions of others don't really matter to them.

Are You an Improver?

True or false?

1. At the last minute your woman's choice of attire can make you decide not to go to a social gathering that you had previously been looking forward to attending.
2. You have gotten far more offended and embarrassed by someone's minor criticism of your mate than she did.
3. You are aware that you have a subtle way of coaching her or correcting her behavior in public.
4. You try to use reverse psychology to get her to choose something your way, so that you can't be accused of being controlling.
5. You feel an intense need to clarify, make a joke of, or do other damage control when she has spoken or acted in a way that embarrassed you.
6. You have a vivid mental picture of the kind of woman you wish you were being seen with, instead of the one you have.
7. There are one or more specific features about her that you find glaringly deficient, and, try as you might, you can't help obsessing over it.
8. You rarely feel lasting contentment with your woman or with yourself.
9. The most significant conflict issues in your relationship have to do with control, personal rights, and acceptance.
10. You are known and respected for your superior taste, style, and creativity.
11. You often wish you were more relaxed and didn't care so much about other people's opinion of you.

12. You automatically give yourself a long mental performance review after you have interacted with someone
you had hoped to impress.

13. Like a chameleon, you are seldom consistent in your
personality or style from one place to another. You get
annoyed when she doesn't shift her "role" to fit yours
without your having to ask.

14. You constantly give reminders and repeat yourself when
explaining your wishes and requests to her.

If you answered true to any of these you could well have
a bit of the Improver in you. The more times you answered
true, the more deeply ingrained and acceptable to you this
significance-seeking love substitute has become, and the more
it shows up in your style of relating to Black women.

All 70 of the Policies and Procedures to come are for you,
but especially those that have the ◆ symbol. Pay closest
attention to them, because for you they are the most crucial—
and the ones you are most likely to deny, resist, or ignore.

Your Dream Woman

You've got a Black woman whose total being, personality,
talents, communication style, visual presentation, and priorities perfectly reflect your taste and the image of yourself you
have designed in your mind. You'd love her dearly because
she'd be receptive to all your molding and shaping—and you
wouldn't even have to hide it. She'll let you make her into a
female version of you.

Your Obstacle to Overcome

Self-conscious insecurity. Your sense of significance is too
much derived from other people's estimation of you. Fact is,

you are the only one who is paying that much attention to you and to what your woman's image means about you. Never quite satisfied that either of you is turning out according to your plan, you can't seem to stop your compulsive improving.

As You Read This Book

The biggest challenge for you as you encounter the Policies and Procedures ahead will be heeding the advice when you can't immediately see how it will enhance, or at least maintain, that fully detailed self-image you have inside your head.

For you, expending effort, especially the hard effort needed to effect change, is only worth it when you can clearly and promptly help your world, and everything in it, rise to your soaring levels of expectation. You only feel truly safe from being looked down upon, ridiculed, or embarrassed when you've managed to put all costumes, props, and scenery in place. You have little time left to meet her needs and nourish her life.

You drive women crazy trying to manipulate them into giving up their way of being, in order to adopt yours. Their sense of security can't flourish in the chilly climate of your discontent. You stay too tense and you make the people around you tense, because it's clear: Enough is *never* enough for you. Your constant subtle requests and your cleverly disguised rewards-and-punishment system, combined with that "well, forget you then" attitude of yours, make it nearly impossible for a sister to know that you absolutely treasure her just as she is.

An Improver gives his woman only one acceptable way of nurturing his significance—willing cooperation with his never-ending efforts to use her to "decorate" himself. It's a price that few Black women are willing to pay for very long. The paradox is that the ones who will let themselves be shaped on your wheel and molded in your image will still have a hard time getting your lasting commitment. Because when it's all said and done, Improvers are turned off by women who "need" so much improving in the first place!

Much of what you will read here about what is truly important to Black women (and not merely get from them for the sake of your image) will be hard for you to buy into. You've encountered women who'd be happy to be your fix-it project and are grateful for the opportunity. This, you may well argue, is proof that "improving" *is* your way of loving, and it *is* beneficial to her, and it would be senseless to change now.

But it is vital that you change. If you don't, the trail of Black women who have been manipulated to conform to your secret designs, or those who have been rejected and insulted by your demanding requirements, will only get longer. And your disillusionment and distaste for your woman, or *all* Black women, will only increase.

Your challenge to change requires that you:

ADMIT that the Improver drive in you has failed you miserably. You are neither giving nor getting the kind of others-centered, mutually satisfying love that you want. You must confront the part of you which believes that image is everything. You'll savor the peace that comes from leaving the land of Me, Myself, and I.

RESIST the urge to elevate yourself above the advice found ahead. Since your constant self-appraisal seldom leaves you satisfied with your woman or yourself, you have a tendency to compensate by pretending superiority. That kind of pride-filled self-perception will only keep you doing it your old Improver way. Just think of yourself as one of us: a man who needs more than his own design to become all he should become. You could use some designs to live by that you didn't create and that aren't just for your benefit.

EXPECT an inclination in you, as you work to follow the advice, to look for a "tit for tat" arrangement with your woman. If you start to perform these nice, new security-nurturing things for her, you could require her to pay you back before you proceed to do more. But that's just more of the same old trick you have fallen prey to, too many times as it is. Now's the time to give up your bargaining, swapping, and bartering policy and begin to do things for her in clear, direct, positive ways that result in a benefit to her. From now on work to do right by her—because it's right to do, not because it pays.

COMMIT to letting go of your rigid, albeit subtly demanded, requirements of her, and the cold shoulder you give when she doesn't comply. Refuse to allow your will to follow your feelings, once again, down the road of obsession over how you are being perceived. Simply decide that for now the Black woman you love is good enough as she is, and she doesn't owe you any improvements.

Blamers

Your favorite line to her: *"It's all your fault!"*
Your favorite response from her: *"You are so right. I'm sorry."*

Nothing drives Kirk crazier than when his wife, Denise, starts insisting that they should see a marriage counselor. She always brings up what she calls their "total breakdown of communication," their strained feelings about their tight finances, and her frustration over not being able to get pregnant. It all sounds to Kirk like his wife is trying to lay all the blame on him. He loudly insists that if Denise would just grow up and stop dwelling on the negatives there wouldn't be any problems that require throwing good money away on some nosy counselor.

Stephan pulled the plug very abruptly on his long-distance romance with Alicia. He concluded that she obviously was not the Black woman for him, after she tearfully expressed her disappointment that he had failed to call, mail a card, or in any way acknowledge her recent birthday. In fact, Alicia was still upset about Stephan's having broken his promise to fly into her city and spend Valentine's weekend with her. After all, she noted, it was his idea in the first place! Stephan felt that there was no way Alicia could be the one for him if she didn't have enough insight to understand these circumstances were not really his fault. A man gets busy and things do come up. Besides, Stephan reasoned, Alicia's fault-finding attitude was a much more serious and destructive problem than any "totally unintentional" mistakes he may have made.

Blamers are the ultimate finger-pointers. They can't bear the possibility that any of the problems or challenges to intimacy in their relationships could ever, in any way, be their fault. To hear him tell it, he's *never* to blame and therefore he never has to assume the burden of accountability and change. Blaming her, "the system," the world, "them," "things," or virtually anything other than himself is what keeps him from having to assume responsibility. And, if he wasn't responsible, then no one can ever say he failed. And never seeming to have failed is how he keeps a tight hold on his cherished sense of significance.

Blamers:

- Have 20/20 vision when it comes to the imperfections of others. They fake blindness when it comes to their own imperfections.

- Possess a built-in "risk-radar." They instinctively avoid at the outset, or later disassociate themselves from, people, places, or pursuits that might make them vulnerable to real or perceived failure. (This is especially true in love relationships.)
- Can't help interpreting their woman's negative feelings or experiences about anything as accusations against him.
- Are perpetually angry and disappointed over what the Black woman in his life does or doesn't do.
- Are skilled masters in the art of self-justification, defensiveness, and rationalization.
- Only experience one-sided relationships where improvement, correction, responsibility, apologies, and vulnerability are her stuff, not his.

Are You a Blamer?

True or false?

1. More than one of the women in your life have accused you of "turning things around to make yourself look innocent."
2. You get uncomfortable when your woman is upset. You don't get comfortable again until she makes it clear she's not blaming you for her problem.
3. You "script" handy excuses and explanations in your mind for future use with your woman, and you keep a readily available mental file of her faults and shortcomings.
4. In heated conflict with your mate you habitually use statements like "Yeah, but what about you . . ." or "At least I'm being honest about what I did, but you . . ." or "The real problem is not about me, it's how you . . ."

5. When you explain your relationship difficulties to others you revise the events or put a spin on your motives that makes you more innocent and her more guilty.

6. You deeply resent anyone (particularly your woman) having a complaint in a given area, especially if you feel you've performed extraordinarily in some other area of your relationship.

7. You employ creative ways to fish for compliments or head off blame.

8. You absolutely love to be apologized to.

9. You have surprised yourself by how violent your feelings and how intense your outbursts are when you are accused of a wrong by your woman.

10. Most people in your life find you far more genteel, charming, and fair-minded than your woman does.

11. At times you have been excessively concerned with who she talks to about the two of you and have gone out of your way to clear your good name.

12. The women in your life whom you have felt strongest about and remained longest with aren't nearly as quick-witted, articulate, insightful, or demanding as you.

13. You believe that usually, when women complain about you, it's because they are the kind who are irrational, judgmental, and unwilling to face their own defects.

If you answered true to any of these you could well have a bit of the Blamer in you. The more times you answered true, the more deeply ingrained and acceptable to you this significance-seeking love substitute has become, and the more it shows up in your style of relating to Black women.

All 70 of the Policies and Procedures to come are for you, but especially those that have the ● symbol. Pay closest attention to them, because for you they are the most crucial— and the ones you are most likely to deny, resist, or ignore.

Your Dream Woman

She's a low-maintenance, high-performance Black woman who feels fortunate to have a man like you. She's only aware of your admirable qualities and never even notices that you have bad ones. As far as she is concerned you're perfect and she is humble and honest enough to realize that if something does go wrong it must be her fault—or anybody's fault—except yours.

Your Obstacle to Overcome

The compulsive need to be right. It's how you get your applause. Blamers secretly struggle with guilt and disappointment with themselves. They are supremely legalistic. If you are a Blamer, you really don't believe you are perfect and guiltless—you believe it takes flawless performance to be a good (not even a perfect) man. In spite of all appearances, your self-confidence level runs at a deficit. Any blame, criticism, or disapproval indicates to you that you are even less than you thought you were. Therefore you can't ever afford to be wrong. Total self-righteousness is the key to maintaining your sense of significance.

As You Read This Book

It could be a real effort for you to continue further in this book at all. Blamers have a way of filtering advice, and the challenge to change, that makes it all sound to them like shaming rebukes and condemnation—the very stuff you're most allergic to. And if you make it to the Policies and Procedures ahead and decide to try them, they could overwhelm you because of your inner compulsion to do everything perfectly, right now, or not try to do it at all. With that mind-set, this book could be dangerous to your mental health—unless you insist that your self-sabotaging mind-set sit down and shut up, then proceed to act in direct opposition to it.

The fact of the matter is, *nobody* in your life except you requires you to be 100 percent blame-free. Most people, and that's likely to include your woman, only want you to own up to your mess and make and keep a commitment to fix it. You may have a hard time believing it, but your woman would rather see your warts and flaws and know you care enough about her and yourself to work on them, than for you to have no faults or failures or blame in the first place. Few people, and none that you should want to be bothered with, toss someone aside simply because they are imperfect but are working toward becoming better.

As you take the steps recommended ahead, virtually everything can be different for you and your mate if you give up hiding, displacing, or ignoring your flaws. Become willing to let them see the light of day. You are keeping yourself so safely protected by your blaming that your woman doesn't get to intimately know huge parts of you. It's like making love with an elegant cashmere overcoat on.

Of course, sometimes you really won't be at fault, and she will. Sometimes you will be falsely accused and unjustly treated. You needn't deny the truth in order to change your ways. It's just that your impassioned crusade, and the way you work over-time to exonerate yourself, make you too much the crafty defense attorney. It has become an oppressive chore, for you, and the worst kind of insult to her.

If you are willing to give up your preoccupation with self-protection in the name of significance, you and the Black woman you love can powerfully benefit from the Policies and Procedures in Part II. You can start by taking the following steps now:

ADMIT that you are a Blamer (or that you, at least, carry some of those traits in your system). Go ahead and acknowledge that it has cost you and the woman in your life way too much already. You won't get anywhere near the more balanced, honest, and fulfilling life and relationship you want if you keep using your "yeah buts . . ." to squirm out of facing the truth head-on.

RESIST that impulse to focus on the Policies and Procedures that you feel you already do well and ignore the ones that challenge you to advance beyond the borders of your comfort zone. You'll need to be ready to do what *doesn't* come naturally—and what could expose some of your weak spots. You'll discover it won't kill you, it'll change you—and for the better.

EXPECT to struggle with the notion that your woman doesn't deserve all these caring, securing behaviors. You may think she sees your kindness as weakness. Remember your old misbelief system is based on the idea that one only deserves good who always does good. Your well-reinforced self-protective strategies have worked hard to convince you that she certainly hasn't earned it. In fact, you have now bought into the idea that all those faults you have projected onto her are somehow true and she *is* at fault. In spite of this legalistic, earned-rewards system, you need practice at giving grace (unearned favor) to her. It'll help you eventually learn to give some to yourself—where it's most needed.

COMMIT to putting these principles into practice, in spite of how messy, awkward, and chaotic it may initially feel. Go ahead and feel all those unsettling feelings—just don't follow them. They'll only lead you back to seeking your significance through the deceptive appearance of perfection.

Givers

Your favorite line to her: *"Just tell me what you want and I'll do it."*
Your favorite response from her: *"You are the sweetest man on earth."*

As a boy, Calvin noticed the way the men in his family treated their women. His father, assorted cousins, uncles, and older brothers often bragged about how much their women did for them and how little they had to do to get them to. Calvin didn't understand it all, at the time, but he did find it strange that the men seemed very proud to describe themselves as "players," "Mack Daddies," and "gigolos," while the women referred to them as "good for nothing" or "not worth a dime." Calvin saw the pain and dissatisfaction in his mother and the others, and was determined to grow up and become, in the eyes of his woman, a truly "extraordinary man," because to him:

- Ordinary men are selfish, egotistical, and insensitive to their women.
- Ordinary men exploit and mistreat their women.
- Ordinary men don't have a clue about the fine points of a woman's needs and desires, let alone what it takes to fulfill them.
- Ordinary men end up with women who hate them and regret ever having gotten involved with their kind.

All grown up now, Calvin tends to go way overboard trying to prove to the Black woman he loves that he's definitely *not* one of those good-for-nothing men. His policy is to guess, ask, assume, or imagine what his woman desires and do whatever he's got to do to deliver it, ASAP. Women start out seeing Calvin as the sweetest, most attentive, and caring man. Later they call him a spineless jellyfish who can only be counted on to make all kinds of promises and seldom make good on them. They swear he set them up by being so unusually attentive and generous at first, then, stubbornly, abruptly stopping—*and*, mysteriously, refusing to explain why.

Antonio thought himself unbelievably lucky to have landed an absolute goddess, like Regina, as his wife. Regina was in a class by herself, miles beyond the colorless, easily pleased women he was accustomed to.

As if to somehow make up for the callous insensitivity he had shown Black women in the past, Antonio went out of his way for Regina. He found her to be so much more *everything*: more beautiful, more popular, more successful and pulled together than any woman he could have ever expected to have. Regina was a thoroughbred, through and through. And if she was a little spoiled, demanding, and nitpicky, thoroughbreds are just a high-maintenance breed, Antonio reasoned. He was so honored to have Regina he made sure to do (or at least appear to do) whatever he thought the lady wanted, with no complaints and no delays. Though he never would admit it, his friends were convinced Antonio's nose was wide open.

Later, Antonio became aware of having mixed emotions about Regina. On the one hand, he was sick and tired of bowing and scraping, overspending, predicting her needs, and biting his tongue. Antonio began to lose respect for himself and to despise Regina for the power he felt she had over him. But, on the other hand, he worshipped her, and craved her presence in his life. There was no way he was going to give her up, or the intoxicating sense of significance her approval brought.

Over time Antonio constructed, layer by layer, a secret world of well-concealed activities, debts, and extramarital relationships. Much of his life was a complete mystery to everyone—including his wife. He found clever, indirect ways of getting back at Regina, without her being able to pin anything on him with any assurance.

Givers are generous, agreeable, and self-sacrificing "servants" who maintain their sense of significance in relationships with Black women they idolize by guessing and satisfying every need, whim, or expectation he even thinks she has. Givers gain their significance by packaging themselves as humble, benevolent men who only live to serve their women. They ask for little and are willing to give everything—except the emotional goodies their women crave, like: direct, unambiguous commitments, integrity, and enough self-respect and assertiveness to say what they really mean and mean what they say—even when NO is what they really mean.

Givers have looked around at the blatantly uncaring and disrespectful manner in which some men relate to Black women and they've listened when the women have expressed hurt and anger about their relationships with men. Givers covet the chance to appear to be that rare, sensitive hero who is everything those other bums aren't. If you're a Giver, manipulating the way things appear is your strong suit. "Have no fear," you'll vow to her, "I'm only here to give, not to take."

But Givers have a big secret: They don't give and give for her sake—they do it for themselves, in order to keep what they feel they need: the sense of peerless virtue and power they gain from their own ceaseless benevolence and the warm glow of their woman's approval. They exalt Black women to a level approaching worship, where disappointing her is not an option—at least not at first. With all his lavish, tender loving care, a Giver usually succeeds at making his woman feel cherished and secure—only to eventually pull the rug right out from under her when she least expects it.

All this work and worship always leaves the Giver feeling:

- *Torn*. You do get a measure of self-satisfaction from presenting yourself as such a wonderfully caring man. But you hate yourself for compromising and for feeling so approval-needy. You want to be free of this, but you don't want to lose her.
- *Worn*. The more you overdo in order to keep her happy and ensure her approval, the more commonplace (i.e., not at all extraordinary) your offerings become, the more giving or guessing or predicting you must do in order to be seen as an exceptional man.
- *Forlorn*. When being your outrageously over-the-top version of a "really nice guy" begins to register to you as self-compromising and one-sided you are likely to retreat to a secret world where you get to be the opposite of how you are with her. As your secret world gets more of your attention and your real life and relationships gets less, your deceptions, mysterious behaviors, and the massive losses you are willing to incur ignite a sense of shame in you.

Are You a Giver?

True or false?

1. You put almost all your energy into finding out what your woman expects and little to none into clearly expressing what you want and expect.

2. You have experienced overwhelming guilt, on more than a few occasions, when she expressed disappointment with something you failed to do.

3. You have some ongoing secret activities, relationships, or major problem (related to your finances, your health, your possessions, or your career) that you work extremely hard to keep her from knowing the complete truth about.

4. You love it when your woman makes dramatic comparisons between your exceptional goodness and other men's no-goodness.

5. You would be more than a little embarrassed if your male friends found out the extent to which you work to please your woman, and some of the inappropriate treatment you've accepted from her without a word.

6. You have gotten a secret jolt of satisfaction when something very important to her fell apart and it could, in no way, be pinned on you.

7. When you are angry with her, you sometimes intentionally procrastinate, ignore, or "forget" commitments made to her.

8. You tend to avoid conflicts and the emotionalism that accompanies them, and are quick to assume responsibility for making the conflict go away.

9. You typically start out exceptionally romantic, creative, and generous in your gift-giving, downshifting later to perfunctory gift-giving and "as required" expressions of affection.

10. You will lie, exaggerate, or otherwise alter the facts if you think it will keep the peace or protect yourself from her finding out you messed up.

11. Though you deny it, you have strategically withheld sex to punish her or to make a point.

12. You hold grudges and seldom forget a slight or a criticism, continuing to replay them in your mind.

13. You have reacted to her ultimatums with either extreme apologies and extravagant promises or outright begging.

14. Though you hate it, you have also envied the relative ease with which your woman can do without you.

15. On at least one occasion you have lost control and gotten physical with your mate.

16. At least one Black woman has broken off with you claiming that your lack of assertiveness, irresponsibility, and secretiveness were real turn-offs.

If you answered true to any of these, you could well have a bit of the Giver in you. The more times you answered true, the more deeply ingrained and acceptable to you this significance-seeking love substitute has become, and the more it shows up in your style of relating to Black women.

All of the Policies and Procedures to come are for you, but especially those that have the ❱ symbol. Pay closest attention to them, because for you they are the most crucial—and the ones you are most likely to deny, resist, or ignore.

Your Dream Woman

She's the world's most exceptional and admired woman who has already been with the world's most horrible men. Rejecting the multitudes of hopeless "bad boys" she picks you. Because with all your exceptional sincerity, sensitivity, and generosity she recognizes that you are nothing like them. She never requires any more from you than what you already give. To her, you will be forever extraordinary.

Your Obstacle to Overcome

The fear of losing out. Your overgiving and passivity cost you your self-respect. But you are afraid that if you stop, or take the necessary steps to bring some balance and limits to what you give to her and take from her, you could lose her and the sense of significance you derive from being seen as exceptional in her eyes.

As You Read This Book

If you're not careful, in your hands, this book could be lethal. Since you are already so deeply invested in woman-pleasing you might be inclined to use the advice found here to help you do it more and better. You'll immediately latch on to the directives that call upon a man's humility and self-sacrificing. You'll skip right over those that challenge you to stand up for yourself, set limits, tell the truth, and be willing to endure some losses.

Just pages from now, you really might be tempted to close this book, shelve it, and go away arguing that this is only good medicine for bad men, and you'll convince yourself that you are such an exemplary fellow already you need none of what's prescribed here. That'll be your cue to go right back to the sweat-soaked song and dance your love life has become and try to escape back to your secret life.

But it really doesn't have to be this way. Your approach to love, self-respect, and the needed sense of significance can be radically transformed by acquiring new motives and new, healthier ways of relating to the Black woman you love. When you stop being so driven by the fear of losing her, to your "please her at any cost" tendencies, you can become a much more balanced and honest man. One who gives because he can and because he wants to. And you'll rightly expect her to give to you as well, because you deserve it no less than she does.

To make that vital transformation you will need to:

ADMIT that you are a Giver and that what you have been

doing for the woman you love has proven, in the long run, not to benefit either of you. If you're honest, you will admit that it has eventually made you both have little respect for you. Don't confuse the terms, your kind of giving is not caring sacrifice, unconditional love, or exceptional devotion. It's people-pleasing—pure giving in order to get!

RESIST the urge to use the advice in the next section as merely different ways to do the same old stuff for the same old reasons. The Policies and Procedures ahead are to empower you to be appropriately responsive to her needs as well as to your own. They are *not* tips on how take complete responsibility for her life.

EXPECT the scalpel to cut deeply as you work to surgically remove the malignant self-centeredness at your core. A sense of guilt and ambivalence about changing your style may tempt you to abort the process. Don't. Even if, as you begin to show signs of changing, your woman accuses you of becoming "just like all those other dogs," you *must* stay on-task. Change is traumatic for everyone, even those who could benefit most from your transformation. You'll learn to live with her temporary displeasure and the self-doubts they stir in you, by keeping to your goals. You'll discover that your worst fear—her disapproval—may hurt, but it won't kill you. And, when it stops having such a powerful hold on you, you'll have no use for your old self-sabotaging love substitute.

COMMIT, throughout the entire process (i.e., the rest of your life), to learning to say no (literally, and loudly) to yourself when you are tempted to say and do things solely to earn her love and her willingness to be with you. Instead, freely offer her the mutually beneficial Policies and Procedures upcoming. It's a trickier task than you might imagine. Having a buddy who has your permission to probe your motives and question your behavior will prove to be an invaluable asset as you apply the principles ahead.

Rulers

Your favorite line to her: *"I am the man here, you know."*
Your favorite response from her: *"Yes, you are the man."*

Curtis was one of the most eligible and sought-after bachelors at his church. A former pro football player turned businessman, he was tall, broad-shouldered, and possessed an intense, no-nonsense demeanor that was both attractive and off-putting to women. Curtis was a thoroughly imposing figure around whom most people felt they were expected to do more listening than talking.

In spite of the fact that Curtis had gone through the church's premarital counseling program for engaged couples three times—with three different women—finding a good Christian woman to be his loving and submissive wife was beginning to seem like a next-to-impossible challenge for him.

Curtis was convinced that the average Black woman was no longer willing to submit to what he believed was a man's God-given right to rule over her. Curtis frequently complained about how each of his mates eventually showed their true colors when they "challenged my authority and tried to be the man in the relationship." Curtis believed that for a marriage to work, his job was to command with absolute, but loving, power. Her job was to defer her ideas, opinions, and expertise and follow his dictates to the letter—and enjoy doing it too!

Jamal's favorite affectionate pet name for his girlfriend Donna was "Daddy's Baby Girl." Though they'd been together only six months, Jamal took great pride in the degree of respect shown him by Donna. He had no problem seeing to her rent, her car note, and giving her a weekly allowance for her kids. How could he complain, he figured. Here was a woman who called him "Daddy" and treated him like a king. She never made the slightest decision without Jamal signing off on it, and she apologized profusely whenever she "talked back" to him and "made him" have to slap her one. In Jamal's mind Donna was a very lucky girl to have a man like him to take care of her.

Rulers are dictators who have granted themselves all rights to the throne in their relationships with Black women. If you are a ruler, you maintain your sense of significance by your authoritative, paternal, and ultimately condescending style of relating to women. Deep down you believe that being a "real man" means being in charge, and you believe that women, bless their hearts, really need you to be. Therefore Rulers of every kind, from the most well bred and mild-mannered to the most raving megalomaniacs, believe that it is in their woman's best interest that he be in control, so he expects her willing submission to his lordship. Ruling can seem like a brand-new lease on life if you have felt put down, dismissed, or "worked over" by some mean-spirited, domineering female only out to reduce a brother to dust.

Rulers employ every conceivable means to rise to power and then to maintain it and the significance jolt that comes with it. At every turn they must draw upon their considerable talents as demanding bosses, convincing liars, frightful intimidators, knowledgeable instructors, insightful psychologists, or pouting, little boys to compel their women to accept and appreciate their man's rule.

At the core of Rulers' feelings of entitlement is the self-applied pressure to know all, be all, and make sure that all turns out according to their own predesigned plans. Rulers are big on getting results.

That's why they don't feel they can afford to share much of the power. They suspect that if they don't run things, then they can't be sure that all will proceed toward the results they have envisioned. If you're a Ruler, that's a tragedy of epic pro-portions, because you need *your* results to get the credit, the applause, and the feelings of significance you yearn for.

Of course, being a Ruler has some extraordinary costs associated with it. Not the least of them has to do with how utterly disregarded and disrespected the women in your life tend to feel. No matter what you say, she knows she only gets to play a bit part, while you have the starring role in the drama that your relationship is. The Black women in your life eventually conclude that you care far less about them, and their security needs, than you care about yourself and what makes you feel significant.

Maybe you can begin to see why the women in your life don't just pack up and politely go, they go with a vengeance, wishing you the worst and delighting in your downfall. Or they stay, too tired or too afraid to pull the plug, but too hurt and angry to keep submitting to your tyranny. They remain with a hardened veneer over their dry indifference to you, your rulership, and your results.

Rather than taking this as a hint that you should consider sharing the throne, you only end up respecting Black women even less, seeing them as overaggressive male-bashers who aren't ready to be loved. The cycle continues because you'll feel the need to rule more firmly and allow for less dissent in your present relationship or your next one. You'll hurt more Black women's sense of security, and their negative responses will diminish your sense of significance, and the two of you will continue to make major contributions to each other's misery.

Rulers:

- Get an elevated sense of self-importance when their woman takes their words, wishes, and whims as her marching orders.

- Believe that the strength of their masculinity assures them of the right to rule, and that the frailty of her femininity necessitates her need to be ruled.
- Are convinced that their sovereignty greatly benefits their mate. But they tend to be suspicious of Black women's motives and deeply resent any rivalry, second-guessing, or "disobedience" from her.

Are You a Ruler?

True or false?

1. You have felt justified in spying, eavesdropping, or in some way monitoring your woman's activities.
2. Apologies are hard for you to formulate. You almost never just plain say, "I'm sorry, I was wrong."
3. You often use phrases like "You just don't understand . . ." when your woman objects to your ruling.
4. You are quick to make mental note of other men's leadership style and degree of authority and compare yourself to them.
5. You constantly reiterate the list of benefits your woman has derived from your being in charge.
6. You are a master of the silent treatment.
7. You have a very hard time when your mate wins or outdoes you at some competition, such as cards, or any contest or shared goal.
8. You have committed a harmful or illegal act in retaliation against a Black woman who crossed you.
9. You have few, if any, male friends who know about all the areas of your life.
10. You are prone to challenging authority figures—subtly or overtly.

11. You tell and highly enjoy jokes that make fun of women.

12. It is especially hard for you to contain your anger when your woman doesn't do something she's agreed to do or doesn't do it right.

13. You'd much prefer your woman obey you because she perceives it as benefiting her, not just you.

14. There is at least one Black woman, when you think of her, you get knots in your stomach and intensely angry feelings.

15. You lavishly reward your woman when she submissively complies with your wishes.

If you answered true to any of these you could well have a bit of the Ruler in you. The more times you answered true, the more deeply ingrained and acceptable to you this significance-seeking love substitute has become, and the more it shows up in your style of relating to Black women.

All of the Policies and Procedures to come are for you, but especially those that have the ■ symbol. Pay closest attention to them, because for you they are the most crucial—and the ones you are most likely to deny, resist, or ignore.

Your Dream Woman

She has a huge amount of confidence in you—but not in herself. She is highly verbal and extremely articulate—but only when she's talking about how powerful and brilliant you are. She's a genius—at least when it comes to understanding that, without you, her life would be so much less than it is.

Your Obstacle to Overcome

The addiction to control. Because men in our culture are often taught from childhood that he who is most man is he who is most in charge, ruling could well be called the significance jackpot. Rulers fear they'll fail to satisfy the minimum standards of masculinity if they don't maintain authoritarian control. Deep on the inside they suspect that something isn't quite right with their heavy-handed approach, but they feel certain they'll lose too much by yielding even an inch.

As You Read This Book

As a Ruler, you are likely to already be nursing the suspicion that this book, and especially the upcoming Policies and Procedures, will prove to be yet another discussion of how rotten Black men are and how mistreated Black women are. Even now you stand ready to shoot holes in the advice ahead because you are sure it doesn't take into account what you see as the absolute necessity of a strong Black man taking a firm hand of rulership in dealing with today's Black woman.

Your greatest temptation as you proceed through these pages will be to only scan the titles, subheadings, and highlighted words and phrases that, when lifted out of context, might help you build a strong case against the advice in the next section of this book. I caution you to be on the alert. There is likely to be momentum inside you propelling you away from taking ownership of the very information that most applies to you. Rulers will instinctively try to sidestep the principles here that have the most potential to transform their rigid, authoritarian love substitute into a strong yet compassionate, sure-of-yourself but yielding kind of love. It is that kind of love that the women in your life have long sought from you. It is love that is not so easily offended or intimidated by the force of her personality, her differences, her priorities, her opinions, and the way in which she expresses them. It's a love that has no problem listening, caring, or compromising, or even completely yielding at times.

Push through the upcoming pages, relying more on your open mind and listening ears than your debating tongue. Sure, you *have* paid the cost to be the boss; but look at the price you've paid. It has made women fear you, despise you, or cling like little girls to their Daddy's knee. And it has reduced your romantic relationship to something very close to an employer-employee one, with little trust or satisfying love flowing in either direction.

Changing your style, for your sake and hers, can happen if you will:

ADMIT that you have definite Ruler tendencies. With your passion for results, you need some compelling motivation to be able to vigorously pursue anything to successful completion. It's especially important for you that you see ruling for what it is, a self-sabotaging love substitute—and that you have been honest enough to see yourself as a man who has used it. When that realization makes you even a little sick and tired, you are ripe and ready to move toward change.

RESIST, for now, your constant attempts to enforce your authority with Black women, or to require her to do anything your way. Determine instead that now is the time to put your self-serving ways on indefinite hold and choose rather to serve your woman by practicing the powerful, but loving, actions suggested ahead.

EXPECT to feel as if you have "wimped out" and that you are now committing to do what you dread more than anything in the world: following someone else's rules. Don't believe it. For you to do what's suggested ahead will be because you have exercised your willful choice and have made a deliberate decision to act in new and more mutually rewarding ways.

COMMIT to allowing yourself time, maybe even a long time, to make the transition from a man who gets his significance from ruling to one who already has his significance and therefore is free to serve and to take pride in how effectively he does. In other words, don't rush so fast to the results stage that you minimize the importance of trial and error, slow but steady movement, and accepting your and your mate's best along the way.

Slow Down . . .
Men at Work!

By now I'm sure it's clear to you that this book is about how to do *The Job:* relating to the Black woman you love with the kind of skill and sensitivity that makes for mutual satisfaction. You really want her to feel satisfied with your love, but you also want to feel satisfied with yourself, and your ability to do the job well. Satisfying her and yourself are both priority one. To aim for either of them alone, and not the two of them together, is out of balance, unrealistic, and makes the prospect of accepting the job far less attractive.

Your summary job description does *not* read: *"Position involves finding out how Black women approach love and relationships and attempting to imitate them."* That's no help to anybody. That's definitely not the job.

Rather, it's about how to offer her the very best kind of love that fits her unique, legitimate needs in the very best ways you possibly can.

You needn't feel any shame over thinking about the way you express your love to her as a job. Often women, whose orientation to love is more abstract and feelings-based, misread your concrete, task-oriented approach as something less wholehearted and therefore less valid. Actually, the things men place the highest value on in life, we approach as a job to do, with goals and objectives, roles and responsibilities—and clearly detailed policies and procedures.

A more accurate summary job description for men in love could read:

Position involves loving a Black woman by:

- maintaining a constant focus on her high-priority need for security,
- striving to accurately "translate" her female communication style,
- choosing to speak when you'd much rather act, and
- keeping an open mind and heart willing to accept the vast differences between her style and yours.

Previous experience is not a requirement, but an unwavering commitment to serve your woman without either over- or undervaluing yourself is vital to your success.

The pages ahead contain seventy straightforward, sometimes challenging, but highly effective ways to love a Black woman. Some of what you will find may seem like "old news," and you'll be very proud of how well you already know and do them. Give them your attention anyway, as they will be useful reminders, helping you to troubleshoot and tighten up your weak areas and blind spots. Then keep reading and you will encounter others that will speak directly to you and your situation, challenging you to live out what is truly effective in loving a Black woman, with more wisdom, more courage, and ultimately, more genuine satisfaction for both of you.

Don't just analyze these Policies and Procedures—perform them. The most effective way to break old useless habits is to replace them with new, more effective ones. These can radically alter the way you and the woman in your life experience love. To adopt even a few of the directives ahead will make a dramatic difference in your life. To adopt most, or all, of them will revolutionize your relationship and, not coincidentally, transform you personally as well.

The Policies and Procedures and You

Give yourself time to carefully read and digest the insights and suggestions given for each of the Policies and Procedures. Pay closest attention to the ones that have your love substitute's symbol at the top of the page.

A brief personal statement "From the Black woman you love" precedes each of these seventy actions. None of them are the exact words of any one woman. The statements are, however, typical of what Black women have shared with me in private counseling, on talk shows, and at seminars around the country. This book is a "translation" in the male language of what women have wanted us to understand about what they need from us. In that they have often conveyed it to us in the female language, we haven't always gotten it. We've ended up filling in the gaps the best we know how.

At the end of each of the Policies and Procedures is an important section called "The Bottom Line" with three essential features. "Men at Work" will help you turn the principles into practice suggesting clear-cut, doable action responses to the insights you have just read. As you know, developing new skills and sharpening old ones require taking bold steps, not just reading about them.

Also included under each "Bottom Line" is a pair of concise statements that answer the two vital questions that are uppermost in a man's mind *before* he'll fully commit to a new task: (a) "If I do this, what are 'The Benefits' I can expect?" and (b) "What are 'The Costs' to get them?"

In every case you will notice that the benefits always outweigh even the most considerable costs.

You have now come to the point in reading this book that separates the proverbial men from the boys. It will, of course, take next to no energy or effort to turn the page here, in the literal sense. But the big question is: Are you now willing to rise to the challenge of turning a new page in your life and in your relationship with Black women?

The advice ahead is not a magic formula. It doesn't come with an unconditional guarantee. Love involves another human being, and wherever there is another human being involved in anything, there are no guarantees because you don't have control over the other person. Influence perhaps, maybe even powerful influence, but never control.

You do have control over yourself. Obviously, you don't have to do a thing you don't want to do. Nobody, not the woman in your life or anyone else, can force you to live what you'll learn here. There's not enough guilt, complaining, or ridicule in the world to make that happen. It's your choice. And if you decide to take the advice, it will be because *you* see Black women as worth it and *you* see yourself as able to do it. In both points, I wholeheartedly agree with you.

Life-changing possibilities do exist, just ahead, for you and for the woman you love. If you've chosen to accept the challenge, now is the time to roll up your sleeves and get down to business. The job—and the genuine satisfaction of doing it well—awaits you.

PART II

How to Love a Black Woman

1. ▲ ■ ● ◆ ▶
Reality-Check Your Expectations of Her

To the man who loves me:
I'm beginning to get the impression that you are judging me
when you look me over from head to toe and as you listen
intently when I am speaking to you or as you so carefully
check out the things I do and how I do them. I'm wondering
if you're looking to see if I measure up—and I'm wondering
what it is that I have to measure up to.

—From the Black woman you love

The hardest part of living real life is accepting the realities
we find there. Even if you've never shared it with another living soul, somewhere in the secret recesses of your mind you
probably have imagined your Ms. Right and how incredible
she'd be in nearly every way. You've seen the way her flowing locks beautifully framed her face or dramatically draped
her shoulders. You've heard her at her most delicately soft-
spoken or sassily outspoken and you know to the smallest

detail of her personality, her level of ambition, and the spiritual depth, passion, style, and humor she possesses. As far as you're concerned she's perfection personified and she's all yours. That is, once you ever find her. I hate to rain on your parade, but unless you reality-check your expectations, the Black woman you seek will never appear or the Black woman you have will never measure up.

Unrealistic expectations set you up for too much disappointment and make the women around you at risk for too much painful rejection. Keep your high hopes and high standards but by all means get rid of those self-sabotaging fantasies of a perfect Ms. Right. If there really is such a thing, she has already been taken by a Mr. Right!

In real-life relationships the man who loves a Black woman does well to reality-check his own perceptions and expectations of her from time to time. You must be brutally honest in answering these questions: Is what I am expecting of the woman in my life based on reality or merely wishes, fantasies, and daydreams? Is it mostly fact or fiction? Is it fair to my sisters that I hold these expectations of them? A reality check requires honest answers and necessary adjustments, which can save you and her some major grief.

Expectations of her that test too high (she needs to score 100 percent in every area of her being, and she never looks, acts, thinks, or makes you feel anything less than perfect) puts any woman at risk of eventual disqualification and dismissal ("You're okay but you're just not the one for me").

Black women have seen it and heard it all before. The let-them-down-easy dismissals, the men who romance them, then come up missing in action, or those who swore to them "You are definitely the one for me" only later to insist "You're not really who I thought you were, you deceived me." Each woman longs to be known for who they are and loved and accepted as they are. Although what they are can be quite impressive, they never will measure up to or continue to measure up to any man's unrealistic, perfectionistic fantasy image. That's too much to expect from love or any lover.

THE BOTTOM LINE

Men at work: Check in with reality. Simplify your expectations of your mate and of yourself. If you keep ending up discovering relationship after relationship, year after year, to have been "not quite what I was looking for," you need to readjust what you are looking for.

The benefits: When your expectations and tastes are based upon reasonable reality-based standards, you are inclusive rather than limited in your choice of mate.

The costs: That nagging suspicion that if you had just held out a little longer you "coulda/woulda" finally gotten your Ms. Right and life would have been right forever.

2. ▲ ■ ● ◆ ❭ *Give Her Your Love in Her Language*

To the man who loves me:
It's not at all a secret. If you pay close attention, I'm showing you all the time the ways I love to be loved. Please pay attention.

—From the Black woman you love

When it's all said and done, much of your success in loving a Black woman finally hinges on your willingness and ability to give her, when you can and as best you can, the kind of love she gives you. Though it's unrealistic for us to demand that we get it that way all the time, human beings love to be shown love that is an exact replica of the best aspects of the love we've shown others. In fact, our tendency is to measure expectations of another person's way of loving by comparing it to the standards set by our own ways. When you are sure that you deeply love someone, it's easy to conclude that the ways that you are naturally inclined to express your love (your "love language") are exactly how your mate will do it too if "she really loves you." Wrong.

Deep inside in the place where we draw conclusions about things, the thinking generally goes something like this: a) Since I am sure that what I feel for you is real love, and b) Since my love prompts me to think, feel, and perform in certain very positive ways toward you, then these ways of relating must be the way real loves works; therefore c) If you have real love for me, then your ways of relating to me should look exactly like the ways I relate to you.

At least three things are true about the foregoing piece of logic. 1) It's what makes women expect that the men who love them (if the love is real) will naturally offer an abundant supply of self-disclosure, emotional expressiveness, collaborative spirit, and intimacy that is constantly shown and reaffirmed through words and feelings. 2) It's what makes men expect that the women who love them (if the love is real) will naturally offer an abundance of goal-oriented, dependable, no-nonsense emotional restraint, a high-performance approach to concrete, pragmatic issues, and trust and respect that is constantly expressed by allowing him freedom and independence. 3) It's what has kept men and women both "speaking" and "hearing" only one love language—their own!

How can the two of you who speak a love language foreign to the other ever be sure each other's love is real? You both must become bilingual of course! For you that will mean you keep on showing love in your native masculine style (to give it up is suicide and an unnecessary compromise) but that you also become a student of your woman's way of loving you in her language. And that you express your love for her in that language as well.

THE BOTTOM LINE

Men at work: Observe the ways your woman relates to you because she loves you. Take note of the kinds of things she likes to tell you, give you, and do for you and how she does those things. These make up her love language. Turn the tables. As often as possible make the deliberate choice to speak, give, and demonstrate your love for her in those ways.

The benefits: It's the closest you can come to hitting the bull's-eye in loving her. It's what most naturally, truly feels like real love to her (that's why she offers it to you) and it doesn't even require that she translate your love language. You'll already be speaking hers.

The costs: The possibility of some mechanical and awkward feelings as you do what *doesn't* come naturally, as well as all the time it may take to learn to do it.

3. ▲ ■ ● ◆ ❭ Expect to Have to Earn Her Trust

To the man who loves me:
It's very hard for me to let you know my feelings all the time
because I'm not always sure what you might do with them.
Actually, I wish I could have a signed guarantee that you'll
handle me right. I don't give my trust quickly or easily, but I
do want to place my trust in you. I just need to watch you
awhile.

—From the Black woman you love

No doubt you've already discovered that women pay very close attention to what is and is not happening in their relationships with their men. She silently, carefully observes you closely, charting the consistency of your words, your disposition, and your behavior toward her. She's constantly assessing both facts and feelings to determine how secure the foundation of your love is.

To your woman, love means giving more and more of herself to you. More physical, spiritual, and emotional access, more of her hopes, her vulnerability, and especially her trust. She won't give these treasures to you if she doesn't trust you. If you want her trust, you have to earn it.

Instinctively, she knows there is much at risk if she deposits too much of her vulnerable self too quickly. She knows she could end up hurt and taken advantage of. Love that doesn't offer her some security is not love at all to her.

It's nothing personal, not arrogant, conceited, requirements she imposes just to keep you busy while she decides what, if anything, she wants to do with you. Measuring your trustworthiness is the necessary and ongoing work she does when she sincerely wants to give herself fully to a loving relationship.

THE BOTTOM LINE

Men at work: You can earn her trust by your commitment to make few promises but by keeping the ones you make, by handling her with sensitivity and respect, and by being consistent, honest, and attracted to who she is now rather than who you'd like her to become. Refuse to show resentment about being so closely watched and evaluated for trustworthiness. Allow it, and behave toward her in ways that stand up to the test.

The benefits: Earning her trust by your consistency and integrity makes her feel secure and frees her to love you and receive love from you unreservedly. The higher her level of trust in you the lower the demand that you work to prove it. Freedom for you. She'll trust you until you give her good reason not to.

The costs: You may feel you are trying to swim upstream against a strong current. You'll discover that it's extremely difficult to undo the painful effects of a previous man's untrustworthiness. You'll have to determine if her trust can be gained, and if all the extra effort to get it is worth it.

4. ◆) Be Responsive to Her Without Taking Responsibility for Her

To the man who loves me:
I am incredibly blessed to have you in my life. I depend on
you being there for me when I'm up against something. My
life can be hard to handle sometimes. I count on you to handle
it with me though, not for me.

—From the Black woman you love

If you think that every burden, problem, need, want, struggle, fear, challenge, or flaw that your woman has is your responsibility to remove from her life, you are going to bite off far more than you can chew. When you take responsibility for the parts of a Black woman's life that only she and God are responsible for, you won't succeed and you'll end up exhausted.

Too often men have bought into the idea that "real manhood" means you must provide the woman you love a pain-free existence, totally unaffected by the harsh realities of her life. When the men who love Black women offer a love that merely buffers, shields, or takes possession of all her pains and problems, to keep her comfortable at all costs, then the love is counterfeit and ultimately an insult to her ability and a hell of a lot of pressure for you.

It can feed your cherished sense of significance and promise great potential earnings in applause when you set yourself up as her safety net. But don't be fooled. The process by which human beings grow wiser, more disciplined, fulfilled, and mature is struggle. Struggle hurts but it strengthens as well. She deserves every bit of the strength that comes from her struggle.

Be responsive to her rather than take responsibility for her. To be responsive means you care and you show it by your concern, your availability, and your support. Responsiveness and responsibility are different in their motives, their intent, and their strategy, even in their vocabulary:

- When she's worried and afraid, responsibility says, "Relax, sweetheart, I'll take over your life from here." Responsiveness says, "I see you're really upset, how can I help you in what you're dealing with?"
- When she's confused and indecisive, responsibility says, "Here, I'll figure it out for you. Just do what I tell you and you won't have to worry about this anymore." Responsiveness says, "I'm your sounding board. If you want to talk, I want to listen. And if you'd like, I'll give you my opinion."
- When she's in conflict with someone, responsibility says, "Let me handle this, I'm going to set them straight for you right now." Responsiveness says, "I know you must really be upset that you and ——— have fallen out. Do you want to talk about it?"
- When she's bored and apathetic, responsibility says, "I promise I will figure out a way to pull you out of the doldrums. Just give me a minute, I'll come up with something, you'll see." Responsiveness says, "It seems like you're itching to do something. I'm available if you decide you want us to do something together."

Everyone who ever learned to live richly, competently, and triumphantly learned to endure the aches and pains that go with taking responsibility for self. Don't rob the woman in your life of her productive struggles. Let her stand on her own two feet—even if her knees buckle from time to time. If you stand with her, in support, you will bless her. Standing for her will surely curse her.

THE BOTTOM LINE

Men at work: Look at your own life where you have seen necessary struggles and have taken responsibility for your life. Haven't you seen that it produces needed growth and maturity and ability for you? Are you helping or hindering that process in the Black woman you love? Make changes accordingly.

The benefits: By becoming responsive to her, instead of taking responsibility for her, you will be able to witness first-hand the leftover traces of "little girl" becoming "phenomenal woman" in the one you love.

The costs: If you stop taking responsibility for her life, you may suffer from a nagging guilt feeling and the self-deflating idea that she doesn't really need you. You could also suddenly be falsely accused by your woman of becoming uncaring, insensitive, and abandoning her in her struggles.

5. ▲◗ *Don't Start What You Won't Continue*

To the man who loves me:
I remember some of those sweet caring things you used to do
all the time just because you loved me. I wonder what it means
about your love for me that you don't do them anymore.

—From the Black woman you love

It may be a well-kept secret but the men who love Black women are more than able to perform the good deeds that demonstrate that love. You've certainly got what it takes to dream up and deliver the right stuff, and if the truth be known you have sometimes shown glimpses of greatness when you thought to do good works as simple as opening the door for her, calling her just to say hi, leaving her a tenderly worded love letter, greeting her with a warm embrace, or remembering her birthday. And you have performed some dramatic fancy gestures as well, like staying bedside with her through a sick spell, surprising her with tickets to visit her mother, or when you moved across the country because of *her* job transfer.

But a word of caution is in order here. Don't start delivering what you won't continue to. Because more important than having started doing a good thing is to continue it with consistency. Over the long haul, when it's no longer cute or clever or convenient to do so. But you keep it up anyway because it is a good work and because it expresses your love, and because you were at some point persuaded that she was well worth it. That kind of treatment, once begun, must continue. To stop (and you are still physically able to continue) sends the message that you no longer find her worth the work. Even if the Black woman you love has a powerful sense of self-worth, believing that her worth to you has diminished feels more painful and lonely than you might ever know. It would have been far less painful for her if you had never even started to offer those endearing good deeds than to have started them and stopped.

THE BOTTOM LINE

Men at work: Think through the little extras—those kind gestures you offer your woman—*before* you start doing them. Require of yourself an honest answer to the question: "Am I willing to keep doing this for her, forever?" If you know you're only willing for a "one-shot deal" and not a long-term one, you should a) Tell her how long she may expect it, or b) Avoid that gesture from the jump.

The benefits: Maintaining consistency in performing both the small- and the grand-scale acts that honor your mate makes your love visible and concrete to her. Your consistency, discipline, and responsiveness here add to the character and quality of your masculinity.

The costs: Like it or not, once you've started it, your behavior indicates an unspoken but binding commitment to continue it. Being bound to anything—even an unspoken relational contract like this—can be burdensome over time. But this kind of commitment can't be harmlessly withdrawn by merely announcing, "Sorry, I just don't feel like doing that anymore."

6. ▲ ■ Accept Her for Who She Is Now (Not Who You Think You Can Make Her Into)

To the man who loves me:
I get the impression that there really is no such thing as
being enough, in your eyes. Just when I start to believe you
are content with me as I am, you raise the requirements
again.

—From the Black woman you love

Loving your woman's potential more than you love who she is now insults her. Black women despise any attempt to shape, mold, or re-create them according to your idea of who and how they should be. Aside from the fact that you have no right to do it, she's most disturbed that how she already is—her looks, thoughts, and the many unique facets of her personality, how she lives her life and shows her love—doesn't rate high enough on your scale. In relationships, some of her deepest hurts revolve around the feeling that your love, devotion, and appreciation for her have to be paid for by camouflaging, or endlessly "refining" what makes her, her. It's like hearing the painful "You are just not enough for me as you are" repeated over and over again. No matter how high her self-esteem is, that's a message that can wilt her spirit; for many Black women it has made dealing with us too hurtful to want to attempt again.

Of course, none of this means you should feel guilty for having observed some things about her that could stand improvement or that you'd like to see changed to suit your personal tastes and preferences. For you to have an opinion is no crime. For you to take her as your mate, then subtly require her to fit your opinion before she can earn your best love, commitment, and affection *is* a crime. That's loving her potential and possibilities more than the person she is. You don't have to establish a relationship with her if the way she is is not acceptable to you, but if you take her, take her because you can love her sincerely and lavishly as she is today. Not because of who she might or might not become tomorrow.

She desires the kind of respect and acceptance that recognizes that change in another human being is something you may lovingly influence, but cannot produce. Not even with all the punishing, withholding, critiquing, coaching, threatening, and manipulating in the world. People change and improve when *they* hunger for it and work toward it, not when you or anyone else has that hunger for them. The Black woman in your life thrives on the assurance that though she's not finished growing, developing, and polishing who she is, she can rest in the assurance that you enthusiastically accept and embrace the woman she is right now.

THE BOTTOM LINE

Men at work: Ask and answer this crucial question: "Can I, will I love and share my best with this woman if in all our tomorrows she stays exactly the way she is today?" If the answer is no, decide what can *you* change in yourself, in order for you to be more fully committed to who she is now. Cease any efforts, both subtle and overt, to re-create her in any way or to penalize her for not becoming your ideal.

The benefits: One of the mysterious paradoxes of real life is that women are most willing to "become" when they feel accepted as they come.

The costs: Living with the possibility that she won't ever become exactly what you had hoped for, or that the process will take too long. You may be tempted to try heavy-handed tactics to "guarantee" she grows into your ideals. That will only make it worse.

7. ▲ ■ ● ◆) *Study Other Men*

To the man who loves me:
Many times I've seen in you some of the best qualities of my father, my brothers, and some of my closest men friends. I've wondered how this could be all wrapped up in one unique individual. It's a fascinating thing to me that you have taken the best qualities of others and made them your own.

—From the Black woman you love

Loving a woman the way she needs to be loved without compromising yourself requires huge amounts of wisdom, stamina, and experience. There is no step-by-step formula, college course, or genetic marker that can make anyone automatically skilled at it. Those who have achieved success got it by on-the-job training. No matter how much you have going for yourself and how well you're already doing at loving a Black woman, you could waste your most valuable resource if you don't study other men who love Black women well. Watch them closely and you'll learn valuable, practical lessons that can only enrich and encourage you as you strive to give and get the most satisfying love.

In everything in which you've achieved success, somebody else's good example, wise input, and generous encouragement helped you to make it so.

Don't be fooled into identifying men who love Black women well, based solely on how many women occupy their lives. As it relates to love, quantity and quality are two altogether different matters. "Quality men" are the ones who are not hung up on proving how much man they are. Not to their women, not to other men, and not to themselves. Quality men have no problem being seen serving their women with humility or protecting them with ferocity or committing to their integrity. They don't just like women for what they can get from them. Rather, they are fascinated by them and truly love them. They have learned how to relate to them in ways that honor women and make them feel adored, cherished, and secure. Take note of them. Listen and follow their example. The quality of your own skill and sensitivity will be enhanced.

Get back some of your time that is too often spent listening to the advice of men who are only bragging, lying, or female bashing. The proof is in the pudding. Where you see no woman in their life or where you see a frustrated, unhappy one, that man should be no mentor for you. Instead, look around for the man who's standing beside a Black woman who is positively glowing with that air of joy and satisfaction, and the man whose face lights up when the woman he loves enters the room. And the one who offers himself and his treasures to her generously, with no hint of shame or selfishness.

If you know one like him, study him. Don't get hung up on how old or young or plain or fancy he may be. Learn from him. If you are one yourself, look around. Some man, or several, could be watching you. Teach them right. Black women everywhere will be extremely grateful.

THE BOTTOM LINE

Men at work: Dare to talk seriously with other men about women and love. Approach the subject with the same kind of interest you show your career, sports, politics, or money. Enlist a qualified "relationship mentor"—an older, experienced "woman-friendly" brother with whom you commit to share the details of your romantic life, and from whom you are willing to accept wise counsel. Be open and honest when you share with him. Then dare to really listen and apply the best of your mentor's advice.

The benefits: The primary benefit is that like in every other area of endeavor your own game will get better when you have the model of a "master" to observe. The secondary benefit is that the woman you love will reap the rewards of the heightened levels of skill and sensitivity you'll get by refusing to be limited to just what you know about loving a Black woman. Other men's relationship success stories can help you become even more of a success story yourself.

The costs: The time and humility it takes to study other men is like the time it takes to study a textbook. To say nothing of the fact that attempting to learn from others makes some men feel as if they're admitting that their own skill level is inferior.

8. ▲ ● ◗
Don't Require That Your Every Move Be Applauded

To the man who loves me:
Maybe it's not fair, but I wish appreciation and respect for
you and the good things you do could be enough. I get the
impression that you really want me to make a big deal out
of every single good thing you do. Could that be true? Every
single thing?

—From the Black woman you love

Whatever you may try to accomplish in any area of your life, you are likely to keep working at it more enthusiastically and ultimately more successfully if you get some acknowledgment, recognition, and applause along the way. It's just as true as you work to follow the advice in this book and show the Black woman in your life the kind of love she most needs. When she notices and commends your efforts, it makes keeping up the good work much easier and more appealing because it's got some personal reward for you.

The real challenge, though, is continuing to do what's right because it's right—even if your woman, or everyone else, fails to applaud you for doing it. When you require that your every positive act be given a standing ovation, or at least some honorable mention, you'll become dependent on her actions to motivate yours. You've got far too much self-sufficiency, tenacity, and initiative inside you to need ego strokes in order to perform. *Want* them? Always. *Need* them? Never!

In a perfect world the woman you love would always be the first one to look you in your eyes and declare with sincerity, "You did that so well" or "I appreciate the respectful way you treat me" or "You keep proving over and over to me that you are an incredible man." In the real world she'll sometimes be too distracted, self-involved, or just plain too tired to applaud you. In fact, she may have more to say about the few things you did poorly than the many things you did well. But when you're motivated from within you, your excellence carries its own rewards.

Get used to applauding and affirming yourself. If you are a good man you didn't become one just because a woman was thrilled by your being one.

THE BOTTOM LINE

Men at work: Let her applause become a fringe benefit, not the fuel you need to live your life, and show your love to the best of your ability according to the highest possible standards. Continue under your own steam if need be.

The benefits: Though the Black woman in your life may love to applaud you and your positive efforts, if she believes you can't or won't function without it, she'll get sick of that real fast. When you are perfectly willing and able to do it for yourself, your woman respects and admires your self-motivated strength—which will be highly esteemed in her eyes and, in one way or another, thunderously applauded by her.

The costs: You may suffer some lonely, underappreciated, and resentful feelings if you have to withdraw, cold turkey, from your addiction to applause.

9. ▲ Tell Her Exactly What Your Commitment Means

To the man who loves me:
I've known you long enough to see. You're a man who doesn't
waste words. I usually don't have to guess where you stand.
Except when it comes to where you stand about us. I'm really
getting confused because I hear you say a lot of words, but
I'm still not sure exactly what you are offering me.

—From the Black woman you love

Ask a thousand Black women what is the most important desire they have of the men in their lives and you're likely to hear repeated a thousand times the word "commitment." Your woman, or the one on her way, wants to know what the two of you are to each other and what that does or does not mean about your future together. She knows she can only speak for herself and her perceptions and desires, and that she can in no way define or demand what your commitment level must be. But you can be sure she's determined to know the truth about the matter and she can only get that from you.

In every phase of your relationship with her, it will be crucial that you clarify what your commitment level is and is not. As much as you may resist the idea of being pinned down to a specific answer, which of course closes off some of the options that being vague allows you, she needs to know.

If she doesn't know she's left to assume. And if she assumes, she's likely to be wrong—over- or underestimating—the seriousness of your commitment to her. If she's wrong, her expectations of you and her efforts in the relationship will be out of sync with the truth. That's a surefire setup for tragic misunderstandings, bitter conflicts, and yet another severed relationship. But even bigger than that, there's then more mistrust, more hostility, and more alienation between Black women and their men. Enough already.

Be thorough and above all be honest. If your present commitment level is such that you're going out with her, and others too, say so. If you're going for broke, offering a serious and exclusive relationship, declare it. If it's only a close friend-ship and running-partner commitment that you have in mind, come clean and tell her that. If your feelings for her run deep, but marriage is definitely not on your mind, again, say so. Then say and do only that which is consistent with your stat-ed level of commitment and nothing else. Don't confuse things by declaring one commitment level and relating to her in a manner that is only appropriate to another. She will feel deceived and taken advantage of. Mismatched or unclear commitment between you and the woman in your life is among the most potentially hazardous areas of a relationship. Best not to play charades with her emotions, waiting until she demands that you make your intentions known. With little to no commitment clarity from you, women are liable to press you for an answer far too early in the game—or way too late.

THE BOTTOM LINE

Men at work: In spite of the fears of disappointing or los-ing her, tell her the truth, the whole truth, and nothing but the truth about what you're offering her, then govern yourself accordingly. The depth of your expressions of intimacy and degree of exclusivity should match the level of commitment you have made to her and the relationship.

The benefits: Maximum clarity means minimal confusion. There is so much more potential for a loving, mutually satisfy-ing relationship when you are both on the same page about your level of commitment to each other. It will keep your woman from giving over too much to you or holding back from you when she is unsure about where you stand.

The costs: Having to think through your commitment level and be pinned down to a precise declaration and demonstration of it. Also, the possibility that what you are offering is something more or less or different from what she has in mind for you. That way, one of you could end up with hurt feelings.

10. ◆❭ *Listen to Her Problems Without Rushing to Solve Them*

To the man who loves me:
No matter how frustrated I may sound when I share my troubles with you, don't be fooled into thinking I'm asking you to make them all go away. I just want you to feel what I'm feeling and understand what I'm going through. I want to know that it is somehow as important to you as it is to me. It's the emotional equivalent of holding my hand.

—From the Black woman you love

When the woman you love flings open the door and invites you into the place where she deals with her problems, questions, and frustrations, you may be surprised to know that she isn't requiring or even requesting that you solve them all. Unless she thinks you are the problem—and she'll certainly let you know that—she's sharing her private struggles and concerns with you because talking it out with someone who cares for her is what women do. It's a crucial step in her way of solving her own problems.

Men's goal-oriented performance momentum is directed toward conquering the problems, not feeling them. Women first need to experience their problems on an emotional level, in effect "trying them on," in order to know how weighty and cumbersome they are. Women tend to feel their problems before they fix them. Talking helps them do that vital feeling work. Your role in all of this is to be her listening ear, allowing her to get at her feelings through her words.

Let her talk. Better yet, encourage her to. As you do, stifle your advice-giving, problem-solving tendency and listen to her with your whole mind and body focused on hearing her out, not rushing to help her out. Offer advice only upon request. Just listen as she talks in circles and stay strapped in next to her on the emotional roller-coaster ride.

Your woman is probably quite able to come up with solutions on her own (remember she had to before you came along), what she can't get alone is the powerfully affirming gift of your nonjudgmental attitude and your listening ears. Work to become her sounding board, not just her advice-dispensing life-management consultant.

THE BOTTOM LINE

Men at work: Practice active listening. Use attentive body language, clarifying questions, facial expressions, and other "I'm listening" signals that make it clear to her that serving her is more important to you than the significance boost you get from solving her problems.

The benefits: You get to put away your hard hat and fix-it equipment and relax. You are free to ignore your compulsion to repair her problems for her. She gets to have your intimate companionship as she processes her situation, in her own way.

The costs: It may be extremely difficult when she needs you to listen to her about problem feelings that have to do with you. You may be tempted to explain or defend yourself or correct what seem to you inaccurate or emotionally overwrought criticisms. Though it may not at first seem so, you'll actually get to the resolution of these matters quicker, more cleanly, and more effectively if you allow her to talk it all out first.

11. ■ ● *Refer to All Black Women with Respect*

To the man who loves me:
I wonder if you even notice it anymore, but there's some really foul stuff that comes out of your mouth when you're talking about women. It offends me. I've always shrugged it off because you never talk about me that way. Finally I realized what I don't think you have: I'm one of them that you're talking about. I'm a woman too.

—From the Black woman you love

Black women are always listening. The one you love is definitely paying attention to your choice of words, the labels you use, and the jokes you tell. She's measuring how much respect you have for her as a woman by how much you show for all women. She knows intuitively that if you are content to use words like "bitches," "broads," "hoes," and all their derogatory synonyms to refer to any female, then you're likely to use them or at least think them in reference to her as well. Above all she knows that if you'll refer to women in a nasty, low-down way, you're liable to treat them low-down and nasty too.

The clearest indications of how little a man values a woman is by how willing he is to:

- Make frequent demeaning and stereotypical references to women and Black women in particular.
- Use vulgarities to describe women that keys in on their physical or sexual attributes and ignores or denigrates their mental, emotional, and spiritual ones.
- Use or allow language that is mostly based on a repertoire of jokes, stories, and sayings at the expense of Black women.
- Settle arguments with her by launching a barrage of cruel put-downs and verbal jabs that he applies uniquely to women but never to men.

Words have awesome power to heal, to elevate, and to affirm. They also have the power to debase, violate, or to shape horribly destructive images. Once spoken they can't ever truly be taken back. What comes out of your mouth reveals the degree of respect and appreciation for your woman that's inside your heart.

Though she may laugh it off, ignore it, or refer to women herself in those vile terms, if you're serious about loving a Black woman according to what they most need and desire most from men, it's important that you develop and employ a vocabulary that refers to women with honor and the utmost respect.

Every verbal reference you make to your woman or any woman will either contribute to more negative, demeaning treatment of Black women or help do away with it.

THE BOTTOM LINE

Men at work: Evaluate your vocabulary, your attitude, and especially the labels and humor you use in reference to Black women. Do away with anything you wouldn't want anybody to use in reference to your mother.

The benefits: Black women have suffered terribly from the damaging and harmful images perpetuated about them through verbal disrespect. When you use only affirming and elevating speech, you send a message to her that she is valued and treasured and worthy of your demonstrated respect and that you can be trusted to give it.

The costs: The discipline and effort it takes to change whatever bad habits you may have developed in this area.

12. Take the Blame (But Only When It's Yours)

To the man who loves me:
What do you think will happen if you take the blame? When it's mine, I'll take it. When it's yours, I just want you to own up to it. It's a bold man who'll do that on his own.

—From the Black woman you love

One of life's biggest time-wasters and frustration-makers is the endless back and forth between you and the Black woman you love over who's to blame for that thing that happened that both of you wish hadn't happened. Whatever it was—an ill-informed accusation, a broken promise, an insensitive response, a bad attitude, or a bounced check—it's out there now for both of you to regret. Since it *did* happen and nothing can change that fact, you'd both prefer to be the victim rather than the perpetrator. Accepting blame can be a terrible assault on your pride, because it means you were wrong. Nobody likes to be wrong.

But when it's *your* imperfection that has shown through and caused some fallout between the two of you, the best thing you can do is take the blame. Own it, repent it, and get over it. Whether it's a little annoyance or a huge disaster, before you get around to any cleanup efforts or to looking for someone else's doorstep at which to lay it—take the blame.

Your strength of character and your boldness to look truth in the eye without being intimidated by it are highly appealing attributes to the woman in your life. When you take the blame that's rightfully yours, without copping a plea, glossing it over, or dancing around it, she sees the power of integrity. It's the kind of power that signals greatness. Women appreciate your goodness, but they absolutely marvel at your greatness, and the privilege of being intimately linked with the man who possesses it. I caution you, however, not to take blame that's not yours to take. When, out of frustration, resignation, guilt, or a desire to placate, silence, or patronize her, you claim guilt where you're really innocent, you are keeping the peace, but by forfeiting the truth. You can't afford to do that.

There is no nobility in taking the blame for what was not within your control or due to your actions. Nothing about being the man who loves her requires you to shift blame that should be on her plate to yours. Start that habit and you'll be digging a deep hole that will swallow you both. Though she may allow you to do it and bask in the vindicating warmth, she'll figure out what you are up to—a quick, hassle-free way to become her hero. Eventually that will erode her respect for you—*and* for your sincerity. Which can do some serious damage to your self-respect as well.

THE BOTTOM LINE

Men at work: When you did it, plainly admit it: "It was my fault, I screwed up . . . I will correct the matter by . . ." (Note: Taking the blame means accepting responsibility, but not punishment, condemnation, or ridicule from her or from yourself.)

The benefits: When you take the blame that's yours and none that isn't, you short-circuit the possibility that she will ever put you up on a pedestal as a perfect, failure-free specimen. If you don't, you'll never be able to afford for your failures to be seen, or you'll come crashing down from that lofty pedestal.

The costs: Claiming responsibility for your wrong can stir up moderate to intense feelings of guilt and failure—what men most hate to feel.

13. ♦ *Never Compare Her*

To the man who loves me:
Have you noticed how often you mention that I'm a lot like
somebody else you know when you are paying me a compli-
ment or when getting on my case about something? Believe me,
I've noticed.

—From the Black woman you love

The woman you love or one day will love wants to experience the joy of knowing that your devotion, admiration, and
affection is based on the unique person she is and the her
and her alone mix of appealing attributes and fascinating
qualities she possesses. Your woman doesn't want to even
think that she stands in anyone else's shadow or that she is
desirable to you because she somehow reminds you of somebody else. Even if she does, you need to keep that bit of
information to yourself. Resist comparing her to any woman
you've ever known at any time.

Though you may mean it as the ultimate compliment
when you point out to the Black woman in your life that she
is "just like . . ." or "on the same order as . . ." or "could be
twins with . . ." any other female living or dead, famous or
infamous, from your mother to Mother Teresa—she is not
likely to be impressed. Rather, what she longs to hear from
you are the wonderful things you've discovered in her that
you have not discovered in anyone else. She yearns to know
that she has, simply by being herself, filled a unique role and
has a unique function in your life. She wants to know that to
you, she is in a class all by herself, not one that's full to overflowing with images of every woman you have ever known.

Comparisons are so handy because they add color and clarity to your conversation, allowing you to make your point concisely and vividly: "My previous girlfriend/wife/lover didn't do it/say it/see it like that . . ." or "You look just like . . ." or (the worst of them) "I wish you were more like . . ." But loving her with skill and sensitivity requires that you work harder to make your point another way.

Black women already find themselves bedeviled by the tendency to compare themselves to too many narrow and preconceived images of feminine beauty, temperament, and conduct—from the super-models of the fashion magazines to the "nasty girls" of music videos to the heroines of fiction and film to the demure, homespun kind of women your grand-mother described in detail, telling you not to stop till you get one like her.

Comparisons make it seem as though she's only as good as Ms. So-and-So or as no good as Ms. Such-and-Such. She treasures her individuality, and if you're not careful she's likely to hear your comparisons as a demand for her to be more like Ms. What's-Her-Name or less like Ms. Whatchamacallit. Black women place a high value on the freedom to be like themselves and nobody else.

Your woman relishes the assurance that on her own terms she is marvelously acceptable to you.

THE BOTTOM LINE

Men at work: Make a mental note to red-flag yourself whenever you use the phrase "just like" in reference to your mate. Back up and make your point to her some other way, comparison-free.

The benefits: The Black woman you *love* will benefit hugely from the assurance that she holds a singular place of honor and esteem in your eyes and not because she's better, worse, or just like anyone else.

The costs: Next to none. Other than losing out on the usefulness of comparisons when you want to communicate something positive about her. Lose the comparisons anyway.

14. ▲ ■ ● ◆ ◗ *Show Her Off*

To the man who loves me:
What really matters to me is not that other people are impressed with me, but that you are. Funny thing is though, when you parade me around and brag all over the place about me, that's how I find out how impressed you are with me.

—From the Black woman you love

A surefire way to make the Black woman you love feel absolutely adored and incredibly secure in your delight in her is to go out of your way to show her off. When your public behavior demonstrates just how proud you are to have her on your arm and in your life, you freshly reaffirm the high value you place on her. Your high estimation of her, how stunning she looks, how brilliant her mind is, how poised, charming, tenacious, talented, and unique she is, means more to her than anyone else's. Women thrive on knowing beyond a shadow of a doubt that you find their inner and outer assets captivating. You confirm it when you enthusiastically present to the "watching world" the woman who makes you proud.

It's boasting to others pure and simple that I'm talking

about. It's your unapologetic habit of bragging about your woman, whose attributes are worthy of your pointing out, declaring aloud, and making a fuss over—and you don't care who knows it. It's pure gold to her and her self-image and confidence in your love for her.

Showing her off is not for the sake of educating others about who you have and what she has going for herself. It's more about taking advantage of the opportunity you have to esteem her as you remind her that she is the woman who, with all her virtues, has stood out among women, and that you are honored that she stands beside you and shares her life with you.

THE BOTTOM LINE

Men at work: Take advantage of every possible opportunity you have to boast publicly about the things that most impress you about your mate. From time to time, go with her, sit in the back and support her in the settings where she performs impressively in her world of activities. Take care to introduce her to others with positive remarks.

The benefits: When you show her off, you dramatically enhance her self-image and her appreciation for your expressive, adoring kind of love. You will do much to ease the aches of self-doubt, any tendency she may have to struggle with feelings of unworthiness.

The costs: Expending the effort to discover and focus on the qualities you want to show off about her when they seem overshadowed by things you don't like about her. The repetition and the pressure to keep coming up with more. And the possibility that her self-image is so poor she'll be uncomfortable with you bragging about her.

15. ■ ● ◆ Give Her the Space to Disappoint You

To the man who loves me:
I can live with the fact that we'll let each other down some-
times. The best I have to offer you is imperfection—but with
my effort toward achieving perfection. I need this to be a
place where letting someone down is not life-threatening.

—From the Black woman you love

Make no mistake, in some ways, great and small, she will definitely blow it and you will hate it. She'll fail to do something she said she'd do (or she'll fail to do it right). She'll forget, ignore, misunderstand, lose it, leave it, or loan it out, and as far as you are concerned it will screw things up big-time. In spite of how much her imperfect performance ticks you off, an advanced-level skill in loving a Black woman is to give her the space to fail and to disappoint you without having to endure your criticism or punishment.

I'm not asking you to pretend you downright enjoyed her mess-up, and you'd love for her to do it all over again. But I am challenging you to pump up your patience and give some grace to the one you say you love. More than likely she'll be tremendously blessed to receive just the degree of patience and grace that you freely give yourself and the friends, co-workers, clients, and virtual strangers who daily mess up a little piece of your world. How is it that they so often get a gracious "That's okay, no big thing . . ." from you, and your woman too often gets a contempt-filled *"What in the world were you thinking about?"*

Grace is love on the highest order, because it's love granted to someone which isn't based on their performance. It's love they can count on from you, even when they admittedly haven't earned it.

Grace:
- Doesn't blindly ignore the failures of others, it just refuses to condemn them for it.
- Doesn't always keep meticulous mental records of the quality and quantity of a lover's every failure.
- Doesn't use "word-whippings" or nonverbal vengeance techniques to scold or demean.
- Doesn't penalize a partner by emotional or physical withdrawal.
- Doesn't lie, sending the message that the mess-up didn't matter, only to later quietly punish the offender as if it really did matter.
- Doesn't pretend your mate's failures are so uniquely different from your own.

Letting you down is one of a woman's greatest personal letdowns. They fervently seek after a harmonious and intimate bond of acceptance and affection with you. Unfortunately, your harsh rebukes or stinging silences can make her feel as if that all-important bond is severed.

THE BOTTOM LINE

Men at work: When she fails and disappoints you, commit to offering her no less than the kind of compassionate response you give yourself or to others who mean far less to you than she does. Watch your mouth, and your mood, in the aftermath of her mistakes.

The benefits: To grant her this kind of patience, understanding, and sensitivity when she blows it will show you to be a man of tremendous compassion. To show grace and compassion to her requires an amazing amount of inner strength and self-assurance. Your compassion for her ignites her passion for you. Also, the more grace you give, the more you're likely to receive when *you* screw up.

The costs: To show grace and restraint will cost you that gratifying feeling of getting to play the role of outraged victim. Often men secretly treasure that feeling because it supports an "I'm right, you're wrong" attitude, which makes ego-boosting activities like indicting, instructing, and punishing her feel completely justified.

16. ▲ ■ ● ◆ ◗
Invest in the Things That Nourish Her

To the man who loves me:
Honestly, there's something I need to know. Do I mean
enough to you that you'll support the things in my life that
give me joy?

—From the Black woman you love

The greater part of building a wonderful relationship has to do with the two of you constantly making every kind of meaningful investment in each other's lives. Love is at its best when it's not all about "I'll get mine, you get yours." Instead it's the conscious, deliberate, and consistent search for ways that your efforts and contributions can enrich the life of the woman you love—and she's busy trying to do the same thing for you. Real love is evidenced by the quantity and quality of things you support in your woman's life and provide for her life to nourish her mind, body, and soul.

Nourishing your woman's life is not a vague abstract concept. It is as practical and specific as the things one must do to nourish any living thing to cause it to thrive and flourish, not merely exist. Feeding, watering, securing, examining, and making provisions for it cause everything in creation to grow, including the Black woman you love.

You nourish her:

- When you invest in the things that enrich her life.
- When you encourage and support her efforts to advance her education, career, or her physical, spiritual, or mental well-being.
- When you accept and make accommodations for the time she needs for adequate solitude, reflection, or revitalization even though it may temporarily take her away from you.
- When you offer her some of the things she doesn't absolutely need but that bring her tremendous joy, like flowers, massages, "the works" at the beauty salon, or a hot bath you've readied for her.
- When you take her most cherished aspirations seriously and rally your own resources to help her achieve them.
- When you insist she go "off duty" and "waste" some time and money on herself.

When you nourish her life in these ways it shows that you place a high value on something simply because the woman you love does. It says to her, "I treasure the things that are special to you because they are special to you." What you are really saying is, "I treasure you."

THE BOTTOM LINE

Men at work: Stay alert to discover what things put a spark of delight in your woman's eyes. Then do everything in your power to provide its consistent presence in her life. Feel free to ask her what's on the list of the most treasured and soul-nourishing things in her private world and how you can help make them happen; listen, then act immediately.

The benefits: She will feel positively adored by you. She'll flourish in the assurance that you care enough about what she cares about to invest in the things that switch on her "pleased, satisfied, and content" button. It's also a beneficial way for you to uphold the value of her paying attention to enriching her own life, rather than only how she can enrich everybody else's.

The costs: Investing heavily in the things that nourish her provides no guarantee that you'll get as much as you give. If you see this as a "contract" rather than a "contribution" with no strings attached, you could easily fall into the trap of trying to keep score of whose turn it is to nourish whom.

17. ■● *Lighten Up*

To the man who loves me:
You look so responsible, determined, and cool, very cool, all
the time. I have sometimes wondered why you have such a
stern, serious personality. I don't know why, but I think there
might also be a laughing, fun-loving boy inside you. At least
I hope there is because I really want to know him.

—From the Black woman you love

If you are the kind of man who always takes care of business, and is a plan-maker and problem-solver, who believes that loving her right is serious business with no room for clowning, you are likely to have impressed the woman you love, yourself, and everybody else. Deep thinkers with their serious-minded approach to life and love are looked up to by everybody. But you are also likely to have driven yourself, your woman, and everybody else crazy with your stiff no-nonsense personality. You might be surprised to know that the Black woman you love hopes that one day you'll relax, lighten up, and laugh a little.

Serious soldiers like you are determined not to be found guilty of finger-popping and good-timing their way through life. They are always stiffly at attention because to stand at ease for even a moment will look foolish and because they fear that something might fall apart if they do. They believe a sense of humor is all right for some brothers, but even better is a cool, unflappable, and thoroughly controlled demeanor. To look and act in the other way could be perceived as being goofy and, worse yet, weak.

But when your actions and especially your attitude display an "all work and no play" mind-set, you have erased out, or safely locked away, one huge part of who you are—your humor. Your sense of humor is your God-given ability to engage responsibly in life and laugh at it, and yourself, at the same time.

As much as your woman may respect your sober-mindedness she would probably love to fall out on the floor and laugh with you, or even at you. Your relationship is not about being "on it" and keeping everything in check twenty-four hours a day. Often it is silly fun and games, and for the two of you to share in that part together adds another dimension to the intimacy of your relationship. You needn't compete with Eddie Murphy, Martin Lawrence, or Bill Cosby. It's not your job to make her laugh. But it is your chance to let the Black woman you love have access to the part of you where pure, spontaneous, unmonitored humor takes over and where you get to smile, laugh hysterically, or even lose it. That'll only happen if, for a moment, you drop your heavy load, lighten up, and let her in.

THE BOTTOM LINE

Men at work: Challenge yourself to lighten your demeanor and laugh more. Simply refuse to hold in, cover up, or flee from your humor or laughter. While you're at it, cease your subtle efforts to silence her humor. Make time for fun with her that doesn't accomplish anything on your to-do list or run the risk of making you feel or look foolish.

The benefits: If you work on lightening up, both of you will gain a new freedom in your relationship with fewer inhibitions and more genuine fun. You'll have another part of you for her to connect with, to appreciate, and to admire.

The costs: The awkwardness and risk of letting down your cool, humorless persona. Your insides insist that doing so will make you vulnerable to criticism and ridicule and the embarrassment they bring.

18. ▲ *Get Serious*

To the man who loves me:
When there is something kind of crazy and laughable going on in my life I usually can't wait to share that with you. With your sense of humor I always know you're going to say something that will make me die laughing. I wish it weren't so, but when it's something kind of serious going on, something that can't be played with, it usually doesn't even occur to me to share that with you.

—From the Black woman you love

The Black woman in your life is counting on you for so much. Your approach to life and every element of it has a great deal of meaning to her. It's what she measures to determine how much strength and character you have stored up on the inside and how wise or unwise it is for her to open her life to you. Though she may admire, and even envy, your footloose, fun-loving style, if that's all you've got, she'll only see you as a nice playmate, not a mature partner she can count on. You'll make her laugh, and she'll have a ball, but when it comes down to the weightier matters of life she'll want you to get serious and get going.

There's absolutely nothing wrong with you not trying to

rule the world or not approaching everything as if it were a life-or-death matter. Your outrageous sense of humor and your delight in the simple pleasures of life are very attractive qualities that catch her eye and win her heart. But if they are not balanced by your willingness to get serious, make tough decisions, and handle the hard stuff that makes life and love work, then giving you the respect that's due a strong, responsible man will be difficult for her. She'll have, at best, the fleeting affection she'd give to a clown at the circus or an old teddy bear on her shelf.

You can stand to add to your serious side if:

- Your spending on toys, gadgets, and good times keeps you behind on your financial obligations or from ever building up any wealth.
- You can't help trying to turn heavy conversations with your woman into jokes that take you off the subject.
- At the end of the day you have efficiently accomplished the tasks you do enjoy and few if any of those you don't.
- You nonchalantly avoid definitive decision-making, constantly declaring "I'm going to . . ." and seldom getting around to it.
- You sail from one relationship to another when your mate's expectations and emotions start getting serious.

THE BOTTOM LINE

Men at work: Identify the few or many ways you use humor and fun to avoid, delay, or deny the serious side of your life and your relationships. Don't wait until it feels right; make serious changes now that will bring balance.

The benefits: Her respect and your self-respect will increase because you prove to yourself that you're a man of substance and seriousness who balances your appealing humor and calm demeanor. She can count on you and admire and enjoy both sides of your personality.

The costs: Decision-making. Confrontation of hard issues and speaking seriously from the depths of your heart, not just your humor, are necessary and beneficial but they are seldom fun.

19. ▲ ■ ◆ *Say "I Don't Know" When You Don't*

To the man who loves me:
One of the first things that attracted me to you was your
intelligence. You are a very wise man. But I'm smart enough
to know that you couldn't possibly know everything about
everything. I hate it when a man tries to act as if he does.

—From the Black woman you love

From time to time the Black woman in your life will ask questions. Probably lots of them. They may be simple yes-or-no ones, probing "how do you really feel about this" ones, or deep intellectual "what's your point of view" ones, and perhaps most frequently, advice-seeking "what do you think I ought to do about . . ." ones. Whatever she may ask, when you have an honest answer, give it—when you don't, admit it: "I don't know."

They may seem like the three hardest-to-say words in the English language. Even though the phrase may feel like a two-ton boulder wedged in your throat—open your mouth and let it out!

Let's face it, there really is something in men that tempts us to believe that if women could come up with the questions we should know the answers—and we think they think we should know it too. We'd actually prefer that our women didn't ask, in the first place, questions that we don't have ready answers to. It really can throw us off when they do. That's why you've probably heard this little scenario, or something like it, over and over:

She says: "Baby, I was wondering, do you think I should_____or not, because you know_____, and I have to___, so that_____."

He says: (here is where "I don't know" should have been inserted. Instead she hears): "Why are you asking me? I don't see why you can't figure some things out by yourself!"

She says (hurt and offended): "All I did was ask you a simple question. You could have just said yes or no!"

"I don't know" can be a very honest and perfectly legitimate response. The truth that can set you free is that you don't have to have all the answers—you don't even have to find out all the answers—and contrary to how you may feel, she's probably not requiring that you do, either.

Fact is, often women are actually trying to demonstrate respect for their men by seeking and valuing your opinions and input. It's yet another way that they try to point out your power and ability—for your sake and for their own, because they feel even more secure when reminded that they are linked up to someone powerful.

Aside from information-seeking, women love to ask questions of the men in their lives because it reinforces for them the idea that we are working on life together—collaboration. Your input is another reassurance that her "us thing" with you is solid and secure.

So when you get a sulky attitude, promise to get an answer, then don't, or just plain ignore her, you break a very meaningful link between the two of you and chip away at one of her key security and intimacy bricks.

For the record, "I don't know" should never be used as an "escape clause," or a handy verbal device to keep from doing some emotional or mental work that you don't feel like doing. If what she's inquiring about is something about you that she can only find out from you and it really is something important for the woman you love to have access to, "I don't know" won't do. Promise her an honest answer, then deliver one.

THE BOTTOM LINE

Men at work: The next time "I don't know" is your honest response to her question, add a "but . . ." statement to it that suggests that although you have no insights, opinions, or advice at the moment, the Black woman you love and her issue matter to you. For example: "I don't know, but that *is* an important question . . ." or "I don't know, but please let me know what you end up deciding about that" or "I don't know, but ask me again tomorrow."

The benefits: She'll admire and deeply appreciate your humility, your honesty, and your concern—she's not likely to forget any of them very easily or quickly. Then she'll move on to get the answers she needs. Additionally, admitting you don't know, when you don't, will relieve you of the self-imposed pressure of "needing" to be the All-Wise, All-Seeing, All-Knowing One, freeing you to just be a good man who knows some of the answers but not all of them.

The costs: When men are sure they have the answers, they feel "more man." When, for whatever the reason, you don't have them, you may feel a little or a lot "less man."

20. ▲ ■ ● ◆ ◗
Tell Her What You Assume She Already Knows

To the man who loves me:
Yes, I am quite intuitive, and yes, I can figure out some
things very well without any explanations. I may know a lot,
but when it comes to you and us, I don't want to just think I
know, I want to be sure I do.

—From the Black woman you love

Don't assume she knows anything about your love for her unless you tell her. Though it may seem to you that your actions have made it loud and clear and that she has somehow figured out your feelings for her by silent observation, she needs the words. She needs you to plainly and repeatedly tell her what you think she should already know. For the Black woman in your life, your skillful use of nouns, verbs, and adjectives, sentences, and paragraphs ensures her more clarity and accuracy in knowing exactly where she stands in your desire, your devotion, and your commitment. Your nonverbal cues—what you do and what you don't ever do—say and are very significant indications of your love. But to your woman, the spoken word wins hands down, every time, because she can at best only make assumptions as to the meaning behind your actions or behaviors. She can't be totally sure of things unless you speak up and spell it out:

- Don't assume that she knows you are thoroughly impressed with her talents and abilities, tell her.
- Don't assume that she already knows you admire her courage and determination, tell her.
- Don't assume that she already knows you love her deeply and you'd hate to do without her, tell her.
- Don't assume that she already knows you are not ready for an exclusive relationship and are still seeing other women, tell her.

For women, an intimate and secure relationship with balance, harmony, and mutual appreciation is the goal. She can be sure of how *she* feels about you, but confirming how *you* feel about *her* is best done with words—your words. When you verbalize those feelings, you erase some of the doubts and insecurities that can plague her in her relationship with you. Work to boost the security of the woman you love. She may not be as self-assured as she appears. She can be especially helped by your taking the time to communicate your reassuring facts and feelings about your pride in her and about how much you care for her.

Your Black woman can give and be and do so much in the name of love when she knows what you know about her. Though she may never ask, she yearns to know with assurance.

THE BOTTOM LINE

Men at work: What are some of the most important facts about your feelings for and commitment to your woman that you hope she knows but you haven't clearly articulated to her? Put them into words. Explain until she gets it just the way you feel it and mean it.

The benefits: To a great extent women are prone to measure much of themselves by the degree to which they have benefited someone else's life. For them being a successful woman has a lot to do with nurturing others. It is not uncommon for them to feel as if they give so much of it, and get so little back. When you clearly make known how much her love means to you, and the depth of your commitment to her, the scales begin to balance. Balance is overwhelmingly satisfying to her.

The costs: The challenge of putting your hard-to-express feelings into words. Trying to find concrete words instead of leaving her to rely upon unverified assumptions and vague unconfirmed thoughts.

21. ▲ ■ ● ◆) *Read Between the Lines*

To the man who loves me:
Yes, I do mean what I say, and, no, I don't expect you to
have to play a guessing game. But I do need you to know
that when I speak to you, everything about what I say and
how I say it has some meaning. Please don't just focus on
my words alone and miss my message.

—From the Black woman you love

Advanced-level skills in loving a Black woman involve:

1. Carefully listening to everything she says to you.
2. Reading between the lines to get her fullest meaning.
3. Confirming with her what you think you heard.

To increase the love and intimacy level between you as well as to keep the lines of communication flowing freely, you'll do well to practice this tricky three-step process until you're a master at it.

When she is satisfied that your love is both plentiful and available, she'll begin to share more and more of herself with you. She'll have a strong urge to communicate her ideas, her feelings, and her desires to the man who loves her. As she does, and as your response makes it clear that you are truly interested, her love builds some more . . . and she'll reveal some more . . . and the cycle will repeat itself. For your woman this is intimacy at its most fulfilling.

The tricky part is knowing that the deeper the bond of closeness grows between you, the more her sharing is likely to flow forth naturally, spontaneously, and often without the benefit of the helpful whys and wherefores, the background information that clarifies what she means. And though her message may have more depth and personal disclosure, it is increasingly likely that it will be harder for you to catch all her meaning from words alone. That's where reading between the lines and verifying what you've read come in.

It's not that you have to be a psychic or a private eye to figure out what the heck she's saying, but you will often need to listen as much to what she didn't say as to what she did. Take note of her facial expressions, the words and phrases she characteristically repeats, the topics she seems to specialize in, and the kind of "vibe" as she speaks. All these will help you translate the message from her mind, as it comes through her mouth and into your understanding.

Sometimes it will feel like you're just guessing at what she means or taking a shot in the dark. Sometimes that's exactly what you will be doing. But reading between the lines is more than that, it's using the sum total of what you know about your woman to fill in some of the blanks. Because for you, where understanding increases, so does your ability to express your love and support.

THE BOTTOM LINE

Men at work: Never fill in the blanks in ink until you've checked with her by telling her what you understood her to have meant and allowing her to confirm, clarify, or revise the interpretation. Don't tell her what she meant as if you somehow know that better than she. Tell her what you understand her to have said, and *ask* her if you were on target.

The benefits: Black women long to be heard and understood to the fullest by their men. It's a big part of confirming your devotion to them. You're listening, then going the extra mile to know her well enough to read between the lines and let her sign off on the accuracy of your understanding. It proves to her that you will gladly receive whatever she's giving of herself to you. And that you are even willing to take steps to get more of her.

The costs: Having to read between the lines will sometimes annoy you. On occasion, you'll just plain not feel like having to decode, decipher, and decide what she might have meant.

22. •◆ *Avoid Analyzing Her to Her*

To the man who loves me:
It's almost like when I was in high school and we had to
examine all kinds of organisms under the microscope and
then had to document all the minute microscopic details
and explain to the class what we had discovered. I'm sure
you don't mean any harm, but I feel as if you are constantly
examining me under a microscope so you can tell me all
about what you've discovered.

—From the Black woman you love

Men absolutely love to get to the bottom of things. They rely heavily on their keen analytical skills to figure out the why of a matter. Arriving at answers to why she is the way she is, why she's saying or doing, desiring or experiencing whatever it is, is not merely for the purpose of satisfying your curiosity about the Black woman you love. You analyze her because it's natural for you to try to break big complex things down into smaller more understandable and thus more manageable pieces. Analyzing her is a man's way of getting meaning and drawing conclusions about what you're hearing and feeling from her. Ultimately, analyzing is what it takes for you to figure out exactly what to do next.

Your woman can have no objections when you're analyzing in the privacy of your own silent thoughts and interpretations. Your thoughts are your business. But when you make it a practice to broadcast the results of your analysis of her to her, you are likely to find she has major problems with that.

I urge you to keep your analysis to yourself and use it for your own benefit in relating to her, rather than offering it, unsolicited, in an attempt to benefit her. Analyzing her to her can make her feel as if she's the subject of your psychological research project and that somehow you now think you're the expert on her. When you try to explain somebody else to them you run the risk of presenting yourself as a more quali-fied authority on them than they are. Even if your findings happen to be accurate, you could come across as arrogant and judgmental. You are sure to hear her most outraged, "How dare you!" more times than you ever want to.

It doesn't matter how tender your tone or how innocent your intent, you belittle intimacy-building when you start giv-ing her a readout about the "hidden meaning" of her behav-ior, what her real motives were, or how she is, in fact, experiencing this emotion as opposed to that one. It only causes distance and sets you up as the man of superior knowledge and her as the woman who you've got thoroughly figured out.

THE BOTTOM LINE

Men at work: It's okay to keep your microscope. Analyz-ing is what men do. But it's best to get rid of your micro-phone; if she wants to know your take on why she is the way she is she'll ask.

The benefits: If you do your analysis, then keep it to yourself, the woman you love will sense that she is free to unfold who she is and how she is to you. She'll be secure in knowing that she doesn't have to live up to, or explain herself out of, the interpretations that you have made, and shared, all too conclusively with her. It means the world to her that you believe and embrace who she is, not who your analysis has determined, and your pronouncements, declare her to be.

The costs: You may be so good at analyzing people and situations that you are sure that your analysis of her could be helpful to her. You may have to work especially hard to keep your unsolicited analysis from seeping into your conversations with her. It'll feel like a waste of such good insights.

23. ▲ ■ ● ◆ ◗ *Call Her by Name*

To the man who loves me:
I treasure everything you do or could possibly do that
reminds me that I'm yours and you are mine. The sound of
your voice saying my name is one of those little reminders.

—From the Black woman you love

The reason clichés become clichés is because they are sayings whose truths are so timeless that they continue to be worth believing and repeating. When you've heard them over and over they can become empty-sounding phrases whose profound, yet simple, lessons can be easily missed because of their boring familiarity. I urge you to give a fresh listen to an old cliché: "In love, it's the little things that count."

One of the "little things" that packs a lot of power in loving a Black woman is for you to call her by name, frequently. It's one of those little things that are really a big thing to the woman you love. Not because she's constantly testing you, to be sure you've not forgotten whether she's a Mary, or a Millie, or a Mabel. Rather it's because women are very fond of the various indications from you that she is *your* Mary, Millie, or Mabel. When her name comes out of your mouth, you symbolically confirm over and over again that she is attached to you, the man who loves her. It can be a revitalizing dose of affirmation that builds her sense of security.

Never be so busy making your point and expressing yourself to her that you give no thought to the "packaging" you put it in. Address her by her name.

None of this means you should repossess those clever, creative, and very private nicknames you've so affectionately given to her. They may have almost become her name to the two of you. She loves them because you chose them, and without even trying to you probably add a certain subtle, flirty, and very intimate flavor to how you say them. Don't stop all that and just call her what's written on her birth certificate and her driver's license. But call her by name, both the ones her mama gave her, and everybody else calls her, as well as the one(s) you created that she just *loves* to answer to.

When you call her by her name, not just "Baby," "Girl," "Sweetheart," or "You" (as in "Hey, You!"), you accomplish two things at once: You of course get her attention *and* you convey in a word that who she is matters to you. That's enough, in the name of love, for you to repeat again and again.

THE BOTTOM LINE

Men at work: Without telling her in advance, work on consistently sprinkling her name (and your most frequently used nicknames) throughout your every conversation with her for a week. Go overboard. When she notices, explain why you are taking care to call her by name.

The benefits: When you consistently practice one of these "little things" that mean so much, the Black woman you love will feel positively adored, which contributes greatly to her self-image as well as her confidence in your love for her. When she feels secure and confident, she is motivated to offer, in return, the kind of loving interaction that matters most to you.

The costs: None, other than the possibility that calling her by name could feel like you're being too stiff and formal, or that it just takes too much time, or that it's too subtle an offering to get you any major applause for doing it. This is a virtually pain-free, risk-free procedure.

24. ▲ ■ ● ◆ ◗ *Touch Her*

To the man who loves me:
Have you ever noticed that little smile on my face when you touch me as you speak? You need to know that, for me, your touch has both tender sweetness and invincible strength in it. It's way beyond skin-deep.

—From the Black woman you love

In loving a Black woman one of your most effective and easily accomplished skills has to do with touch. Of course it's true that women tend to love words and it's probably also true that they want a lot more of them from you. But words can come up short in expressing the kind of closeness, affection, approval, affirmation, tenderness, desire, reassurance, devotion, and concern that touching her can. Black women cherish their men's gentle touch.

I'm talking here about your basic, uncomplicated, reach-out-and-touch. Caressing, stroking, and fondling are fine and not to be avoided in the appropriate context. But I'm attempting to sell you on the liberal use of "plain wrap," generic touch. Women know that when you touch them, especially spontaneously and unsolicited, you momentarily interrupt all that momentum propelling you toward your next project, obligation, or destination. When you touch them as you speak or listen or think, they, for that moment, *become* your cherished project. They feel elevated to a singular place of honor among all the things that matter to you.

But how much touch and when and how exactly she wants it are questions that loom large in the mind of an action-oriented man. To get the answers you'll have to ask and experiment.

No two Black women are exactly alike in their capacity and their appreciation for touch. For some, a little here and a little there go a long way. For others, there's no such thing as too much. You'll need to adjust the measure and your methods according to the feedback you get from her.

Unfortunately, some Black women, maybe even the one you love, have experienced the indignity of being mishandled, through physical and sexual abuse, and other violations of their bodies, minds, and souls. For them physical displays of affection, sometimes even simple touch, can feel intrusive and undesirable. Don't take it personally if she is not as receptive to your touch as you would like. Best to let her request more of it than to give more than she can comfortably handle.

THE BOTTOM LINE

Men at work: Nearly anytime reach out and tenderly touch the side of her face, her shoulders, hips, or hands as you converse. Keep it light and nonsexual. From time to time ask her if she's getting enough touch (or too much). Adjust accordingly. Experiment, ask, adjust.

The benefits: When you touch her as you speak, she'll surely be more attentive to you and what you're saying. Touch often effectively conveys through your hands what's in your heart that may be hard to put into words. Your touch will constantly reconfirm, nonverbally, that she is a valuable treasure in your world.

The costs: It may take some work for you to alter your natural style in order to touch your mate more. In some cases your woman will be uncomfortable with the amount of touch you give. So not only won't you be shown the major appreciation you'd like, you could be asked to tone it down or cut it out.

25. ▲◆ *Do Your Best, Then Be Yourself*

To the man who loves me:
If it has ever seemed like I've required you to become some-body that you're not in order to live up to my fantasy, for-give me. And if you've ever fallen for it and tried to become my fantasies, I forgive you.

—From the Black woman you love

Even if you are truly a good man, you'll never be a perfect one. As you work hard to live up to your highest potential, you'll find that at various points along the way you will both disgust and impress yourself and the Black woman you love.

There's nothing sorrier than the sight of a man who has stopped trying to become something more and better than he was yesterday. A better husband, lover, father, friend. A better leader, servant, or team player. A better human being.

But as valid as it is that you keep striving to become more excellent, you must pay close attention to your goal. If you're attempting to live out the best of your unique identity authentically and honorably, you'll try to perform in every area of your life to the best of your ability, consistently doing the most you can, with what you've got. But if your goal is to become (or appear to become) everything she may fantasize her man should be, then your goal isn't worth very much.

A loving relationship with a Black woman should never mean you give up the perfectly legitimate elements of who you are (and how you are) to match her (or anyone else's) unrealistic notions. Often women, especially those who during their childhoods didn't have the benefit of ever-present, real-life models of manhood from their fathers, develop a pronounced hunger for masculine love. It's a legitimate hunger, but one that has been distorted by unrealistic ideas about the package it should come in. She may be completely unaware that what she expects and requires from the man in her life is way beyond what is reasonable and is closer to myth, legend, or wishful thinking.

Add to that the fact that men can easily fall prey to the performance-driven, approval-seeking temptation to fulfill those fantasies. It's an attempt to gain applause and the self-esteem perks that go with it. It's also a setup for disaster. Offer her who you are, not the fantasy role she may cast you in.

Though you may possess certain of the fantasy role's qualities, you are not, nor do you ever need to become, her knight in shining armor, her stern but loving father, or her smooth-talking leading man, her twenty-four-hour delivery boy, or "the one who will make me complete." It's not your place to be all that, and if you act as if it is, you'll be disgusted with yourself. Efforts at fantasy fulfillment do major damage. They invite shallow, unsatisfying relationships that are based on what one or both of you think you ought to be, rather than what you are. There's no way to keep it real under these conditions. That's why so many Black women and their men end up throwing each other away, only to begin the long wait and the endless search all over again.

THE BOTTOM LINE

Men at work: Stop and carefully consider the most consistent desires, requests, expectations, and "requirements" your woman expresses to you—especially the ones you seem to keep failing to fulfill. Were they realistic in the first place or have they emerged from her or your fantasies and unrealistic notions about what a good man is or does? Whenever you suspect it's fantasy, discuss it with her honestly and plainly. Let her know what she realistically can expect in your personality, your performance, and what you have to offer her in the relationship. It's up to her to revise her fantasy. It's up to you to work to give the very best of yourself to her—authentically and sincerely—no more, no less.

The benefits: When you boldly offer your woman the things that make you, you, it will do away with much disillusionment and disappointment between the two of you down the road. You'll bring the measure of your love and commitment down to the realistic, the achievable, and available. Which means you can give and she can finally receive real-life love from the real-life man in her life. Not an often impressive, but inconsistent, fake.

The costs: If you believe women are always the most qualified experts on loving relationships you may have a hard time turning down her fantasy as your goal. You're apt to believe that her fantasy-filled expectations are valid. And that to challenge them, or fail to live up to them, is wrong. You can expect feelings of failure and dissatisfaction under these circumstances.

26. ▲ ■ ● *Own Up to and Express Your Fears*

To the man who loves me:
Your whole life is important to me, including the things that make you afraid. I don't care how courageous you look, every-body feels some fear sometimes. I can only assume that you do too, because you don't go there with me. I wish you would.

—From the Black woman you love

Being a good man is very hard work. Focus, sensitivity, courage, wisdom, and ingenuity are the necessary ingredients if you are to accomplish all that you and the Black woman you love are counting on you for. If you are succeeding at loving her, taking care of yourself, and seeing to the myriad responsibilities of a man's life you probably feel like you're juggling a hundred plates at one time—and any minute all of them could come crashing to the floor. Even if you are extremely proud about how well you're doing, life and love can be intimidating.

Fear is a natural part of living. Those who succeed at anything big, do so in spite of fear. Not because they had none. Fear of failure, fear of loss, fear of powerlessness, ineffectiveness, being mistaken, misunderstood, or ignored. Fear that you will never achieve what you aspired to, and fear that you will fail to maintain what you have achieved. Fear is common to both men and women; neither has a monopoly on it. But when it comes to acknowledging and expressing fear, men, especially when in the presence of their women, can have a particularly hard time. That's unfortunate because Black women crave the opportunity to share in all that's hidden inside you. Sadly, your fears are inaccessible to them if you hide, deny, or call them something other than what they are.

The easiest trick in the world is to camouflage your fears. Rather than admitting that there is some anxiety, self-doubt, intimidation, embarrassment, or some other kind of fear troubling you, you opt to hide it by expressing what seems more acceptably masculine: anger, indifference, blame, or sarcasm. When you do that she can easily get the impression that you are not so much a fearless, unshakable model of masculinity, but that you are a selfish soul who's out of touch with his feelings and who therefore couldn't possibly handle hers very well.

Owning up to your fears means you are the kind of person who is well balanced and emotionally secure enough to refuse to measure yourself by some ridiculous macho stereotype. You're the kind of man she can bring her love, support, and encouragement to and know you'll accept it. When she's not allowed that, the relationship sorely misses the mark to her. It's emptier and less fulfilling than one where she is valued as the person to whom you can show the bitter and the sweet of your insides because you're man enough to own up to and express your fears.

THE BOTTOM LINE

Men at work: When you are aware of feeling tense, angry, embarrassed, or anxious, try to identify the origin of those feelings. Do they involve something between you and your woman, or some other facet of your life? Boldly, honestly access the degree to which some fear, uncertainty, or insecurity is really what's bothering you. Acknowledge and (when appropriate) admit your fears to your woman rather than keep them stuffed in by employing rage, finger-pointing, frozen silence, or feigned indifference to camouflage them.

The benefits: You can gain her support, encouragement, and understanding when you need it most. She gets the fulfilling opportunity to share one more part of your world that she has previously been barred from. You'll not waste so much time and energy hiding from your fears or deflecting them onto the woman you love or something else.

The costs: Taking the risk of a new level of vulnerability and the possibility that she'll condemn your fearful feelings as a sign of weakness. Or that she'll make the mistake of trying to take control of your life, to rid it of any of its potential risks.

27. ▲ ■ ● ◆) *Let Her Know When You're Headed Underground*

To the man who loves me:
To me, being in this thing with you is all about us giving each
other what we need in order to be at our best. It seems there
are times when you really need me to be patient with you and
willing to wait. I'm willing to give you that. But I need you to
let me know when that is what you need from me.

—From the Black woman you love

Women can have a very hard time with the secrets men keep. Even if you're not intentionally trying to keep a secret, your brooding silences, unexplained mood changes, and eternal "everything's okay" responses can be mysterious and frustrating to her. She experiences them as unclimbable walls and uncrossable miles that separate the two of you.

All she has to go on is the knowledge that when women have anxious concerns, nagging questions, or important decisions to deal with they tend to want to talk them out with each other. So she'll tend to try, immediately or repeatedly, to make that happen with you. And immediately and repeatedly she'll find that it just doesn't work that way.

Partnering together around deeply emotional issues is completely natural to them and greatly appreciated. She may not know that men don't do it that way. In fact, what sends her to a "talk it out" partner to dialogue, discuss, and decide usually sends men into private thought and silent contemplation. One style is no better or worse than the other as long as eventually the processing and reporting back with each other happens.

But unless you tell her otherwise, she is likely to assume that when you descend into your "underground" where you temporarily kick back, zone out, and shut down (so you can process your feelings) it will feel to her like you've suddenly hung up the phone on her in the middle of a lively conversation.

For the sake of her feelings and your need for some quiet solitude to figure out how you're feeling, why you're feeling it, and what to do about it, tell her when you're headed underground. Do it honestly, do it simply, do it unapologetically—just make sure you do it. Otherwise, she won't be sure what your silence means and at first she'll struggle with the feeling that something's wrong and she is somehow at fault. Then she'll ache to know what she can do to heal the separation; and because you're deep in the silence of your underground (and because it's not about her anyway) she won't get answers. And then she'll really be thrown off and tempted to demand you break your silence—immediately! Or she'll offer you her silence in return. It's a nasty little process that can be short-circuited at the outset if you let her know that your travel plans include an immediate trip underground. But always round-trip, not one way.

THE BOTTOM LINE

Men at work: When you need the time and freedom for some private processing, warn her in advance by saying something like "I've got some figuring out to do, I'm headed underground. When I've got a handle on it, I'll be back and I'll let you in on it."

The benefits: Informing your woman before you head underground frees you to take the time you need to process, analyze, and clarify your thoughts and feelings. Promising to return to her with your findings makes it clear to her that you aren't trying to shut her out. In fact, you're doing what you need to do to be able to include her.

The costs: No man wants to feel as if he has to "get permission" to be alone with his own thoughts. But the fact is, it may be difficult getting the downtime you need to figure out your feelings if you don't clarify what your apparent withdrawal does and does not mean.

28. ▲ ■ ● ◆ ◗ *Tolerate Her Rambling*

To the man who loves me:
Would you just let me make my point. If I take five minutes, or five years, to do it, I'd really appreciate it if you'd just let me make my point my way.

—From the Black woman you love

One of the key ways women respond to the complications of life and love is to talk. For women, sharing, relating, and dialoguing help them to clarify and process what they feel, what they think, and what they need to do. The Black woman in your life, or the one on the way, will naturally tend to think out loud, and in the company of someone else who cares. The more emotion-laden the issue, the more she'll need to talk to be able to successfully respond to it. Like it or not, she'll most want to talk with you.

Though you may be the sensitive, caring, gracious kind of

man who welcomes his woman to share her heart and bare her soul, you may soon find her words too long and your patience and attention span too short. At those times, you'll need to sit tight and tolerate what will sound to you like pure rambling repetition with no bottom line in sight. Your heart will beat faster. You'll grow restless and your brain will begin to feel overworked and underpaid. In spite of it all, for her sake, you'll need to tolerate her rambling. In fact, you'll be even more helpful to her if you encourage her to keep on talking until she's talked it through and figured it out.

There are few things that rate higher on a woman's list of what a "good man" does than affirming her by listening to her and giving her room to explore her feelings with you without having to put it all in alphabetical order and without it being concise, articulate, practical, or profound (i.e., just the way men like it to be when they speak or when they have to listen!).

THE BOTTOM LINE

Men at work: Be receptive to her talking through what she's going through with you. Allow her to move in and around the issues in her own possibly "all over the place" style. Offer your woman your interested, attentive body language, as well as verbal encouragement (like questions that prove you're listening, comments that express your understanding and empathy for her feelings, and summarizing her message back to her in her words) while keeping any unsolicited advice to yourself.

The benefits: If you'll tolerate her rambling and even lend her your verbal as well as nonverbal assistance to help her keep talking, you'll witness her ability to work out her own difficulties quite ably. Then you won't have to struggle with feeling you must take on the burdens and responsibility of "fixing" her life. You'll find her self-sufficiency very attractive and she'll be captivated by your sensitivity and your acceptance of her and her style of processing issues.

The costs: Your urge to get as quickly as possible to a logical, concrete conclusion can make listening to her circular, detail-filled, and not necessarily goal-oriented discourse unbearable at times. You'll have to put up with the blood-pressure-raising reality that to employ your analytical, advice-dispensing, "get on with it" style is only likely to cause her to shut down, detach, and get the support and affirmation she needs the way she needs it—elsewhere.

29. ▲ ● ◆ *Never Run from Her Tears*

To the man who loves me:
I understand my tears can be a problem for you. I wish they weren't. I wish your heart would stop beating so fast and your body wasn't so tense when I'm crying in your arms. Without even trying to, I usually count to see how many seconds will pass before you let go of me and leave me to cry alone.

—From the Black woman you love

Women cry. Some only rarely, others quite frequently. Most of them understand that the shedding of tears is a perfectly acceptable and highly effective response to a wide range of emotions, including, but certainly not limited to, disappointment, joy, fear, anger, surprise, and fatigue. Contrary to what you may think, her tears are not a signal that you are expected to solve something for her. That's a burden that could make you want to run for your life. So relax and don't check out on her. You needn't run from her tears.

A good sincere cry is her body's way of paying tribute to what has already deeply touched her heart and soul. It's one of the most natural and honest human expressions. Though the Black woman you love expends effort and energy doing it, her tears are not meant to solve, settle, or signify anything. For her, crying is 100 percent genuine present-tense feeling. No more than that, and no less. Your best bet in loving her is to give her the space to feel and express what she's experiencing without running the risk that you'll soon be plotting your escape. You don't have to punch a time card, roll up your sleeves, and get busy working to get her all dry and happy again.

When she cries, men who are big on "doing," and "undoing," for their women often struggle with the suspicion that a) You messed up something, and she wants you to undo it; b) She messed up something, and she wants you to take care of her by taking care of it; or c) She has a baffling situation or decision and she wants you to solve it.

Warning: You can be so distracted by this guilt and feeling of responsibility that you can't tune in and support her fully in what she's going through. Lonely for her. Even if there are issues that need to be fixed, for the sake of the woman you love, don't shift so fast into fix-it mode. Avoid saying or doing anything, especially with an expression on your face that says you find her tears immature or inappropriate. At those moments don't play her psychologist, fairy godfather, or the voice of reason. Instead, give her your patience and your listening ears (and your crying eyes if you've got them). It's definitely not the time for you to work on being more verbal with her. The worst thing you could do is withdraw mentally, physically, or emotionally from her tears.

THE BOTTOM LINE

Men at work: Offer your concern, your patience, and your presence when she is emotional to the point of tears. Fight the urge to take blame or feel guilt for her feelings (unless you really are to blame). Focus on her. Don't silence her or try to fix her when you can hold her and just wait it out. Use everything you've got that confirms to her that you understand how she could feel the way she feels.

The benefits: When you refuse to detach from her and her tears, you put the "gentle" in "gentleman." She'll absolutely flourish knowing she has the kind of man who can silently, tenderly, patiently practice emotional intimacy rather than abandon her in response to her tears.

The costs: You may experience that awkward, impotent feeling that comes when you believe you should be doing something but you're not sure what, and you're not sure it would do any good anyway.

30. ▲ ■ ● ◆ ◗ *Remind Her Daily of Why You Love Her*

To the man who loves me:
There are some things I only need you to say or do once and that's enough. The benefit will last forever. But telling me about your love for me is something I can never get too much of.

—From the Black woman you love

God knows you've got your reasons for loving the Black woman in your life. But does that woman know? I mean really *know,* not suspect, hope, or assume. Today, at this very second, does she know beyond a shadow of a doubt how much you love her and why? If you're counting on her knowing because of the wonderful words you uttered, or the things you did yesterday, don't. Today is a brand-new day. She could use some new reminders. Best to act as if every one of yesterday's reminders and reassurances expired and need to be replaced with a fresh supply.

You can never tell the Black woman you love how much you love her and why, too much. If your declarations are sincere and flow steadily, even if they are a little repetitious, you nourish her soul and firm up the very foundation of the relationship: her assurance that you unconditionally love her and day by day you choose to continue. Constant daily reaffirmations of that fact speak peace to that part of a woman that is prone to struggle with self-doubts and insecurity about your love and commitment. Those nagging doubts and insecurities are just as real and normal as yours are about your abilities and accomplishments.

Whatever your feelings about her and commitment to her may be, the reality is you have made a willing choice to love her. It was not an accident or an involuntary reflex. Yours is a deliberate decision based on an assortment of whys and wherefores. Every day go out of your way to remind her and yourself of what they are.

Is it because of her strong but gentle and nurturing spirit? Is it the faith she has in you and the supportive, respectful way she shows it? Is it her one in a million outer packaging and her even more phenomenal inner beauty? Is it the wisdom with which she speaks and her knowing use of silence? Or is it her iron-willed determination and infinite patience? Maybe it's the flirty sway of her hips as she walks toward you, the way she never fails to pray for you or the way it feels when she gently strokes your face. Is it any of these? Maybe all of these and much more. Whatever they are, they are hugely important to her. Important enough for you to remind her of them every day.

THE BOTTOM LINE

Men at work: Never be so busy building a future together that you fail to revisit the reason that you loved her in the first place. Simply tell her out of nowhere, making use of those unscheduled moments you have together. Turn to her and say, "I love you so much because you . . ." Whether you write it, phone it, fax it, e-mail it, or sing it out loud, remind her constantly.

The benefits: Your daily reassuring reminders of why you love her are your most practical and effective strategies for communicating your desire for her and commitment to her. It's how you can contribute to keeping her doubt and insecurity level low and her faith in you and your love high.

The costs: It may feel like a bothersome daily obligation that will get old fast. Deep on the inside you'd rather she just know you love her today and every day until you tell her otherwise. The possibility also exists that when you tell her she won't appear to make a big deal of it. Believe me, if you sincerely mean what you say, it will be a big deal to her, whether she shows it or not.

31. ■◆ Be Willing to Sacrifice Your Schedule for Her

To the man who loves me:
I know you have a million and one things to deal with every
day. I can understand that. I do too and believe me I'm not
trying to get you to stop taking care of business. But those
times when you shift your obligations around or cancel
something just so you can be with me mean so much to me.
I treasure those times.

—From the Black woman you love

Black women are born with a built-in nurture radar that makes them alert to how they can make someone else's life easier, more comfortable, and more secure by their sacrifice. They are willing to do it for all those they deeply care about, including their children, friends, co-workers, and the men in their lives. They are no strangers to the expression of love and commitment through self-sacrifice. Their giving to us frequently involves giving up something for us. They've usually done it willingly with few regrets, but they've noticed how their sacrifice has richly blessed our lives. They long to bask in the warmth of your sacrifices on their behalf as well.

What sends the most persuasive love message to her is when you show a willingness to sometimes sacrifice what you cherish most. Women know men cherish their schedules dearly. We men tend to be inherently goal-oriented and masters of the outer world with all its ambitions, pursuits, deadlines, and limited time constraints. We thrive on knowing what we've got to do, having what it takes to do it, and getting it done as quickly and perfectly as possible. Our schedules are our efficient ways to organize what we cherish most—accomplishments. Accomplishment is what it's all about for men.

You freshly, powerfully affirm her worth to you when you temporarily toss off the demands of the outer world and in the name of love give in to a delay, temporary shutdown, or hiatus. It's giving her a portion of the time that you already had scheduled for conquering new worlds, in order to spend time with the Black woman you love pursuing a richer inner world of intimacy.

Sacrificing your schedule says to her that you are indeed very busy and that you are available to her in spite of that fact. It means a lot when she asks for the sacrifice and you grant it. It means even more when you grant it without being asked. It may be as little as your regular everyday half-a-second kiss being expanded to a long passionate embrace, or making an unscheduled (an uncharacteristic) "hey how's your day going" phone call. Or as much as sacrificing one of your normal basketball, bowling, or "by yourself" days to spend in her company. Or a last-minute vacation together at the height of your busy season. You'll know you are right in the zone when it feels like you are sacrificing your time for something in which little concrete and result-rich is happening.

Your willingness to slow down your life for her (truly willing counts even when you are not truly able) brings relief to the parts of her that have been wounded by things like the discouraging ratio of Black women to Black men, the feeling of being ignored or coming up short compared to women of other races, body types, skin and hair types, and so on. It's an action-oriented, creative way of loving her that "speaks" of your esteem for her. Though nonverbally expressed, it speaks loud and clear.

THE BOTTOM LINE

Men at work: Be specific. Tell her how much or how little time you have. And, great or small, give it to her with your undivided attention. Don't be afraid that if you do it once she'll begin to require more than you can afford to give.

The benefits: Ironically, when she is confident of your willingness to sacrifice your schedule, she will be less compelled to make "test" requests for it. That's the nature of sacrifice: It gives based on what will bless someone you love today, not what it might cost you tomorrow.

The costs: Efficiency, productivity, and the powerful sense of control that strict schedule-keeping affords you may be jeopardized by sacrificing in this way.

32. ■ ● ◆ *Follow Her Lead Sometimes*

To the man who loves me:
I really appreciate it when you are secure enough to
acknowledge that sometimes you don't know the way. I
appreciate it even more when you are willing to go with me
when I do know the way.

—From the Black woman you love

The way the Black woman in your life got to be in your life at all is because you saw in her some impressive qualities and characteristics. She possessed some strengths and virtues that made you sit up and take notice. Doubtless you discovered that owing to her background, her experiences, her interests, education, or God-given ability there are some things in which she is more expert than you. It could be in managing the checkbook, setting the schedule, organizing the project, disciplining the children, closing the deal, or any one of countless other things. If she's demonstrated she's got more interest and effectiveness, you'd both be foolish not to follow her lead in that area.

You've got your strengths, she's got hers. Wisdom requires that you both become good at leading and following according to your abilities, interests, and expertise rather than based on tired stereotypes that require men to know it all and lead the way in order to maintain their masculine honor. With that kind of foolish setup, women, in order to be considered respectful and submissive, are only expected to take the lead when it comes to cooking, cleaning, or raising the kids.

The very strengths which you first admired and appreciated in her, her resourcefulness, her know-how in specific areas, or her competent approach to the tasks at hand, can, if you don't watch out, quickly become unappreciated and ignored by you. It can be hard to follow her lead if you feel that relying upon her expertise means you're not living up to what it means to be a man. In addition, when women perform functions effectively they are gratified by knowing that their efforts contributed to the betterment of an entity larger than themselves, as in the relationship, their family, their team, their organization. It's a part of the natural relational dynamic that pervades the feminine psyche.

Each time she is hindered or not allowed to make use of her full resources and abilities, for the benefit of the two of you together, a little piece of what motivates and fulfills her is snuffed out. It's a tragic and unnecessary waste. To say nothing of the loss to you and that thing that needed to be taken care of by somebody in the know.

When you submit to her lead sometimes, she gets to see that you recognize, value, and rely upon her unique strength. If you don't, she'll feel like she's a stranger that you've never taken the time to get to know. That's a million miles away from where she wants to stand in your eyes.

THE BOTTOM LINE

Men at work: Confess to yourself and your mate areas in which you have stubbornly resisted following her lead. Work on changing your mind-set. Ask her to let you know when she feels you are holding back or taking over in that area again. Above all, point out to her the areas of her knowledge, ability, and skill that you recognize and respect.

The benefits: Acknowledging her expertise and following her lead is yet another extremely powerful way you testify to her as to what you find desirable and impressive about her. In this way you again answer that all-important question: "Why do you love me?"

The costs: If in any way your masculine identity was tied to always being the one who leads and having a woman who meekly follows, becoming more role-flexible here may be a painfully ego-crushing experience.

33. ▲ ■ ● ◆ ◗
Initiate Physical Affection That Doesn't Always Lead to Sex

To the man who loves me:
There is a way you hold and kiss me that makes me feel as if you're giving me a very special gift that's for me and me only. Then there are other times when your touches and kisses feel to me like they're mainly for you to get something from me for yourself. I think you should know that when I get enough of the first kind I can enjoy more of the second kind.

—From the Black woman you love

If the Black woman you love gets the idea that every time you display affection by hugging, kissing, holding, tender talk, and gentle caressing you are leading up to having sex, you might become confused and annoyed at how unwelcome your affection becomes to her. Women tend to be suspicious of love play if it always turns out to have been foreplay.

Though she may have a healthy appetite and appreciation for you and for sex, she wants very much to be sure that's not all or even mostly what makes her desirable to you. Typically, women view sex as something that they do, a meaningful, beautiful, delicious thing they do to express their love, but it's not an expression of their identities. For you to desire the pleasure of her sexuality doesn't necessarily mean to her that you deeply desire her as a person. Sex makes the most sense and holds the most value to her when she has the deep assurance that outside of sex she is already cherished, approved of, and delighted in. When you initiate physical expressions of your affection for her and consistently demonstrate sex is not required, she begins to believe what can sometimes be hard for her to believe, that you truly value her for her sake. Not just for the sake of the physical pleasure she can make you feel.

T H E   B O T T O M   L I N E

Men at work: Frequently initiate affectionate, physical expressions like hand-holding, passionate kisses and embraces, caressing, and cuddling that are nongenital, nonsexual, and appropriate to the commitment level of your relationship. Don't let her have to initiate all nonsexual displays of affection and you initiate all the sexual ones.

The benefits: There is a bond of closeness and comfort that comes from your nonsexual affection that can only be gotten there. You make it clear that she doesn't have to "give it up" to be able to receive love from you. Ironically, when you offer sincere physical affection that doesn't lead to sex, you are likely to find her even more responsive to your sexual advances.

The costs: As a man, her sexual desire and the expression of it means as much to you as your nonsexual affection does to her. You may sometimes feel frustrated and a bit deprived by stimulating love play that doesn't find its release in sex. That kind of sacrifice can be costly to you, yet tremendously rewarding to the woman you love.

34. ■ ● ◆ ◗ *Share Your Insides with Her*

To the man who loves me:
I want to know you so much. What I see on the outside pleases
me no end. Come on now, take me further. Tell me what I
don't see. Show me your heart.

—From the Black woman you love

She really wants to know you literally inside and out. She
wants to know the past, present, and future of your experiences, your thoughts, and your desires and what you're
absolutely assured of and what completely baffles you. She
wants to know your feelings, motives, and fears, and the way
the world looks through your eyes. Knowing the entire inventory of your heart, mind, and soul matters to her far more than
you may imagine. And she'll work hard, some men complain
too hard, to gain access to your private inner world and get
the treasures that are stored there.

Her need to know should not be taken as a sign that she
is just plain nosy; she's probably not "fishing" so she can use
the information she gains to back you into a commitment corner. It's not her attempt to unearth some good reasons to criticize or condemn you. She is on a search expedition because
women feel freest to give the best of their love and themselves to the man they know thoroughly—from the inside out.
It is only when she feels secure that she knows you (not just
the historical facts about you) that she feels truly connected to
you in secure love and intimacy.

Knowing your insides has a lot riding on it for her. The
best move you could make is to not only invite her into your

private world, but to take the initiative to reveal that rich part of you to her on purpose rather than to make it a restricted area with limited access and a "don't ask, don't tell" policy.

As challenging and unnatural as it may seem to commit to sharing your insides with her, you do it by:

- Not waiting for her to ask how your day went, but from time to time offering her all the boring details before she requests them.
- Taking the time you may need to process your thoughts and feelings about an issue between the two of you and coming back to share those feelings without her having to make repeated requests.
- Relaxing your compulsion with keeping your business to yourself at all cost.
- Refusing to buy into the unnecessary requirement that the length, style, and content of your sharing has to match hers. Be thorough, but do it your way.
- Incorporating specific emotion words (like sad, glad, discouraged, enthusiastic, angry, intimidated, embarrassed) into your self-disclosure rather than only hinting at or completely hiding your actual feelings.

THE BOTTOM LINE

Men at work: Take the woman you love on a guided tour of your private inner world. Work on sharing yourself by your honest and thorough verbal expression. You'll get better at talking about yourself by choosing to do it, and she'll get better at listening to you, understanding and accepting you, by having to.

The benefits: It keeps her desire to love alive. When women don't get access to your private thoughts, feelings, and experiences—your inner world—their sense of a vital, secure bond of intimacy with you is lacking. She's likely, then, to "go through the motions" in the relationship, only offering and expecting in return a frail, superficial love.

The costs: The vulnerability and awkwardness of sharing more than you feel like sharing and the risk that she'll misunderstand, judge, or attempt to change you when you do share your inner self.

35. ▲ *Expect to Love Her Out of Both Desire and Duty*

To the man who loves me:
You continue to offer me the very best of your love, even when our feelings for each other are not at their best. I am grateful that your love is so sturdy and determined.

—From the Black woman you love

If all your images of what love is come from sexy R&B ballads, Hollywood movies, the pages of fiction, lies from the locker room, or your favorite recurring daydream, you're likely to believe that real love is just a feeling: passion. But if that's your working definition of love, you'll require that it always flow from your passion all the time and when your passion grows thin so will your love. That's unfortunate and unnecessary.

Love and passion are not the same thing. Passion is only a fringe benefit of love, a fabulous, though often temporary, emotion that, just like Christmas, comes and goes and can come and go again.

But real-life love is fueled by discipline and duty far more than by passionate feelings. Though discipline carries more weight and substance than passionate desire does, passion has discipline and duty beat when it comes to exhilarating feelings.

Sadly, we live in a feelings-obsessed culture where if you're not careful you'll be sucked into believing that when the feelings are not intense neither is the love. That ain't necessarily so!

Accept the fact that ongoing love for the Black woman in your life will emerge from your disciplined commitment and desire. You simply don't always have to feel so lovey-dovey to be able to love her and be loved in return. Don't require it.

Passionate desire, intoxicated romantic feelings of being "in love" with your woman are like the waves of the sea, they flow in and they flow back out again. You really don't have as much control over your feelings as you may think you do. They can change like the weather. The "how you feel" part of love is constantly based on a million things that may or may not be going on in your life, her life, or your love life together. Believe me, whether the passion is at high tide or low, *this too shall pass.* No need to sweat this fact. Enjoy it when intense desire is present, remain disciplined and committed when it's not.

Discipline is the willful choice to do what love requires without needing that it be fueled by the energizing thrust of your passionate feelings. Discipline continues to speak words of love and perform acts of love because discipline has fought and won the battle to keep love from being enslaved to our constantly shifting feelings.

Love that doesn't guarantee the uninterrupted presence of passion, fierce attraction, total compatibility, and constant positive feelings may sound dull and dreary. It needn't be at all, because if you keep working at the disciplines of love—respect, affection, sacrifice, and patience—they will sustain you through the comings and goings of your waves of passion.

THE BOTTOM LINE

Men at work: Stop evaluating the worth and overall rightness of your relationship based on less significant factors like feeling "in love," maintaining "want-to feelings," 24/7, or other vague on-again, off-again variables. Chemistry, compatibility, electricity, and passion are not all true love is about. Consider your love, and hers, to be acceptable when it flows from "choose to" rather than "want to."

The benefits: Your willingness to commit to constant love without requiring constant passion is the best safeguard against needlessly throwing away a potentially great relationship (especially a marriage). When you take your feelings down from the number-one priority spot, you become less vulnerable to the oppressive perfectionism that can keep you starting and ending relationships merely based on the rise and fall of your emotions.

The costs: You may feel like a hypocrite acting lovingly toward your woman based on your willful choice and your discipline rather than spontaneous desire. However, to act in accordance with your true identity—as her _committed_ lover—is not hypocritical, it's consistent.

36. ▲ ■ ● ◆ ◗ *Protect Her*

To the man who loves me:
I've been watching over my shoulder and peeping around
corners to look out for myself for so long that I almost didn't
notice that you're right here with me. I need your strength
and your concern for me and for my well-being. When I
have them I feel even safer.

—From the Black woman you love

It's not that you have to be the Man of Steel because she's a frightened and defenseless little girl in harm's way. In fact, Black women have stood tall and fared well, going toe-to-toe against some of life's most threatening adversaries. They have victoriously withstood savage exploitation, cruel injustice, bitter loneliness, and violent abuses against their own physical and emotional well-being, and against their families. They are fighters and often they are conquerors. Yet none of this takes away from the fact that she deeply desires that you care enough about her to protect her.

Don't be fooled by her confident, "take no mess" exterior, the hardness of her speech, and the boldness with which she responds to a challenge. Your woman has probably learned to deal with those who would harm her, alone and as best she could, because too often she had to, not because she wanted to. She'd love for you to join her and in many cases to assume the responsibility of protecting her. She wants to relax in the assurance that you won't easily tolerate those who would speak to her disrespectfully, strike, mishandle or threaten her, or otherwise act with malicious intent. If she's the woman you love, she longs to know beyond a shadow of a doubt that you've got her back.

To protect her may sometimes only mean that you show up with her, proving that she's not just a woman alone, she's connected to a man who treasures her, and who will protect what he treasures, by any means necessary. At other times, it may mean that you'll have to discreetly, but firmly, confront those who step over the line with her. Whether it's a smart-mouthed cashier or a drunken fool in the streets—or in your own living room! At all times protecting her will mean taking care that you are never the one who disrespects or demeans her by your own words or deeds.

THE BOTTOM LINE

Men at work: Take a position and respond with the necessary show of force to those who in any way pose a threat or have mistreated your woman. Keep ego and showmanship out of it. Protect her for the sake of her sense of security. Resist the natural inclination to ignore or minimize what she sees as threatening. Even if you think it's something she can and should take the lead in handling, let her know why you do, then walk supportively with her as she handles the issue.

The benefits: To be protective of the woman you love demonstrates to her that you take her security and well-being seriously. You make it clear that she is not alone in this world. She knows that men fiercely defend and protect what matters most to them.

The costs: You definitely won't be able to take away all threats, risks, and dangers from her life even though you may feel you should. In fact, some of what feels threatening to her will feel that way to you as well. Stir up your courage and do the best you can. Also, there will be areas of her life in which she doesn't need, or want, your protection. In fact, she may

resent your attempts to handle challenging problems or people that she wants to handle herself. You'll have to rely on
your instincts and her feedback to learn which kind are
which.

37. ▲' *Be Conservative in the Promises You Make*

To the man who loves me:
When you promise me you'll do this, that, or the other, I
admit I'm thrilled at first. But promising me the world is not
necessary if you're not absolutely sure you're going to keep
those promises.

—From the Black woman you love

Since the Black woman you love doesn't have X-ray
vision and she can't read your mind or accurately predict the
future, she has to gauge some pretty important internal things
about you, as in your character and commitment, by observing some external indicators. Perhaps none of your externals
are more telling than the promises you make and your record
at keeping them.

When you get right down to it, the way you handle
promises is the vital indicator to your woman of how much or
how little of her trust she can safely bestow upon you. There
has probably never been a time in the history of the world
when Black women have more yearned to be able to trust the

men in their lives. Sadly, some of her deepest wounds and most crushing disappointments were because of someone's broken promises to her.

Simple, consistent promise-keeping will always be more meaningful to her than fancy, overzealous promise-making. Making few promises but following through on the ones you make will dramatically increase the level of her trust and security. But to make an abundance of promises—even well-intentioned ones—and only keep a few counts for little and in fact will eventually erode her trust in you and her respect for you over time. When it comes to promises, you're always better off a conservative rather than a liberal.

Instead of putting your lofty dreams, appealing possibilities, and extravagant ambitions into the form of promises you make to her, come down to the more earthly commitments that you already have the desire and the ability to keep. Otherwise your promise is only a maybe. Maybes are great as personal goals, but they are lousy as oaths to someone else. A commitment to conservative promise-making and consistent promise-keeping should apply to all matters—across the board. From as serious as the promise to marry her, down to the promise to pick her up at 7:00, not 7:30 or 8:00.

THE BOTTOM LINE

Men at work: Only promise what you mean to perform and can perform. If something unforeseen and uncontrollable delays or prevents you from keeping your word, don't assume she'll know that. Take the initiative to offer an explanation—and an apology. Note: You can always go ahead and do incredibly impressive and much appreciated things for her without having made a promise to do them.

The benefits: When you make few promises and keep the ones you make, you set a high standard of integrity and sensitivity in your relationship. The woman you love won't have to wonder about the weight of your words or the worth of your character. You won't have to spend your life constantly defending, justifying, and explaining why you broke your promises.

The costs: You give up the strategic use of overly extravagant promise-making as a means of impressing, consoling, or manipulating her. You may have to work hard to find other ways to accomplish those goals.

38. Never Beg

To the man who loves me:
My brother, please get up off your knees. You don't belong there and I can't stand to watch you do that to yourself.

—From the Black woman you love

Maybe you do need to work on being less demanding, harsh, stubborn, loud, or any number of other "mannish" ways of being. Finding the proper balance in how you relate to the Black woman in your life is crucial. You obviously want to, or you wouldn't have made it this far in this book, but even if you are on a mission to tone down, mellow out, and soften the edges of your style, never let that tempt you to become a man who begs.

Begging is the desperate, humiliating extreme side of requesting. When you beg you throw off your dignity and your self-sufficiency to plead for your woman to give you what you want, how and when you want it. Men who beg think too highly of her (she's a woman, after all, not a goddess) and they think too little of themselves.

Begging your woman for anything, whether it's approval, understanding, money, time, freedom, sex, or whatever else, is a big-time setup for disaster. When you make it obvious that you see yourself in dire need and dependent upon the provisions of your mate in order for you to survive, you diminish yourself in her eyes. Even if your insides scream out that that is true, it certainly is not. You may be in major *want* but you are not in *need*, so don't beg.

Needing another human being is actually an altogether false concept. You need food, air, water. You desire (maybe even strongly desire) your woman and the things she brings to your life, but you don't need her or them. When you act as if you do by begging, you're living a lie. One that will eventually make you resentful and ashamed of yourself. You're never truly free to love someone when you believe you need them. That only reduces them to an object, a substance, or a tool to meet your need.

THE BOTTOM LINE

Men at work: Ask for what you want. Ask again if need be. But by all means don't act as if your life is her responsibility.

The benefits: When you refuse to beg, you gain self-respect and you tone up your courage and discipline muscles. In addition, the Black woman you love will see your courage, discipline, and self-respect as strength. Strength is high on her list of desirable masculine attributes.

The costs: If you give up begging, you are likely to suffer the nagging question as to whether or not you missed out on something from her that you really desired, and may have gotten—if only you'd begged for it.

39. Rock the Boat When Necessary

To the man who loves me:
I need a strong man in my life. I need to know that you are
not afraid to bring up hard things that we'd rather ignore if
it means our relationship can be better.

—From the Black woman you love

No matter how much you and the Black woman you love have in common, how comfortably and compatibly your lives seem to connect, the fact is you are and forever shall remain two separate individuals. Individuals who were brought up in two different homes, have taste preferences, experiences, and priorities that differ either a little bit or a lot. And you are subject to see one issue in two vastly different ways.

None of this has to be a problem. Loving each other doesn't mean you have to be a perfect match in everything. In fact, if you think it does, you're likely to do anything to deny, avoid, or ignore conflict. And if you do that, your relationship will be safe, peaceful, and very superficial. Real intimacy requires that you be willing to rock the boat.

Rocking the boat involves standing up for your valid opinion even when it's contrary to hers, or sensitively but firmly challenging her inappropriate behavior even if she doesn't appreciate your doing so, or voicing your disagreement with what she may have assumed you were in agreement with, or saying no when yes would have gotten you more goodies, or bringing up that issue that the two of you hate to talk about but that you really need to.

Certainly seeing things eye-to-eye is more comfortable than having conflicting points of view, especially over something important to both of you. But because you are different, you will see, desire, and conclude differently and when you do you must be willing to say it even if it causes your love boat to drift from calm seas to choppy waters.

Fear and laziness are at the heart of a refusal to rock the boat when necessary. Fear and laziness are the enemies of love, and though they may powerfully tempt you to complacency and the comfort of unchallenged silence, they are rusty anchors that keep you and the relationship stuck in neutral and slowly sinking.

THE BOTTOM LINE

Men at work: Put away the fear-based notion that sensitive, unpleasant, or potentially volatile issues should never be brought up between the two of you. But first evaluate your timing, accuracy, communicator style, and, most important, your motives. Then where appropriate and necessary to the health of your relationship, unapologetically risk rocking the boat by raising the issue.

The benefits: If you willingly rock the boat when necessary, you and your mate will find that disagreement, conflict, and confrontation are not only honest and natural, but your effectiveness in handling them will grow with practice. Also, a significant fringe benefit is the mutual respect for each other's courage and integrity that you will gain as you sensitively, yet boldly, risk rocking the boat when needed.

The costs: Upsetting the status quo by exposing and confronting your differences is risky business. You can expect to feel at least a little unsure as to whether it's worth the risk of challenging or offending the woman you love when you'd much prefer to maintain her constant approval and admiration.

40. ■ ● ◆ Monitor Your Complaint Output

To the man who loves me:
To you it may be just your way of venting and getting things off your chest, but when you complain too much and it turns into this big evaluation of my performance where I grade myself, I completely turn off and make space between us. Neither way is very helpful at all.

—From the Black woman you love

You've got just as much right as your woman or anyone else to open your mouth and voice your complaints. It's not that you are demanding perfection of your mate and your relationship or any other part of your life, right? It's just that if things could be better than things already are how can they get better if you don't say something. There's nothing wrong with your noticing what you'd like to see changed, improved upon, or terminated, or even your having a serious beef about it, but there could be something terribly wrong and ultimately destructive with voicing your every complaint every time.

A major component of your woman's self-image and her passion in life is derived from feeling approved of and wonderfully acceptable to you, the man who loves her. She thrives on knowing you have not only accepted what you can see of her with your naked eye, but that you have looked beneath the surface into her private interior where her motives and intentions, her tastes, opinions, values, and character—her true self—reside. And she wants to be sure that even there you find her not only acceptable, but impressive. Your opinion of her matters more than anyone else's besides her own (in fact, to some women your opinion matters far more than it should).

When there is an all too steady flow of complaints and criticism from you (especially when there is not at least twice as much praise), she begins to believe that you see her as damaged goods. When that happens for too long her capacity to love you and receive love from you as well as her courage to respond to even your valid complaints diminishes. Intimate relationship with you becomes to her a dangerous place where your disapproval and her shame threaten to overwhelm her.

Even if all your complaints aren't directed at her, the nurturing, care-giving tendency in women sometimes crosses the line into feeling responsible somehow to make all your complaints go away. Women are prone to internalizing blame that's not theirs and that you never meant for them to have in the first place.

THE BOTTOM LINE

Men at work: You can forever wonder why she is the way she is and why you need to monitor your complaint output, or you can, at great sacrifice, sensitively and wisely keep your lesser complaints to yourself. If your complaint is merely motivated by a desire to let off some steam, moan and groan over a pet peeve, or enforce your nitpicky standards, swallow it.

The benefits: Monitoring your complaint output keeps the air cleaner between you two and it makes the complaints you do raise get taken more seriously, because you won't be considered a man who gripes all the time.

The costs: Having to figure which complaints are acceptable and which aren't, and allowing to stand uncorrected some minor beefs about her or your relationship.

41. ■ ● ◆ *Adjust Your Tone of Voice*

To the man who loves me:
When you raise your voice at me, I shut down. Then it's hard for me to even care what you're talking about. I don't want to shut down, but I don't want you to manhandle me with your mouth, either.

—From the Black woman you love

To a woman everything means something. Obviously *what* you say communicates to her, but *how* you say it does too. As a matter of fact, your tone of voice can make all the difference as to whether your words are truly heard. The volume, inflection, and the general attitude behind your words always say something—be it positive or negative—about her and about your relationship.

She can't help but be attuned to how you speak to her, whether it's full of hard edges and loud noises or steady restraint and well-modulated tones. You may need to adjust your levels to get away from the former and closer to the latter.

Don't forget she is descended from foremothers who were uprooted and brought to a land where they were verbally abused and commonly addressed as "Gal," "Mammy," or "Auntie." Later, they were made to feel shame for staying home to tend to babies and keep house and badgered into the workplace. Once they got there they were loudly criticized for doing so well and thus "undermining their man's ability to succeed." Even now, no matter how great their efforts and their contributions, they too often have to endure some fool somewhere disrespecting her or her sisters with boisterous demands, ridicule, or offensive labels.

If you fail, even infrequently, to keep a sensitive, respectful tone of voice with her, it can have a devastating effect on her ability to trust that, when all's said and done, you mean her well.

You see, every time you open your mouth to say anything to her, she has to gear up for what could be a tone that blesses or one that curses her. Believe me, it matters to her which one it is. By adjusting your tone you have the power to decide.

THE BOTTOM LINE

Men at work: Never raise your voice to a point that offends or frightens her (her eyes will confirm it for you). Avoid stinging sarcasm and condescending remarks intended to set her straight. Wait until you have complete control over your anger before you discuss volatile matters with her. Temporarily interrupt the conversation if your tone gets salty. Don't make excuses or apologies for your anger or hurt feelings. Always apologize for the inappropriate attitude or actions that result from it.

The benefits: Keeping an agreeable and appropriate tone of voice when speaking to her can help undo some of the destructive effects of the verbal disrespect your woman may have experienced from others. You'll show yourself to be a man of respect and self-control. She will not only admire and appreciate you for that, she will feel secure and esteemed in your presence.

The costs: You may feel restricted and a little less spontaneous by the need to monitor your mouth.

42. ■ *Share Her Load*

To the man who loves me:
Help . . . !

—From the Black woman you love

Everything about loving a Black woman is not centered in passionate feelings, romantic gestures, and sensitively speaking each other's language of love. As important as all those may be, if your love for her doesn't express itself in mundane, practical, day-to-day affairs of life, your love is too high in the clouds. It needs to be brought back down to earth.

There's nothing more intimate or loving than choosing to bear or share some of the responsibilities and obligations that make her days full and her nights weary. Wherever you can, as much as you can, share in or take over some of the demanding tasks on her personal to-do list. Especially those that benefit you as well.

The worst thing you can do is to get hung up on non-issues like "that's woman's work." If you buy into that foolishness, you could easily end up with a woman who's doing a "man's job" eight hours a day, earning a "man's check," and then coming home to another shift doing "woman's work"— not fair. By all means, share her load.

Though many women seem to be handling it well, keeping the pace and balancing all their demanding responsibilities, they are too often sacrificing adequate self-care, rest, and recreation in order to keep up. In the short term they look like highly efficient, ultra-organized superwomen. In the long term, much to their men's disappointment, they often because exhausted, resentful, passionless souls who just want to be left alone.

No question about it, you are certain to be quite busy yourself, and to do what I'm suggesting may mean some of the items on your to-do list may get delayed or completely erased. In a word, I'm talking about sacrifice and by definition that means it will cost you. Do it anyway. Help lighten her load. Lower some of your expectations and requirements of her and, by all means, decrease the frequency of your requests and complaints. Let her see that your love for her is willing to show up and help out where she may least expect it.

THE BOTTOM LINE

Men at work: Permanently, if you can, or temporarily if you can't, assume some of the work in your relationship that has been exclusively, or mostly, hers. For example, do some shopping sometimes, or cook, or find the baby-sitter, or clean the house, or make the travel arrangements, or keep the appointment . . . Don't require that she lavish praise or gratitude on you. Just take on the tasks willingly and regularly.

The benefits: As you work to share her load, you will learn firsthand the rigorous demands on her life, which will stir you to new levels of respect and appreciation for her. She will feel tremendously supported by your efforts and your selfless attitude. She will develop new levels of respect and appreciation for you. The result—mutually satisfying love.

The costs: The expenditure of your already heavily extended time and energy. You may also resent the possibility that if you share her load she'll see it only as your doing what you should have been doing in the first place rather than a special act of love worthy of some form of recognition.

43. *Let Her Help You*

To the man who loves me:
You'd probably be surprised by how much I do that truly
benefits so many other people in my life. I still don't know
what would be wrong with your being one of those people.

—From the Black woman you love

Unlike men, who measure real strength by how much they can accomplish on their own, women are more apt to measure it by how much they can get done together. The Black woman you have has or once had and can recover a sincere desire to share in the responsibilities that grab your attention, consume your time, and stimulate your abilities. She wants to help you do what you do because helping you is one vital way she experiences herself as a part of you.

In minor matters like balancing your checkbook or unpacking your luggage or reminding you of your appointments or organizing your closet, and in major ones like getting your new business up and running or working out your IRS problem or settling a breach between you and your children, if she loves you, her two goals are:

1. To help your life work easier and better.
2. To merge with you in the intimacy of making another "you alone" activity become an "us together" one.

Though that may be her intention, to you it can feel like she's hovering over you, doubting your ability, interrupting, interfering, and trying to take control. All of which are complete turnoffs for you. Granted there are some Black women who *are* doing just that and it understandably makes you want to keep your business to yourself. But they are not the norm. More likely the woman in your life yearns to experience the joy of offering her help to you and knowing you'll accept and value it.

You know firsthand how satisfying that can be, because men love to give assistance to their women. They just feel funny when women try to return the favor. Now is the time to change the lopsided arrangement. You can be sure you need to change if:

- Your most common response to her offer to help you is "That's all right I've got it covered," or
- You say yes to her help, then take the task back over that she was performing for you, or
- You try to keep your most challenging responsibilities a secret from her, or

- You can't fully enjoy your accomplishments if she gave you a helping hand, or
- Your woman never offers to help you anymore.

THE BOTTOM LINE

Men at work: Because to your woman it's not just a job that needs to be done, it's the opportunity to share love with her man by being active in the things that make up your life, look for ways to include her and solicit her help. Or sometimes take her up on her offer to assist you. You'll miss out on what she can offer if you only show appreciation for her abilities, instead of making comments about how you love working together.

The benefits: Practically speaking, you'll get help to get done what's important to you, which will make it possible for you to be even more productive and efficient. But even more importantly, your woman will get the vital emotional benefits of being welcomed into your private world of responsibilities. Your willingness to depend on her is yet another indication of the bond of closeness that exists between the two of you. It's what she thrives on.

The costs: It may be hard for you to appreciate your own accomplishments when you know you had help. Also, it could take some extra time and effort to show her what you're trying to do and how she can and cannot be of assistance. You also run the risk that she'll add her touches and the results won't end up exactly the way they would have if you did the whole thing yourself.

44. ▲ ■ ● ◆ ◗ *Resist Procrastination*

To the man who loves me:
Sometimes I just watch you, you get so busy planning and
preparing yourself to go for it, then when it's time to make a
move—any move—you start planning and preparing all
over again. That's when I want to ask so badly, "Baby what
are you waiting for?"

—From the Black woman you love

The good news is women are beginning to more fully understand and appreciate that a man's love is often expressed by what he does and what he doesn't do, rather than by nouns, verbs, and adjectives. So your actions have become vital to her trust in your love. The bad news is when you don't quite get around to the doing of things, your love begins to smell like a fake. Procrastination is recognizing the need, desire, and opportunity to meet a goal, having a strategy to accomplish the goal, rallying your resources—and then delaying on the follow-through.

When men fail to follow through, especially when they habitually fail to follow through, their women stop trusting them. When they can't trust you, their sense of security diminishes, and when their sense of security dies their love for you has lost its foundation. It's especially important in loving a Black woman that you not commit to action and make promises that you are not willing come hell or high water to act on. It's okay to dream, to contemplate, and to consider out loud, but when you do, call it that. To imply that it's something you *will* do and then you don't is not taken lightly or easily dismissed by the woman you love even if it feels like no big thing to you.

Fear of failure (which often only means fear of missing perfection) is at the root of procrastination. It can keep you meaning to act but waiting endlessly for the "right" conditions (i.e., the advance guarantee that all will go perfectly). The pain of past letdowns, failures, and disappointing performances can often tempt us to hesitate on follow-through. Nobody wants to rerun a failure, so we tend to avoid the situations where we've already experienced some failure. But for your sake and hers, you must try again. No one succeeds who's not willing to fail.

So go ahead and pay the bill, make the appointment, keep the promise, fix the thing, clean up the misunderstanding, make the apology, return the call, do the job, sign up, pay up, show up, or speak up. Throw off your procrastination and follow through.

THE BOTTOM LINE

Men at work: Identify three to five things you need to do and have been procrastinating on. Put them in order from the most to least challenging. Share your list with the woman in your life (only if yours is a fairly significant relationship) and your time line to follow through (sooner beats later hands down). Start with the least challenging, do it, and move on to the next. Note: Don't require that your mate be thrilled and impressed in order for you to be motivated to continue to follow through.

The benefits: You get things done that are important to you and the woman you love. Also, acting, instead of avoiding, will help you to shake off the vague, shadowy fears that bind you to inactivity. You'll also help foster a sense of security in your woman, which ignites her respect for you, which in turn enhances your self-respect.

The costs: To resist procrastination is to choose to walk into the anxiety-inducing unknown, where you can't be 100 percent sure of the outcome and where you're likely to be confronted with your own faults, fears, and self-doubts.

45. ▲ ■ ● ◆ *Be Patient*

To the man who loves me:
I have found out again and again that if I wait for you it
will usually be well worth the wait. I guarantee you it works
the other way around too. Give me the time I need and
you'll be glad you did.

—From the Black woman you love

When you merge men's concrete, goal-oriented style and women's more intuitive, feelings-oriented style in a balanced, well-integrated way, it's amazing how much the two of you can accomplish together. Your two strengths are halves of a highly efficient, mutually benefiting whole. Each approach, though, has its pluses and minuses, the bitter and the sweet. To get all the good of your woman's style, you'll need to put up with what you'll see as the drawbacks. You'll need to exercise patience or end up missing out on the vital positive contributions that emerge from your woman's natural style.

Abstract-thinking "feelers" can be slower to take action than concrete-thinking "doers," just as concrete-thinking doers can be slower to know and share feelings. In a multitude of ways the Black woman you love will, by her internally driven approach as compared to your externally driven one, seem to be slower than you'd like her to be when it comes to deciding, strategizing, and acting. When you want hard answers and competent choices, she may still be firmly planted at the think-it-through, feel-it-out-and-talk-it-over stage, getting a handle on what's happening inside herself about the issue. All the while you're ready to do what it takes to get the matter quickly crossed off your list so you can move on to the next item.

But when you rush her, requiring that she merely consider the cold hard facts alone in order to make a move, you stifle what's natural to her and demand she act like you—and that she be quick about it! Just like you may need loads of extra time to process internal stuff like definitive answers, final choices, and her course of action, she won't necessarily be ready to give you her bottom line just because you're ready to hear it.

Be patient with her. She needs time to analyze the matter and what to say or do about it by breaking it all down to at least three parts: the emotional, the intellectual, and the intuitive. Then she'll need to put them all back together again before she can wholeheartedly commit to action. The weightier the question, decision, or behavior, the more time she may need to be able to make a move.

Your standing over her tapping your toes nervously on the floor or making any attempts to coerce her to a "facts only" conclusion will just frustrate her and come across as insensitive and unsupportive. All of which will at the very least slow down her processing time, and perhaps even shut down the entire process altogether.

THE BOTTOM LINE

Men at work: When you need her input, choices, answers, or commitment to action in a matter that's important to the two of you, approach her not just with the facts but with your feelings and the process by which you arrived at your choice as to what to do. Patiently entertain her questions and allow her to think out loud without using pushy, hard-sell tactics. Ask her, "At what time or on what day will you be ready to give me a bottom-line answer on this? And how can I help you get one?" If, at that moment, she delays giving a conclusive response, then repeat the process with a good attitude as many times as is necessary.

The benefits: She'll bring to the table the strength of her thoughtful, intuitive nature, which can be beneficial when added to your "just get it done" approach. By being patient you give her space to do it her way—in spite of how different her way is from yours. Your woman sees that as truly loving sensitivity and respect for her.

The costs: All the extra time that you'd rather not have to invest in just trying to get some answers or in action.

46. ▲ ◆ *Keep Your Fascination with Passing Women to Yourself*

To the man who loves me:
Please, don't accuse me of being insecure or jealous when I say this. Being out with you anywhere makes me feel proud. Proud that we hold such love, respect, and desire for each other. But when you gaze so long and hard at some other woman, it seems like a piece of your love, respect, and desire for me has been loaned out to her.

—From the Black woman you love

It can happen anytime. Even when it's the last thing on your mind and you're in the last place you'd ever expect it to. As if out of nowhere she enters your field of vision—on the elevator, at the mall, on TV, at a stoplight, or even in church on Sundays, just as you open your eyes from praying. She's one of the dozens of eye-catching and worthy-of-a-second-look beauties who innocently cross your path daily, and whom you innocently (at least at first) can't help but notice.

A few of them *are* drop-dead gorgeous and everyone in the place stops what they're doing for just a second or two to pay tribute to her. More often, though, she is not the type you'd find on any magazine cover, but she does have some attention-arresting quality, like a fabulous physique, or thoroughly hooked-up attire, or a sharp "do," visible poise and confidence, a multimillion-dollar smile, or she plain drips with some indefinable, highly charged sexual energy. Whatever it is, when she passes, you notice her, and for a moment, your eyes linger and that mechanism inside your neck makes your head swivel to follow her, as your jaw drops open and a barely (or loudly) audible "umm, oomph, oomph, oopmh!" sounds forth from your mouth before you can stop it. (We won't even go into the sweaty palms, the racing heart, and elevated blood pressure that afflicts some men at these times.)

When all this occurs it means that, for a second or two, you were fascinated by the visuals—and *usually* that's all it means. That brief moment blows over and your life goes on.

But when you are in the company of the Black woman you love, and your eyes wander, at the very least it is likely to annoy her, or it could possibly wound her deeply. To her, even the little bit of time you invested in following your fascination was time and attention you gave to a woman who was not your woman. Though you may have no intention of letting anything else wander but your eye, you will have "innocently" given away what your woman wants most from you.

That means, if you're not careful, several times a day you could, in an instant, chip away at your woman's trust, security, and the respect for her feelings that to her define love. Your best bet is to keep your fascination with passing women discreetly to yourself. Because the truth is, looks *can* kill.

THE BOTTOM LINE

Men at work: If your admiring looks are in fact brief and harmless (i.e., not flirting or fixating), practice making them even briefer by downscaling to an imperceptible side-glance as she passes. Restrain all your "fascinated" body language and sound effects. Better yet, let her come to your eyes rather than your eyes going to her.

The benefits: If you discipline your eyes and keep your fascinated moments few, you'll save yourself a lot of grief. Most men don't mind big arguments over what they see as big issues. But you'll get frustrated in a hurry by how big a fight can arise just because of one lingering look.

The costs: You may resent this advice—and the Black woman who wants you to follow it—because it'll seem to you that she's being way too needy, insecure, and demanding. And you might feel deprived, like you're missing out on something important.

47. ■ ● ◆ ◗ *Hold Her Even When You Don't Have To*

To the man who loves me:
When you hold me I can figure out so much. I can tell if everything is all right with us or if there's something we need to clean up. I can tell if there's anything weighing on you heavily of if you are excited or if you're content. What thrills me most is knowing that you'll reach out for me and hold me tight regardless of the state of your feelings or our circumstances.

—From the Black woman you love

Most men have learned to live with the fact that the women in their lives generally can appreciate being held or embraced nearly any time. The feel of your physical presence wrapped, joined, clasped, bound, or otherwise connected to hers is one of her most treasured natural experiences. There are few, and for some women no, circumstances under which she would not delight in simply being held close by you.

Many Black women, maybe even yours, would love to get far more holding than their men give. And even though they have learned to live without it and seldom make requests for it anymore, they yearn for it deeply.

Often men feel as if they have their hands full with what should, ought, and must be done, in the million and one parts of their fast-moving lives. It's easy to only think to hold her when you "have to," like when she outright says hold me and you suspect it will cost you if you don't, or those times when you feel as if you should say *something*, but you don't know what to say so you have to hold her.

But holding the Black woman you love only when you must makes you merely a reactor to her spoken or implied requests, or to your own crisis-averting instincts. Reactors don't initiate, they just respond.

Actors (not in the phony role-playing, but action-initiating sense) take steps, not just to avoid or remedy a problem, but to give a good thing because it's a good thing and they have all the power it takes to give it freely.

THE BOTTOM LINE

Men at work: To her, deeply satisfying love is made up of the frequent intimate, caring "micro-moments," rather than every now and then major events. When she least expects it, tell her, "I'd love to just hold you close for a moment, is that all right with you." Practice telling her briefly why you choose to hold her.

The benefits: When you hold her without being asked or made to she feels cherished and is freshly and powerfully reminded of your delight in her. It communicates intimacy, acceptance, and commitment. It will appeal to you because it is a thoroughly uncomplicated way for you to express a whole lot of your love in a little bit of your time. And you're not likely to ever be chided for doing it too much. There's virtually no such thing as "excessive holding."

The costs: Don't hold or caress or any of those nonverbals instead of talking out an issue between the two of you. Your holding can become too mechanical and automatic if you're not careful.

48. ■ ● ◆ *Surprise Her*

To the man who loves me:
For you to be a man who's stable, dependable, and consistent means a lot to me. But it sure doesn't mean that you shouldn't feel free to shake things up a little. I trust you. Feel free to surprise me sometimes.

—From the Black woman you love

One of the richest things about love is the fact that when it is at its best you are willing to offer your partner what is highly treasured by her, *because* it's treasured by her. Even though it may be something that means very little to you.

Most men learned a long time ago that most women love surprises offered for love's sake. It's a good bet that the Black woman in your life is included in that number. It's also a pretty good bet that surprises don't mean anywhere near as much to you. Being caught off guard and the suspicion that you will be required to spontaneously show some big, loud, shocked, pleased, and appreciative emotion is probably not your idea of a good time.

But to her the totally unexpected, caring, usually unrequested presentation of something from your creative mind, or your generous heart, or your caring hand, ranks among her greatest joys. It's not even about how much it cost or how impressed anybody else might be with the surprise, it's that you, with all the things you could have done with your time, energy, and resources, considered her and brought some joy to her life. Above all she's utterly taken by the obvious fact that you did it just because you wanted to. As often as you can, surprise her.

You needn't wait for the "expected surprises," occasions like birthdays, holidays, and anniversaries. Whenever and as often as you decide to is the right time:

- Surprise her by doing something for her that she expected to have to do herself (fill her gas tank, run her errands, cook her dinner).
- Surprise her by calling, writing, faxing, or e-mailing a one-liner like "I am so unbelievably blessed that I woke up this morning with you in my life."
- Surprise her with a fresh rose on her pillow or a bouquet sent to her at work.
- Surprise her by doing something *her* way for a change.
- Surprise her by sharing some of your deepest thoughts and hidden feelings without being asked to.
- Surprise her by showing up exactly when you promised and not a minute later.
- Surprise her by giving her two surprises in one day.

THE BOTTOM LINE

Men at work: Keep your creative juices flowing (and any tendencies toward self-centeredness in check) by blessing the Black woman you love with frequent and varied surprises. At the bare minimum, never let a week pass without making at least one happen.

The benefits: Beyond all the appreciative laughter, her delight at being caught off guard, and her anticipation of just what you might come up with next is the powerfully affirming fact that you went out of your way for her. In that glorious moment you caused your sweet, creative surprise to come out of nowhere and land in her life. By doing so you simultaneously hoisted her up on a pedestal, and reminded her, once again, that she is a precious treasure to you.

The costs: The risk that she'll turn the tables on you and expect you to show the same level of enthusiasm and appreciation as she did, or you'll have hurt feelings to deal with.

49. ▲ ▶ *Let Her Romance You*

To the man who loves me:
I would love to see you sit back and relax and let me show
you the kind of romantic evening that you'd never forget.
One of these days I guess I'll be able to once I figure out how
to keep you from beating me to the punch.

—From the Black woman you love

If given half a chance, Black women are perfectly capable of romancing the men who love them. In fact, they are not only capable, many of them have no shortage of the creativity and the desire to express themselves romantically. Be assured you are not solely responsible for designing and financing all the dates, coming up with all the surprises, or initiating all the imaginative displays of affection. She can do it too and she will if you let her. Somewhere along the way men and women made an unspoken agreement that men must be the romancers and women must be the romanced. Many men got really good at the job, and their women were altogether thrilled by it. But always, when a really good thing only travels on a one-way street, somebody ends up overworked and somebody else ends up lazy. Romance needs to travel both directions.

Many women have come to believe that only men can be the pursuers, so they sit and wait, and sit and wait some more for men to notice and pursue them. These women are convinced that it is somehow "unladylike" for her to approach an attractive, desirable man. Obviously there are some right ways and some ridiculous ways to do it but both of you should do it.

Often men who love Black women suspect that if she expects you to arrange all the sweet romancing and you don't do it then you'll be brought up on charges and convicted of gross negligence. Liberate yourself and your woman. Declare it's a new day where all is fair in love. You may be surprised to discover that she'd love to ask for your number, or take you out to dinner, or send you flowers, or tickets to the game, or a romantic CD or . . .

You'll also discover that there is no shame in the game for you to absolutely love it when she romances you too.

THE BOTTOM LINE

Men at work: Say yes to her attempts to romance you. Give up responding with anything like "Baby, you don't have to do that"; instead focus on encouraging her to be creative. Enjoy yourself thoroughly and applaud her romantic efforts lavishly.

The benefits: You get to relax more and experience the deep satisfaction that comes from seeing how much the Black woman in your life truly desires you, as evidenced by the way she puts her feelings into action. She gets the benefit of being freed to develop and express her romance repertoire.

The costs: If you let her take some of the romantic responsibilities you will have to share the credit and the applause for those fabulously romantic goings-on. Also, if all you two do is completely flip from you do it all, to she does it all, you will still be out of balance and no better off than before.

50. ▲ ■ ● ◆ ◗
Tell the Truth

To the man who loves me:
I know what it's like to be lied to . . . little white lies as well as huge completely uncalled for ones that take me by total surprise. The fact is, our relationship can't ever be the real thing if we don't give each other the truth. I make that commitment to you. Please, give me that in return.

—From the Black woman you love

Your life is probably much more complicated already than you would like it to be. The simple day-to-day things that you have to deal with to keep your world moving forward and not sliding backward already take up more of your thought, energy, and effort than you'd prefer. So when it comes to relating effectively to the Black woman in your life, the way to keep complications to a minimum is to simply tell the truth. Always. Period. When it's convenient and when it's not. She doesn't need to know everything on your mind or every detail of your existence, but whatever you do share for her sake and yours let it be the bold-faced 100 percent, genuine truth. Telling her the truth won't always get you applause, admiration, and appreciation. In fact, sometimes the truth will cause her pain, sadness, or anger, because the truth may be disappointingly different from what she wanted to believe about you and about the two of you together.

But when you lie, you're using words to offer the woman you love a counterfeit version of reality. It may make her smile, calm her fears, and temporarily increase your approval rating, but ultimately when you're found out it will destroy what matters even more to her, and that is her trust in you. No matter how much you gain in the short term by not telling the truth, in the long term lying to her insults her, and creates distance between the two of you.

Lies, exaggerations, creative deceptions, false promises, denials, and conveniently left out facts and figures can be tempting to use from time to time. They can handily pull us out of a jam or put us into a sweeter situation. You're probably not trying to hurt her with a mistruth. More likely you're shrinking or stretching the truth to keep her from getting hurt. But no hurt you save her from by deception is as devastating as the pain of discovering that you were willing to let her live with a lie in the first place. She'll feel foolish because she'll know that, for whatever reason, you "played" her. And she fell for it.

Even if they were little white lies about what you consider lightweight issues, you could end up doing heavyweight damage. Because when you play fast and loose with the truth, you have an unfair advantage over her that makes her vulnerable. Her survival instincts warn her that if you're a lover who'll lie, you have the power to devastate her life—before she'd even know what hit her! That's too dangerous a position for many women to tolerate. They'll want to flee to safety before little lies become giant ones that could cause her major losses.

THE BOTTOM LINE

Men at work: Even when it won't put you in a more favorable light or guarantee your most desired outcome, commit to telling the truth and nothing but the truth.

The benefits: When you tell the truth, she gets an accurate picture of who you are and how you operate. She finds security in the knowledge that though you are not perfect, you are honest, and your honesty demands honesty in return. Also, by telling the truth you never have to go through all the complicated changes of adding more lies to keep the original one in place.

The costs: The truth may hurt. You run the risk that what you honestly report could disappoint her or disgrace you. Telling the truth is always the most moral choice, but not necessarily the most comfortable one.

51. ●◆◗ *Explain*

To the man who loves me:
I am ready to care, to listen, to understand, and maybe even
to agree. But that won't matter much if you won't tell me not
only where you're coming from but how you got there.

—From the Black woman you love

Black women and the men who love them seem to come from two different planets when it comes to their communication styles. Men are naturally focused on how the story ends. Getting to the point quickly is what's most important to you, not messing around with the boring details. Women do just the opposite.

Communication is not about right ways or wrong ways. It's about effective ones or ineffective ones. Whatever works, works. With a Black woman explaining the details, not just announcing the bottom line, works.

Everyone wants to be heard and not just heard but understood. Women hear and understand you best when you take the time to explain the step-by-step and blow-by-blow details of how you arrived at your bottom line. Unless you explain the whys and wherefores, the thoughts, circumstances, feelings, and motivations that shaped your ultimate decision, perspective, or remark, women are likely to 1) feel barred from entry to the most vital and appealing part of you—your thoughts and feelings; welcome access there is what intimacy is all about to her; 2) assume you really didn't put any thought into making the decision or drawing the conclusion, which could lead her to have little respect for your approach to thinking through issues. Unless you clue her in, when you unveil your bottom line but give no details, they'll never know you may have been carefully processing the details for days before you even uttered a word.

When you leave out the details and tell her only your point, for example: "I've decided we should take a break from each other for a while." Or, "Would you be my wife?" Or, "On the first of the month I'm quitting my job," you can expect to see that dazed, confused, hungry look on her face that says, "Hold on . . . Wait just a minute. Would you please back up from Z and explain the details from A, B, and C to me?"

Women are notoriously process-oriented. They enjoy sharing with each other all the rich details of matters that concern them. Don't assume that they lack the ability to reason objectively, draw logical conclusions, and make concrete decisions. Yes, they are "thinkers" too, and not "feelers" only.

But the more intuitive side of them traffics in details. The more vivid and comprehensive the details, the greater their ability to grasp and respond to the issue. The work of probing, clarifying, and analyzing details is so important to them that they may go overboard sharing the process with you, and making you have to wait to interrupt to ask for the bottom line. They may expect you to be the way they are and misinterpret what it means that you aren't.

Men are notoriously performance-oriented. If you must, you'll tolerate the annoying details and seemingly inconsequential nature of a matter just long enough to figure out what to do about it. You're looking for the all-important bottom line. To you, this is the streamlined, efficient approach. And you're more than willing, at the end, to share with your woman what you came up with. But if you really want her to hear, understand, and respect your bottom line, you definitely need to give her the details along with it. You needn't feel you must defend your position, but you should explain it.

THE BOTTOM LINE

Men at work: The more important the issue, decision, suggestion, or problem, when you share your bottom line with her, take the time to summarize what led you to it. Be willing to respond to her many questions about it, knowing she is probably not trying to shoot holes in your conclusion, but is only expressing her process-oriented, details-seeking style.

The benefits: When you give the details along with your bottom line you open the door for her to your private world of thoughts, feelings, and motivations. All of which communicate a special kind of naked trust and intimacy to her. Also, it's the only way to make sure that she has accurately understood your point as you meant it, rather than as she interpreted it after she filled in the blank spots you left.

The costs: It will feel so inefficient, time-consuming, and intrusive to have to articulate details to her that hold little value or interest to you now that you know what you plan to do.

52. ▲ ■ ● ◆ ☽ *Keep Her Secrets*

To the man who loves me:
I deliberately take the risk of sharing with you what I kept secret from others. I love the idea of your wanting to know me fully and that you won't take those deeply private parts of who I am and carelessly display them for the world to see.

—From the Black woman you love

Her secrets are your woman's most private possessions. She carries them in a safely guarded place inside her where absolutely no one has entry—except that rare companion to whom she grants it. Once she begins to trust that yours is a love with some weight and substance to it, she'll want to share her secrets with you. She longs to be open, vulnerable, naked and not ashamed, because she can have faith in your integrity.

No matter what you hear, what you think, or how you feel about it, what's crucial here is keeping her secrets as if they were your own. Though there should be room for some failings in any truly loving relationship, I assure you, keeping her secrets is the last place you should ever be caught failing.

Her deepest, most fiercely protected secrets are probably not very different in nature from the kind you have. They have to do with the various twists, turns, and detours of her life. The private thoughts behind her public image. Her fears as well as her faults. Her hopes and yearnings. Her freshest scars and her oldest regrets. The things that cause her to laugh or weep even when no one sees her do either of them. Though some of her secrets may shock or offend you, most will only add detail, definition, and vivid color to your image of the Black woman you love. Knowing her insides will help you discover the target places to apply your love.

For women, open, vulnerable self-disclosure is an essential ingredient for building intimacy. As risky as it is for her to unwrap, unveil, and uncover her business to you (especially to you), the idea of being able to is tremendously appealing to her. It's not that she delights in danger for danger's sake, it's that making herself vulnerable to the threatening possibility that you could use the secrets she volunteers to destroy or dismiss her is far outweighed by the deeply rewarding possibility that you will handle her secrets with the utmost care.

When you do, you honor her with the kind of acceptance and support that confirms to her that, even in the shadow of her secrets, she is not alone.

THE BOTTOM LINE

Men at work: When it comes to hearing her secrets, be receptive and nonjudgmental and permanently closed-mouthed about them. Never let them slip out to others for the sake of building a case for yourself or telling a juicy story. Never throw her secrets up in her face again as payback or punishment.

The benefits: Knowing and keeping her secrets is by far one of the most meaningful ways that you could ever confirm and demonstrate your love for her. They provide you the opportunity to do what is naturally and deeply satisfying to men, protecting the women they love.

The costs: To know her secrets and refuse to criticize, publicize, or criminalize them means you lose out on being able to use them when you need ammunition in a conflict with her. Also, you'll never get to conveniently use her secrets as a way to explain or excuse your own failures in the relationship.

53. ■ ● ◆ ◗
Resist the Urge to Punish Her

To the man who loves me:
When you are angry with me, your punishing ways really
sting. I feel as if I have been left alone out in the cold. Pay-
back doesn't become you. I can actually feel it suffocate my
love for you.

—From the Black woman you love

If your relationship with a Black woman has any depth to
it, and even a brief history, you can count on the fact that she
will at some point make you angry. In fact, if she's the
woman you love she'll probably make you more angry than
anyone else can. When she does—as your jaws grow tight
and your collar gets hot—please be sure not to give into the
temptation to punish, scold, or condemn her. Do deal with
the issue. Let her know that she has royally ticked you off
when she has. But get a grip on yourself, or the urge to punish and pay back could get the best of you.

There's no other person with whom you have so fully
invested yourself and exposed your insides than the woman
you love. That means there's no one who better knows where
your buttons are—and how to push them—than she does.
When fears or frustrations overtake her, she may express it by
giving you major mouth or what you consider an all-too-salty
attitude. She may start making a valid point, but in the escala-
tion of emotions and volume levels, your response or lack of
response may lead her to step over the line and say or do
something that thoroughly works your nerves.

Punishing paybacks include withholding affection, threats
of retaliation, harsh verbal attacks, sabotaging or shaming her,

and general meanness. Punishment is focused on revenge and one-upmanship. Neither of which has any place at all in your relationship.

As justified as you may believe yourself to be, it is never okay to use your power (whether verbal, physical, psychological, or otherwise) to punish her for her "sin." No matter how tough she talks, the fact is, you have the power to humiliate her. When you are angry, hurt, or embarrassed, you could be tempted to do just that, with the intimidating punishment of a big bully or the cold, detached, indifferent payback that silently yet forcefully declares "as far as I'm concerned you no longer exist." Don't give in to it.

THE BOTTOM LINE

Men at work: Don't let her, anyone, or anything else become your justification for punishing. Talk together about what she's said or done that ticked you off. Take the risk of telling her not just how wrong it was, but exactly how you were hurt by it. Don't insist that she endorse your every accusation and offer herself up for your rebukes and chastisements.

The benefits: By refusing to give in to the urge to punish your woman when she has angered you, you powerfully demonstrate the kind of love you have for her. It's a love that exercises self-control and offers her a tender yet truthful response even when provoked, disappointed, or enraged.

The costs: You'll sacrifice the short-term satisfaction that getting angry and getting even provide when you feel you've been wronged.

54. ■● *Season Your Criticism with Praise*

To the man who loves me:
I have never pretended to be perfect. You have helped open
my eyes to some things about myself and how I handle
things that I could stand to improve. I appreciate that you
are so direct and honest. But maybe you could sometimes
also tell me directly and honestly what I'm doing right.

—From the Black woman who loves you

Have you ever experienced times when your comments, criticisms, or complaints directed at the Black woman you love ended up packing far more force than you intended? You certainly did intend to make a point. A point you considered quite valid. A constructive criticism about the way she did or didn't handle something. What you did *not* intend was for your point to wound the woman you love. But by the look in her eyes and the droop of her shoulders and the tone of her voice you realized that your criticism did more tearing down than building up.

To women, words tend to have more nuances, secondary meanings, and implications than with men. Women rely heavily on words to convey meaning when they speak to each other. There are complex levels of meaning behind their phrasing, intonation, and choice of words. When they speak, they are not just trying to deliver news but they are very attuned to the effect on their listener of the emotional and relational dynamics behind the words.

Men, on the other hand, tend to use words to perform more basic and direct functions. You are bottom-line-oriented and pick words, tone, and body language for the simple functional purpose of making your point about the issue at hand.

These differences between men and women have led to men viewing women's communication style as too wordy, indirect, and vague. And women finding men too blunt, insensitive, and thoughtless.

When it comes to voicing a criticism to the woman you love, your best bet is to add some sincere words of praise, commendation, and encouragement. Otherwise, your criticism, as legitimate and constructive as it may be, could be met by her defensiveness or angry dismissal of you, your criticism, and your motives. Your approval and acceptance mean the world to her. When you pour on the criticism and leave out the praise, it makes it too easy for her to feel cast out from the place of your approval.

For example, don't just say, "You've overdrawn the account again. I wish you'd pay closer attention to the balance before you write a check." Add to it something like "And I really appreciate how you've been making sure lately that all our bills have been paid on time."

Don't just say, "I've told you, I don't care for surprise parties. I wish you hadn't done this behind my back." Add to it, "I am amazed at all the work and trouble you went through for my birthday."

Your words of praise go a long way in helping your words of criticism be heard and given the consideration they deserve.

THE BOTTOM LINE

Men at work: Go overboard for a while adding a B part (praise) to your A part (criticism) with the woman you love. Keep at it until the awkward, inauthentic feelings in you subside, and the injured, discarded feelings in her subside.

The benefits: She'll begin to trust that your criticism doesn't mean condemnation and cruel rejection. It just means you have a negative but necessary concern that needn't threaten her sense of security about your love.

The costs: When what you really want to do is throw a fit and prove a point to her about something negative, you might feel that having to add some praise will "water down" the strength of your message. You'll be worried that she'll ignore the criticism and only hear the praise.

55. *Don't Cheat on Her*

To the man who loves me:
How could you? . . .

—From the Black woman you love

The quickest way to inflate a man's ego and deflate a woman's trust is by your unfaithfulness. If your love for a Black woman does not offer the sincere commitment of your total faithfulness, then your love is only a pale imitation of the real thing. At the heart of an intimate, committed relationship with another person is the promise of exclusivity. It means that there are certain personal treasures (like your physical, spiritual, and emotional nakedness) that you just don't make available to any other living soul under any circumstances, because you have already pledged them to your mate. It belongs to her because you gave it to her.

Unless you are officially serving notice to the woman in your life that you are repossessing your love so that you can offer it elsewhere, be faithful to her at all costs. You do that by keeping your flirtations few, your promises sincere, and by all means keeping your zipper up. What might be the most intense pleasure of "a little harmless messing around" or the major emotional gratification of a super-secret thing on the side, your infidelity will do more damage than you can imagine to the woman you say you love and to your future together—to say nothing of the fact that being unfaithful causes your lying, cheating, and manipulating muscles to develop at a rapid pace. You could become so good at it that you are no good to any woman at all. Here, as with anything else, practice makes perfect.

Let's face it. Even if you are genuinely committed to a serious, exclusive relationship or marriage, sex is all around you. The vast numbers of available women and the comparatively small number of available men has resulted in making this a "buyer's market" for men. If it's simple, low-commitment, high adventure, part-time romance and readily available sexual opportunity that stir your hormones and weaken your will, you could repeatedly end up in big trouble. Because unless you settle the temptation issue in your own mind and heart, your groin will eventually call all the shots.

You can be sure that there will never be anything outside of you that will make you say *No!* and walk away. Fidelity, and the self-restraint it demands, comes from within. And if discipline, integrity, a rock-solid moral center, and an unshakable devotion to the woman you love aren't in you, faithfulness will be a foreign language and cheating a way of life.

Nearly any mess-up, even the most calamitous, in a relationship can be cleaned up if the two are willing to work, to change, and to forgive (not ignore, deny, or excuse, but forgive). But even one occurrence of infidelity—whether your extracurricular involvement was a way too physical thing or a way too emotional one—can destroy the very foundation of your woman's trust in you. Playing fast and loose with your already-committed affections will also cause her to experience the pain of rejection and abandonment in a way no one deserves to suffer.

Though your secret fling may have seemed trivial to you (*"It was purely a sexual thing. She didn't mean a thing to me."*) or justified (*"I know what I did was wrong. But you know you drove me to it."*), don't count on your woman believing that what you gave away was only the scraps of your passion and that she still has the best of your love.

Instead, your willingness to go behind her back will argue convincingly that she holds little value to you. Even if she is eventually willing to forgive you, how will you ever persuade her that there's no need for her to question your commitment—and your whereabouts—in the future? After your cheating has become for you a faded memory of the distant past, you are likely to look into the eyes of the Black woman you love and still see remnants of her hurt and mistrust. Her eyes, even more than her words, will constantly remind you that it really wasn't worth it to have roamed in the first place.

THE BOTTOM LINE

Men at work: If you are in, or sincerely working to build, a serious intimate relationship, avoid all high-risk people, places, and activities that you know invite the temptation to cross the faithfulness line. Enlist a male friend who knows all the gory details of your personal life and who has no problem challenging you—forcibly if need be—to get out of the path of temptation before you get in way over your head. Caution: temptation does not always come wrapped up in sexual packaging. Often it's in the innocent-looking, emotional bond developing between you and some other woman who is fast becoming your most intimate confidante/advisor, your best friend and the constant occupant of your uncensored thoughts.

The benefits: You won't need to constantly look over your shoulder, juggle your lies, or wrestle with sleep-stealing guilt about where your affections have inappropriately been deposited. Your signed, sealed, and delivered commitment to faithfulness means you'll avoid destroying the very thing that you may never be able to rebuild.

The costs: You'll deprive yourself of the thrills you could have had but chose not to.

56. ▲ ■ ● ◆ ◗ *Show Your Love by How You Handle Your Money*

To the man who loves me:
Money seems to be one of those things that gets far too much of your attention sometimes, and at other times not enough. I can't help but notice the way you are with your money. Believe me, it says much to me about you.

—From the Black woman you love

Like it or not, money really does have meaning and power. Contrary to what some believe, it doesn't mean the world, and it certainly isn't *all*-powerful, but it is what you use to make happen many of the things that matter most to you and the Black woman you love. How you handle—or mishandle—it will speak volumes about you to her, much more persuasively than what you could ever say about yourself. Handling your money with care, discipline, and maturity builds a strong case that you are a caring, disciplined, and mature man. Those, of course, are the very character traits that hold the most weight to her and elicit the highest level of respect from her.

Balance is the key word when it comes to your approach to finances. If you are a man of extremes—either too cautious or too irresponsible—you'll fearfully hoard it all, or foolishly spend it all, completely obsessed with your bottom line and cash flow or totally unmoved by your zero balance and past-due bills. Either way, you spell danger to her. She'll surmise that if your relationship with money can be so out of balance, so can your relationship with her. She'll see you as not only a credit risk, but a commitment risk who makes a mess out of what most deserves to be handled with care.

Before you even jump the broom, while your money is *your* money, she doesn't get to go over your bank statements and your credit report, but she does need to know that you are both responsible and motivated enough to take care of business with consistency and balance. She will figure that out by what you actually do with your money, not what you say about it.

After vows are said and rings are swapped, your money and her money become "y'all's" money and the very currency intended to provide the financial stability of your union. Now your money-management style will directly and dramatically affect the degree of security or insecurity she will experience with you—and not just in the dollars-and-cents areas of your relationship!

THE BOTTOM LINE

Men at work: Give your spending, saving, and paying habits a brutally honest examination. Take steps to get a handle on what's out of control in your finances and within yourself. For her sake, as well as your own, begin (or continue) to operate in a responsible, consistent manner that she can count on.

The benefits: When you handle your finances sensibly, the woman in your life can breathe easier and trust you more fully. Every way in which you help to strengthen her sense of security, and decrease her anxiety and tendency toward self-protectiveness, makes her feel safe, and free to be more receptive, passionate, and affirming—the stuff you love.

The costs: To benefit from this advice may require the rigorous and often painful process of overhauling your approach to money and things. It can be traumatic, because the work must start inside you, with your attitude, discipline, and motivation. It will require courage and patience, as you're bound to unearth some excess baggage that may seem too challenging and embarrassing to face, let alone work on changing.

57. ▲ ■ ● ◆ ◗
Become and Remain Clean and Sober

To the man who loves me:
Because I love you I can't stand watching how you are tear-
ing up your life. And, in ways I don't think you even know,
you're tearing up mine too. I don't think I can keep on like
this with you.

—From the Black woman you love

Love is not merely an emotion, an intention, or even a commitment. These only become love when one essential ingredient is added to them—action. In other words, love is not just feeling something, it's doing something. And the kinds of somethings it takes to love another person require an amazing amount of physical, spiritual, and emotional resources.

Substance abuse is a surefire way to destroy those resources, paralyzing or short-circuiting the possibility of a mature, mutually satisfying love. The sad truth is too many Black women have been caused too many tears over too many men whose love was taken back and given over to a high. It's a tragic plague that has left both Black women and the men who love them broke, devastated, and deprived of each other's love and trust. It's the worst kind of bankruptcy.

If you're caught in the smothering quicksand of depen-dency on drugs, alcohol, sex, or any other out-of-control plea-sure pursuits, nothing will change yesterday's broken promises and broken relationships. But today you have a fresh opportunity to take action in the name of love that surely can change the course of all your tomorrows. I urge you to get and remain clean and sober. Do it first to save your own life but also to regain the hope of being able to love without being too preoccupied to show it honestly and dependably.

The Black woman you love or loved will not be able to do it for you, nor should you expect her to continue to bear with you if you don't do it for yourself. It's likely her love won't up and leave overnight; but eventually, having you in her life will cost more than she can afford to pay. You can be sure that being with you has kept her caught up in, or headed to, a world of constant losses, bitter disappointments, and nightmarish insanity. Though she may truly wish it were not so, loving you up close is just too costly.

THE BOTTOM LINE

Men at work: Get help. Contact a counselor or a minister, or perhaps a friend who has succeeded in recovering from an addiction. Enlist their help in accessing an appropriate twelve-step program such as Alcoholics Anonymous or Cocaine Anonymous. Focus first on getting your life together, not trying to please someone else.

The benefits: You can be liberated from the bondage of your dependency. Spiritually, physically, emotionally, and relationally, you can regain your life. You can step out of your lonely, secret, and self-centered world of addiction and into the bright possibilities of mutual love and self-respect.

The costs: Admitting to yourself and to your mate that you have a problem will be hard on your sense of self-worth. Feelings of failure and discouragement and the likelihood that rigorous honesty here could cause you to lose what you value the most: your reputation and your relationship. Also, a very real fear that sobriety may be an impossible goal to attain.

58. ▲ ■ ● ◆ ♪ *Change Your Running Crowd*

To the man who loves me:
Some women swear they can tell right away if their man has
been in the company of another woman by the way he looks,
acts, and speaks afterward. I don't know about that, but I
can always tell the quality of the guys you've been hanging
out with by how you look, act, and speak when you return.

—From the Black woman you love

There are two basic varieties of running partners—the kind that are a positive influence on you and who help you rise to your highest potential in all the various areas of your life. They are your brothers, who, though imperfect, keep you grounded and remind you that a good man doesn't merely talk the talk, he must walk the walk. They are committed to walking that walk and a million different ways of helping you walk it too.

The only other kind of running partner there is, is the kind that doesn't bring anything particularly good into your life, and instead is a draining, destructive influence on you. They too come in all colors. They live everywhere from high up in the hills to down in the valley and across the tracks and everywhere in between. Even if no one else knows it, if you're honest, you know your character and your conduct go down at least a little whenever you run with them. You may hate to admit it, but they are no good for you and what you are trying to build with the Black woman in your life. Another powerful way you can add to, or subtract from, your woman's sense of security is by the poor caliber of company you keep. No, she absolutely does not have the right to dictate your list of friends, but she does see the fruit of those friendships in your life, and sometimes it's rotten to the core. Consider the following:

- If you must lie to your woman or keep secret who you are spending time with, you need to change your running crowd.
- If your friends disrespect, by word or deed, the woman in your life, you need to change your running crowd.
- If you always mean to help your partners become better men but instead you keep ending up worse, you need to change your running crowd.
- If you're committed to keeping your buddies and hiding the woman you love from them, you need to change your running crowd.

Changing your running crowd is not for the sake of gaining her love, but it's because you take seriously setting up the right conditions for your relationship to flourish. If your running crowd doesn't help that or actually gets in the way of it, you can't afford that crowd.

THE BOTTOM LINE

Men at work: Be honest with yourself about your friends. Stop being available to run with the wrong crowd. Tell the brothers you have absolutely no business spending time with why you must pull back, even though it's hard to do.

The benefits: Taking the bold step of rethinking who your friends are for the sake of yourself and the health of your relationship is the kind of willingness to sacrifice that demonstrates sincere commitment. Sacrifice and commitment are the means by which you develop true intimacy.

The costs: To remove yourself from the people and activities that get in the way of your growth as an individual and

as a relationship partner may feel like you are selling out your
buddies, depriving yourself of some fun, or being manipulated by your woman's taste in friends for you.

59. ▲ ■ ● ◆) *Apologize with Words*

To the man who loves me:
When you've let me down, your apologies mean a lot to me.
It takes a real man to say "I'm sorry." Though there are a
million ways you could show me how sorry you are, I really
do want to hear you say those two little words to me.

—From the Black woman you love

Let's be real about it. At some point—probably at several
points—you will blow it. You'll try to do something in the
name of love and for the sake of the Black woman in your
life and you'll fail—perhaps miserably. She'll feel let down or
angry, or weary, or a combination of all three, and you'll feel
guilty, embarrassed, and exposed. Rotten feelings all around.

There are countless ways that human imperfection shows
itself in a loving relationship. You, and every man or woman
on the planet, can be counted on to disappoint, offend, or
disgust each other at some time. But we also need to be able
to count on each other to acknowledge our mess-ups and
apologize for them too. Like it or not, it's a job that is most
effectively done with words—and plainly spoken, nondefen-
sive words, at that!

Women tend to be verbal. They place a high value on words, spoken and heard. Men, on the other hand, are often very content to rely heavily on nonverbal expression. With apologies, leaving it at the nonverbal level seldom works in her best interest or yours. Use words.

When, instead of *saying* "I'm sorry" (and why you are), you resort to apology alternatives, like doing something especially nice for her as a kind of penance, buying her something as a payoff, or just privately committing to yourself to do better next time—you leave out the essential ingredient that matters most to the Black woman you love: humility. Because humility is exactly what it takes to open your mouth and admit you were wrong. Pride and arrogance are opposite of humility. They require men to take an oath of silence after a mess-up. As if the failure somehow didn't really happen if you don't mention it.

One of the things men most hate to hear women say is that their men are full of pride, arrogance, and insensitivity. When they've said it, believe me, a big part of the hurt that motivated it was around their man's failure to adequately apologize. To her that can feel like a worse offense than the original one, because it adds insult to injury.

THE BOTTOM LINE

Men at work: A "good man" puts down his fear of being seen as a failure and chooses to love his woman by saying "I'm sorry" when he really is and when he is committed to a different course of action the next time. Work on both speaking the words and changing the offending behaviors. Never settle for just one or the other.

The benefits: Verbal apologies are actually the quickest and cleanest way to communicate what you are sorry for and how much your woman's feelings mean to you. The possibility of your mess-up lingering around in the shadows, providing her ammunition for future attacks against you, is dramatically lessened. If you'll get it out, you'll get it over with much quicker. It's not attaining perfection, but how you handle your imperfections that shows you to be a man of courage and integrity.

The costs: You'll feel like there's a little meter inside you adding up each and every "I'm sorry." It'll make you not want to say it before you feel you have too many.

60. ▲ ■ ◗ *Resist the Sugar Daddy in You*

To the man who loves me:
Now, don't get me wrong. I do enjoy all those wonderful romantic things you do for me and everything you've given me. You're very generous, and I'm very impressed. But maybe you've been generous for the wrong reasons. Maybe you think it takes all that to keep me. Wrong!

—From the Black woman you love

Having stuff and being able to give it to your woman can be tremendously appealing to men. There is such a satisfying jolt of power and significance to be gained from dispensing material goodies to the Black woman you love. It is the ego stroke of being Santa Claus, her wealthy benefactor Daddy, and "The Bank" all rolled into one. And when that's what it's all about, then it's not about her very much at all. It's about you and your conscious or unconscious search for significance by casting yourself in the role of her Sugar Daddy.

Some women may love it and they'll give you loads of admiration, approval, and applause in exchange for the various baubles, bangles, and beads you dole out to them. But eventually you'll get tired of "love" that costs so much and returns so little. In fact, many Black women couldn't care less about your trinkets. These days they've managed to get those for themselves. Instead, they want you, your devotion, your companionship, commitment, and affection far more than they need your stuff.

Quiet as it's kept, Sugar Daddies would much rather be loved for who they are, not just for what they hand out. If you're one, and you suddenly terminate your Sweet Daddy Macking and change the dynamics of the relationship, you may discover, however, that with some women it *was* the gifts she was after and not the giver. But if you keep on being Big Daddy Greenback you'll lose respect for yourself and begin to despise her, when you see that her love for you only reaches as far as what you've got in your hands or your pockets.

Resist the Sugar Daddy urge anyway. To give generously to your woman with the goal of blessing and benefiting the person you love is one thing. But to do that exact same giving with the number-one goal being to get more of her awe and admiration, thus boosting your sense of significance, is not only expensive, but it's selfish, and more than a little foolish. Selfishness and foolishness have no place in your love life.

If you've got a bit of the Sugar Daddy in you:

- Learn how to show up without having to bring something in your hands for her every time.
- Don't take all her financial complaints as hints that you must do something about them.
- Don't make promises that are based on what you only hope you can provide her but currently have no way to do.

- Don't lie to yourself about who your Sugar Daddying is really for. First, last, and always, it's for you.

THE BOTTOM LINE

Men at work: Go ahead and have that dreaded conversation with yourself, and with your woman, where you acknowledge, and assume all responsibilities for, your Sugar Daddy ways. Lovingly, yet firmly, announce that you are through shopping for significance by paying for love.

The benefits: You and the Black woman in your life will be able to clear away the superficial material "tokens" of love and get down to the real thing, love that is based on the emotional and spiritual bond between a man and a woman—rather than the one-way flow of cash and commodities.

The costs: If you stop playing Sugar Daddy you run the risk of finding out how little you mean to her and how much your stuff does.

61. ▲ ■ ● ◆ ◗ Never Play with the Word "Marriage"

To the man who loves me:
Marriage, marriage, marriage. I've heard you use the word
over and over now. Over and over I still wonder what exactly
you have in mind when you say it.

—From the Black woman you love

As you work to get better and better at putting your private thoughts and deepest feelings into words for the Black woman you love, I urge you to pause and truly hear this word of caution: Don't even think about uttering the word "marriage" to her until you're dead serious about it. Even if you think you might perhaps, one day, some way, we'll see, be headed that way, wait until you know you know or otherwise you'll be playing with the idea and she'll begin to think you're playing with her.

- Don't drop hints or raise her hopes.
- Don't play-act the possibility. Say it and mean it, then either do it, or don't.
- Don't use the word to manipulate, reward, or pacify her.
- Don't try to talk yourself into it by talking about it with her.

Marriage is the ultimate, intimate, exclusive, and long-term commitment between a man and a woman. For a woman, intimacy, exclusivity, and permanence are the three essential elements that confirm the strength and security of your love for her. When you start talking marriage and you're nowhere near marriage-ready, you've started constructing a high-rise building in her mind without bothering to lay the foundation. When it comes tumbling down, she'll be buried in the rubble.

Of course it's important to have some dialogue on the subject of marriage before you're down on your knees with a ring in your hand and a proposal on your lips, but at the just-talking-about-it stage, it's best to keep your words few and resist the temptation to spout anything that she could take as a promise. Because men are so goal-oriented and task-driven it seems that if you really are feeling strongly about her and the relationship, you really should get busy identifying a goal, looking at the possibility, and watching to see what develops.

And when men are in that mode they get a lot of satisfaction from talking about their ideas in order to analyze, troubleshoot, and evaluate them. It's fine to do that, but it's foolish to do it with her. Watch it: You may hear your words as an idea that you are considering. She may hear those same words as an idea you have confirmed.

THE BOTTOM LINE

Men at work: Do some serious initial observation and assessment of you and your mate's marriageability and marriage-readiness before you begin to talk matrimony with her. Until it's more than a maybe with you, explore the possibilities and think aloud about marrying her only in the company of your own support network, and separate from your woman. If you do broach the subject even in the most preliminary and commitment-free way, take pains to clearly communicate where you are and where you aren't about marriage (only daydreaming for now, or curious but cautious, or serious and inquiring, and so forth).

The benefits: Clarity. Avoiding premature or indefinite marriage talk will circumvent one of the most potentially destructive kinds of misunderstandings. This way you can't be found guilty of "relational fraud" and violation of an implied verbal agreement. You'll both be reading off the same page about marriage. She won't have to endure the pain and embarrassment of feeling set up by your careless words that offer her a vision of matrimony that may never materialize.

The costs: If you resist toying with the idea of marriage, you will sacrifice all the fun of playing pretend games with your woman. It really does work for you to try an idea on for size first, and speculating about it out loud helps you do just that. But it can cost your woman far too much in unfulfilled hopes and emotional upheaval.

62. ■● Stop Comparing Paychecks

To the man who loves me:
I sometimes wonder who first came up with the idea that
how much money we make gets to determine who we should
love and who we shouldn't. I hope we both continue trying
in our own ways to be successful people. But even if the level
of success we each achieve differs, that shouldn't have any-
thing to do with us staying together. Please don't let it.

—From the Black woman you love

One of the walls that separates Black women and the men who love them has come about because somewhere along the way many of them started practicing a very destructive habit: comparing paychecks. As if little numbers on big checks is the way to decide who deserves respect and who has the most rights and privileges in a relationship.

Lately, this obsession with measuring how much is in one's heart and soul by how much is in his or her pocket or purse has made some Black women afraid to admit and celebrate their material successes. It's also made some of the men who love them become humiliated and embarrassed when their numbers don't match or exceed their mate's. The fact is, the true value of a man or woman, and the relationship between them, is measured by the character and qualities of the two individuals, not the job they do and how much they earn for doing it. When you get hung up on those superficial matters, you'll fail to look deeper at a potential or present mate and you'll fail to discover the amount of character and commitment they possess within. And if you don't know their riches or poverty within, you'll stay distracted by the blue-collar/white-collar, "first and fifteenth," dollars-and-cents differences that may tempt you to disqualify yourself from such a woman. Or as bad is pursuing and remaining with a character- and commitment-poor Black woman *because* she's a high earner. Either way it's an insult to one or both of you.

Careful, every prosperous Black woman isn't damning you because you are not equally prosperous. Nor is every Black woman who has little materially requiring that you "bring the bank." Certainly there are some like that, but that is not the norm. You'll have to stick around and look around awhile to know which kind you're dealing with before you draw that conclusion about her and move forward or pull back from her.

THE BOTTOM LINE

Men at work: Work as hard as you can to excel at what you do and the compensation you get for it. Don't compare your earnings to hers. Define success as doing the best work you possibly can and getting the most you can for doing it. Compare your paycheck to your own effort, potential, and opportunity, and nothing else.

The benefits: Resisting paycheck obsession prior to marriage gives you a wider range of potential mates because you're not using pay stubs, credit reports, and investment portfolios to qualify or disqualify a potential partner. In a marital relationship, you can enjoy the closeness and interdependence that comes from living as if all the dollars you make are not his or her dollars but "*our* dollars."

The costs: Because men tend to define themselves largely by what they do, and the rewards they get for it, keeping paycheck measures of financial success secondary may be difficult for you. It may not be easy to switch to some other measure of your success.

63. ▲ ■ ● ◆ ◗ _Take Good Care of Your Kids_

To the man who loves me:
I enjoy so much watching you with the kids. You know them so well and just how to talk to them to make them feel loved and cared for. You can look in their eyes and tell that they know they can always count on you. You may never know how much that means to me.

—_From the Black woman you love_

If you've brought children into this imperfect and sometimes threatening world, you have signed on to be the most important man in the world of another living soul. It's neither part-time nor temporary. It's not just about what you do, it's about who you are before them. It's a long-term commitment to protect and to provide the resources—material, physical, spiritual, and emotional—that they will constantly need in order to flourish.

No matter how they got here or where they live, your children deserve your attentive, consistent, self-sacrificing presence in their lives on a daily basis. When you give them that, and not just your tender emotions and well-intentioned promises, your love for them becomes and remains alive, active, and visible—to them and to the Black woman you love.

The way you take care of your children reveals to your woman like nothing else can the depth of your capacity for love and commitment. Should you have little concern for your own flesh and blood she may reasonably conclude that you couldn't possibly have that much for her either.

These days the vast number of Black women raising children alone or with the father's "maybe today, maybe tomorrow" involvement has left many women exhausted, deeply disappointed, and full of mistrust.

You provide a healing touch to your woman and to Black women everywhere when you allow absolutely nothing to stop you from working toward perfection in caring for your children. Without excuses, in spite of distractions, and free of selfishness and blaming.

THE BOTTOM LINE

Men at work: If it's not possible to live in the same household with your children, at least live in the same town with them, even if it requires radically altering your life. That way you are available for daily, face-to-face interaction with them. Reestablish, recommit, or consistently maintain the highest possible levels of physical, spiritual, emotional, social, and financial involvement in their lives. Let what you promise to your children and to your woman (about your children) be what you actually deliver, and keep delivering, no matter what.

The benefits: Aside from the obvious benefits to your children, you will offer the woman you love the most compelling evidence that you are a man whose love can be trusted to include sacrifice and long-term commitment.

The costs: Having to work so hard to demonstrate your love for your kids' sake as well as your mate's sometimes will feel like too many people needing too much from you. Also, expect it to be harder to maintain a high level of commitment and involvement with your children when your woman and your kids' mother are not the same person. It can mean dealing with envy, strain, and a tug-of-war over your time and attentions.

64. ■ ● ◆ *Remember the Big Events*

To the man who loves me:
Thank you so much. I know I get excited as the kids do about all our special occasions. And I know they don't necessarily mean as much to you. But I get so much joy out of the way you let me go completely berserk celebrating and you join right in.

—From the Black woman you love

Most of the dates she has circled on her calendar may mean far more to her than to you, but if you're the man who loves her, you'd do well to remember them and enthusiastically celebrate them as well. The big events of course are her birthday, your anniversaries, holidays, the first day of this thing or the last day of that thing, and other milestones in her life or in the history of your relationship. To the Black woman you love these special occasions and the rituals and traditions that go with them are the perfect opportunities to celebrate what matters most to her: the joy and the significance of your shared life together.

When you remember the big events and honor them with your enthusiastic participation, you confirm to her that in this fast-moving life there are moments that belong to the two of you alone, and they hold status far above all other days. The big events are symbols of some of the specialness of your lives on this crowded planet. When you remember by yourself, and don't have to be reminded every time, you are in position to take some initiative in the way the occasions will be honored. That's much better than merely following along as a silent partner who appears as if he couldn't care less what, if anything, happens on these occasions.

Like it or not, a part of her identity is wrapped up in the big events of her life. When you remember and celebrate them you recognize and reaffirm those parts of her that the big events represent. Her birthday: the one day when you reaffirm that she is the leading lady, the queen, the hero of your life. It's about her, and when you recognize and celebrate it she knows it's fine with you that it's about her. Valentine's Day and your anniversary: when you recognize and reaffirm your love for each other as well as celebrate from whence you've come together and where you're headed.

Don't let the rituals, traditions, and ceremonies that go along with you and your woman's way of celebrating slip away. As the years fly past keep creatively and enthusiastically involved in observing the big events. It's not how much money you spend, it's all about the zeal you bring to the celebration.

THE BOTTOM LINE

Men at work: Mark your calendar well in advance and you be the one who first brings the big events up and makes plans for them to be bigger and bigger.

The benefits: Celebrations that you don't get swallowed up in because of your guilt or have forgotten or not planned anything; instead you have some creative input and thus some control. You win and so does she.

The costs: Big events seem never to end. When one goes away another is just around the corner.

65. ■ ● *Become Her Best Mirror*

To the man who loves me:
I don't care much about what "everybody else" has to say
about me and how I look. Knowing that you, my man, find
me beautiful and what you find beautiful about me are
what really matter to me.

—From the Black woman you love

Even if she's the most secure, self-assured, and popular Black woman, knowing that the man who loves her is impressed with what he sees when he looks at her means the world to her. But what she prizes even more is when you tell her about the beauty that you see. If you're willing to become her best mirror, you'll be more than any looking glass where she'll most delight in seeing her image reflected. It will be found there in your approving eyes and admiring words.

The Black woman you love, or one day will, relishes every kind of reminder and reassurance that she is desirable to you. It's not need, insecurity, or sheer vanity that makes her yearn for your approval and appreciation of her outer beauty. It comes from that part of a woman's nature that delights in knowing there is one person on this planet to whom she can boldly bring all the various parts of herself and that they can be found wonderfully acceptable, desirable, and pursueable.

You're her favorite mirror when you consistently:

- Rush to point out her most attractive features rather than criticize her flaws.
- Notice and commend her efforts to enhance her beauty.
- Brag to others, especially in her presence, about how gorgeous she is.
- Find her completely embraceable before she's made up her face and "whipped" her hair.
- Don't make her have to assume, guess, or imagine that she's attractive to you, but tell her instead.
- Don't compare her looks or attributes to those of any other woman.
- Encourage her about a part of her appearance about which she's very sensitive.
- Thank her for making you look so good.

She shouldn't have to look like Whitney or Naomi or Tyra to merit your highest praise, any more than you must look like Denzel, Wesley, or Billy D to get hers. You needn't lie to her. That will get old fast. Rather, find the many or few marks of her beauty and tell her over and over what you see.

THE BOTTOM LINE

Men at work: Find out at least one major and two minor things about her appearance to compliment each day. Keep one or two ready for when she asks you for them. Should you be given the opportunity to make a suggestion or voice a constructive criticism about her appearance, sandwich it between two glowing compliments.

The benefits: A woman who is confident that she is attractive and desirable to her man carries a unique and powerful self-confidence and openness. She'll perform at higher levels within and outside her relationship with you. Your praise helps her to become the kind of self-assured, high-performance woman most attractive to you.

The costs: It will be hard for her to fully appreciate your compliments about her outer beauty very long if you seldom (or never) mention what you find attractive about her inner beauty. Also, you will find it difficult to reflect her beauty to her when she makes appearance choices that you hate (like hairstyle, clothes, weight). The fact is, the more you lavishly and sincerely praise what you do like, the more attention she'll pay to the things you'd like her to change or improve.

66. ▲ ■ ● ◆) _Don't Let Pride Rob You of the Help You Need_

To the man who loves me:
It's not criticism, it's concern. Believe it or not I love you and I can't sit comfortably by and watch you go under when you don't have to. You and our life together mean too much to me for me to be able to stand that.

—From the Black woman you love

One of the things that has made Black women sometimes reluctant to put their full confidence in the men who love them is the men's often stubborn refusal to seek help when it's clear they desperately need it. Women instinctively tend to call out for specialized help when they are in a specialized jam. They are bewildered and frankly scared to death by the man who's willing to go under and take her with him before he'll acknowledge a need and ask guidance or assistance from someone who has something or knows something that he doesn't. If you've ever known such a man or seen him in the mirror, you know he's got PRIDE written all over him.

Pride is image-obsession fueled by false and ultimately self-destructive notions of what it means to be a man. The pride that keeps men from seeking help is based on the lie that a man ought to be able to handle every facet of his life (and especially his love life) by using his own resources. If he can't, pride erroneously argues that he's a failure and not a real man. Men instinctively avoid people, places, or things which might make them feel like a failure. Unless you recognize pride's lies and deceptions for what they are and accept the truth that sometimes needing someone else's help is a given, you'll be robbed of the opportunity to get exactly what you need, when you need it.

It's hard enough for some men to ask a friend for something as simple as help in solving a transportation problem or some assistance in polishing up a résumé or figuring out the best job option. Your woman grieves for you and for herself as she witnesses you opting to do without, rather than reach out, in these plain, everyday matters. But her grief is multiplied a thousand times when in the crisis you won't seek needed professional help like that of a financial advisor, a doctor, a therapist or a marriage counselor, a minister or an attorney. Instead, you're willing to suffer and allow her to suffer with you the slow death or rapid decline of your finances, your health, your emotional well-being, your relationship, or your family. And all this to save face and avoid any damage to your ego's lust for significance through supreme self-sufficiency.

The pride robs you of far more than it benefits you. It costs you in terms of her resentment, anxiety, and misery. It costs you directly because when you fail to seek help, you're likely to keep suffering multiple, irretrievable losses and ultimately the loss of your own self-respect.

THE BOTTOM LINE

Men at work: Don't deny, pretend, or tolerate the paralysis of analysis. When you need help (or even think you do), say no to your pride and get the help you need from the best possible places you have access to. Demonstrate to your mate that you love her too much to allow your undealt-with needs to become a crisis for her.

The benefits: Freedom from the bondage of prideful image-protecting. The benefits you'll derive from other people's expertise and abilities. Your woman will feel more secure, knowing that you are the kind of man who gets what he needs to take care of himself and those he loves.

The costs: That uncomfortably humbling feeling that comes with admitting you have a need and pursuing someone else's help to meet it.

67. ▲ ■ ● ◆ ◗ Love Her in Ways You Want Your Son to Imitate

To the man who loves me:
No matter how hard it gets, just don't give up trying to make
our relationship solid. We can't afford to screw up at this.
Like it or not, our children are becoming who we are.

—From the Black woman you love

It doesn't matter whether any of them are your actual flesh and blood, or whether they live at your address, or call you Daddy. Our sons are watching you. They are paying close attention even when you're not paying attention to what you say, how you say it, and what you actually do in the name of love for the Black woman in your life. For some "man-in-the-making," or several, you are their teacher, textbook, and role model on the subject of how to love a Black woman. Like it or not, these boys will learn more from how you live the lesson than from whatever you might say about it.

Treating Black women with dignity, tenderness, truthfulness is what it takes. It requires the application of wisdom, creativity, and skillfulness before our sons can be turned loose on the next generation of our daughters. Aside from the essential rightness of loving your woman with care, aside from how it edifies her and benefits her, is the grave obligation you have to equip your son, and all our sons, to do it as well. Will he get it if he patterns himself after you?

Too often your brothers of this generation did not have the benefit of constant, up-close role models around to demonstrate the finer points of:

- Listening to a woman when what she's saying is true, but embarrassing or ego-deflating.
- Speaking about her, even in her absence, in ways that honor and esteem her.
- Protecting her from mistreatment.
- Honestly telling her your limitations, but always giving her your best.
- Not being intimidated by her strength.
- Letting her have welcome access to your innermost thoughts, feelings, and aspirations.
- Adding to rather than taking from her sense of security when you can, and always being sensitive to what makes her sad or afraid.
- Valuing and accepting her as exactly who you want in your life, even if she's not exactly what you wanted.
- Keeping your complaints few and your expressions of affection frequent.
- Measuring love by what you give, not just what you get.

THE BOTTOM LINE

Men at work: Constantly ask yourself and demand an answer to this question: "Am I treating this woman in a way that I'd be proud for my son to imitate?" Make changes accordingly.

The benefits: The joy and satisfaction of working hard to become the best kind of man to the Black woman you love and literally shaping the life of the next generation by raising a high standard of masculine love.

The costs: The awesome burden of influencing somebody else's life other than your own, and, having accepted that, the tendency to ache with guilt over your past failures.

68. Don't Let Your Love Life Become Your Whole Life

To the man who loves me:
I used to be flattered by the feeling that I was the center of
your universe and that you didn't seem to need anyone or
anything else in your life. Now, to be honest, your needing
me so much feels like a heavy weight on my shoulders. Some-
thing's not right with this.

—From the Black woman you love

For a healthy man in a healthy relationship, there are two parts of you that together make the whole. One is your desire for the sense of connectedness that sharing your life with your woman brings. The other is your need to stand separate and apart from her in the independent side of your nature. Your desire for intimacy is not a curse. Your craving for independence is not a crime. But if either of the two is out of balance all kinds of problems can and will result. If most everything you value, pursue, or accomplish in your life is connected to, or initiated by, her, you have surrendered your identity as an individual. And if you are not able to be happy, whole, and content apart from your relationship with her, she will eventually find you to be more of a burden than a blessing. Because when your love life becomes practically your whole life, you don't have enough life of your own to share with anyone else.

It's not intimacy, it's dependence that has a man seeking virtually all his identity, self-esteem, and companionship needs from one source, his woman.

You'll know if you're dependent on her if her approval, her expectations, and her constant presence are your preoccupations, if they are nearly all you think about, talk about, and do anything about. If these are all connected to pleasing or keeping her, your world revolves too much around her, and the smothering effect of it will turn her off, and eventually run her off.

Black women admire and are highly attracted to signs of strength, reasonable self-sufficiency, and self-confidence in you. Though they want to be included in your life and hold a highly cherished place in it, they don't want the burden of having to give you a life. When you march to her drumbeat and not your own, that indicates to her that you are a needy man with insufficient internal resources. You will at best elicit her motherly devotion and sympathy but never her romantic love, admiration, and respect. To show her otherwise and, more importantly, to open the narrow confines of your life:

- Make and keep some friendships of your own, not just ones you inherited from her.
- Discover and pursue the things that will enhance your personal, professional, and spiritual life without waiting for her direction or motivation.
- Resist the pursuit of her total agreement and endorsement of your every idea, opinion, and plan in order for you to act upon them.
- Strengthen your ability to tolerate being alone. Your social and recreational life should not be limited to her company or her arrangements.

THE BOTTOM LINE

Men at work: Maintain a healthy independence along with the shared life of intimacy with your woman. Never abandon one for the other or you'll end up losing both.

The benefits: If you refuse to allow your woman and your relationship to become or remain the sole focus of your life, and you maintain some of your independent interests and pursuits, you are far more attractive to her than the man whose whole life revolves around her. For your sake, you'll stop using love and your lover as a drug, lulling you to sluggish inactivity. You will regain the balance between your purposeful independence and healthy intimacy by choice, not by necessity.

The costs: Your woman could be resistant to your changing your style on her abruptly, even if she has secretly loathed your dependent ways. It may have turned out to be a sign to her of your all-consuming devotion. She may feel threatened by any manifestation of your independence. And when she feels threatened, you may have to fight the urge to give up your life again and put her back at the center of your existence.

69. ▲ Stay

To the man who loves me:
When it's all said and done, a love that's here today and
gone tomorrow is just not worth it to me. I know that if we
really plan to be with each other there will always be good
times and not so good times. I can deal with that, but only
if I know you plan to be here, in this with me, through
whatever comes our way.

—From the Black woman you love

Even if you could perfectly perform all the advice in this book making available to the Black woman you love the best your mind, body, and spirit have to offer, in the final analysis it wouldn't matter very much if you are not a man who sticks around. Sometimes the hardest expression of your love for your woman will be rising to the challenge to stay when you feel that powerful urge to drift or flee. Choosing to stay anyway is your love at its most disciplined and determined. Staying involves keeping your focus, and maintaining your efforts on behalf of the relationship instead of letting yourself become distracted or "gone" without actually leaving.

There are an endless number of reasons why your staying power may wane at certain points as you work to build and maintain a relationship. Though all of them aren't justifiable reasons to pull up stakes and move on, they are real and persuasive, and you would do well to pay attention to them. Otherwise they are sure to try to control you rather than you controlling them. Don't be surprised if you get "itchy feet" when:

- You're bored. It may seem you know all her little crooks and crevices and there's little possibility of thrilling discovery and exciting conquest left to be had together. You're simply tired of her and want new frontiers.
- You're disappointed. It turns out she actually does not fulfill your perfect fantasy of what your woman and your relationship were supposed to look like.
- You're tired. When your relationship begins to feel like way too much work and like the burden of it is all on your shoulders, you will yearn for a vacation, perhaps a permanent one.
- You're distracted. The grass looks greener elsewhere. Some other woman or goal or way of life grabs your attention and beckons you to come and bring your all. You feel confined: The daily demands and discipline of your relationship with her sometimes make it seem like you're serving a life sentence in a cramped cell.

Your feelings are real and they may even be based on some actual flaws in your woman or your relationship, but feelings alone shouldn't be allowed to dictate your decision to stay or to go. If they do you'll become (or continue to be) somebody who spends his life packing and unpacking—promising your love, then taking it back.

When many Black women have been willing to be painfully honest, they have admitted that some of their worst fears about loving us is the possibility that your staying power will dissipate.

They end up crushed by the idea that they weren't enough to make you want to remain in spite of the inevitable challenges and restless feelings that tempt you to go. That kind of rejection, perhaps having been rerun countless times before, has led many Black women to put up a protective veneer, become suspicious of you and openly derisive of all men, and of Black men in particular. Your departures—even your logically and sensitively explained ones—wound them deeply. Not unlike the way their criticism and disrespect wounds you.

All courtships are not destined to be permanent relationships. And, no, you don't have to give your life away to a girlfriend who's all wrong for you and you for her. But stick around long enough to know exactly why you're choosing to leave and to make sure it is a mature decision driven by truth and wisdom and not just your impulsivity and self-centeredness.

To those men who have already vowed till death do us part, I'll make it simple: Put your feelings in their place and recommit to stay and do all you possibly can to make the marriage the best it possibly can be. There should be nearly nothing that changes that.

THE BOTTOM LINE

Men at work: Examine your own history and your patterns of entering and exiting relationships with women. Consider how much self-centeredness and a "never-satisfied" attitude have played a part in your departures. Honestly, diligently work to do the opposite in your current or next relationship.

The benefits: Aside from the obvious benefit to your woman's sense of security, making a serious commitment to stay will model to other men and our sons a love with that all too rare staying power.

The costs: Feeling the restless feelings and not automatically "medicating" them by leaving the premises.

70. ▲ ■ ● ◆ ◗
Keep on Loving Her Even if You Don't Always "Get It"

To the man who loves me:
I suspect we'll never have each other completely figured out.
I don't think I even want us to. If the way I am sometimes is
hard for you to understand, let's not worry about that. We
may wonder about each other sometimes, but then we'll
never bore each other.

—From the Black woman you love

Even if you carefully memorize every piece of advice contained in this book and follow it to the letter, you will find Black women (and especially your own) will still, from time to time, stare at you with a furrowed brow and an exasperated tone and declare: "You just don't get it, do you."

And because it will still sometimes be hard to figure out what she is talking about and what in the world she wants, you could be inclined to agree with her and answer back: "You're right, I *don't* get it!"

In some sense the ways of women and what it takes to love them will always be a mystery to you. They will eternally possess some confusing "X factors" that you just won't understand. Don't sweat it. You can love them just fine even when you don't always "get it."

Men can't stand not being able to thoroughly explain the things that baffle them. That's why little boys eventually break open their favorite toy to explore its insides and find answers to the mysteries of how the thing works. To men every question ought to have an answer. And if a man has a question, he feels he'd better get the answer, or he'll melt, evaporate, or pass out and die of "terminal bewilderment." The truth is there are some things about women for which no neat, tidy answers exist. They are, and to some extent will always remain, a mystery to men.

One of the greatest attractions between men and women is the fact that they can never fully sum each other up. No matter what profound discoveries you make, on some questions you will still be left groping in the dark for answers. Getting bored with each other is much less likely to happen when a little mystery remains between you. Learn to tolerate it.

Don't get nervous. Don't bang your head against the wall. Don't give up on Black women or on yourself. When you can't understand her *and* love her, then just love her.

Relax. Some answers to her mysterious ways will come later and some not at all. If you accept that, not being able to "get it" about something she did, said, or meant and why and what she really wants from you won't be so frustrating. Keep right on loving her anyway. She'll prove to be just understandable enough to grab your attention and just mysterious enough to keep it.

THE BOTTOM LINE

Men at work: Work on loving your woman in spite of her unexplainable ways and the mysterious differences between her style and yours. Whenever you become baffled, impatient, or at a loss to make sense of her, say to yourself, "I don't get it. And, at this moment, that'll have to be okay."

The benefits: Relief from the burdensome pressure to fully comprehend every minute detail of your woman's personality, behavior, motivation, and style of relating to you. You give her the liberating permission to remain somewhat a mystery to you and you give yourself permission not to have to turn romance into research.

The costs: Feeling slightly stupid that she accuses you of not understanding her, and having to agree that, at that moment, you really don't.

For Booking Information

How to Love a Black Woman and *How to Love a Black Man* were inspired by the many men and women throughout the country who have experienced powerful transformations in their lives after attending one of Ronn Elmore's highly popular seminars.

Dr. Elmore is much sought after for conferences, seminars, communications skills workshops, and other speaking engagements inspiring his audiences on a wide range of topics related to love, marriage, the family, and personal success.

To schedule an event:

The Ronn Elmore Group
The Trinity Building
333 W. Florence Ave. Suite 212
Inglewood, CA 90301

Attention: Booking Manager
(213) 732-0250

What You Can Do With an

Arts

Degree

OPPORTUNITIES FOR CANADIANS IN A GLOBAL ECONOMY

Dave Studd
Philip Schofield

Trifolium Books Inc.
Toronto

Published by arrangement with Hobsons Publishing PLC.

Canadian Cataloguing in Publication Data

Studd, David, 1941-
　What you can do with an arts degree

Includes bibliographical references.
ISBN 1-895579-95-3

1. Humanities - Vocational guidance - Canada.
　I. Schofield, Philip. II. Title.

HF5382.5.C2S88 1997　331.7'0235　C97-930848-8

Printed and bound in Canada
10 9 8 7 6 5 4 3 2 1

Cover and text design: Rick Eskins

Ordering Information

Orders by Canadian trade bookstores, wholesalers, individuals, organizations, and educational institutions: Please contact General Distribution Services, 34 Lesmill Road, Don Mills, Ontario, Canada M3B 2T6; tel. Ontario and Quebec (800) 387-0141, all other provinces (800) 387-0172; fax (416) 445-5967.

Trifolium's books may also be purchased in bulk for educational, business, or promotional use. For information please telephone (416) 925-0765 or write: Special Sales, Trifolium Books Inc., 238 Davenport Road, Suite 28, Toronto, Ontario, M5R 1J6

CONTENTS

How to Use this Book   1

What Subjects Are Covered by Arts?   1

1   WHY STUDY AN ARTS SUBJECT?

     1 The Value of Studying Faculty of Arts Programs   6

     2 Why Choose Arts?   11

     3 Trends in Arts Graduate Employment   20

     4 Adding Value to Your Degree   32

2   CAREERS USING YOUR DEGREE SUBJECT

     5 Teaching Your Subject   48

     6 Careers Using English   58

     7 Careers Using Archeology   73

     8 Careers Using History   78

     9 Careers Using Languages and Linguistics   83

    10 Careers Using Art and Design   91

    11 Careers Using Music, Drama, and Dance   98

12 Careers Using Political Science,   110
    Psychology, and Sociology

3   CAREERS OUTSIDE YOUR DEGREE SUBJECT

13 Careers in the Public Service   116

14 Careers in Uniformed Services   126

15 Careers in Management   136

16 Careers in Financial Services   149

17 Other Options   163

4   SOURCES OF ADVICE AND INFORMATION

18 Sources of Advice   178

Appendix Additional Information Resources   184

Source Notes   186

Index   187

HOW TO USE THIS BOOK

Whether you are thinking of studying for an arts degree, are already doing so, or have recently graduated, this book is for you.

As you have probably discovered, arts degrees are often seen as having limited vocational value. This book aims to dispel that myth and to describe the enormous variety of career opportunities open to you.

The first section of this book starts by looking at the value of arts studies, and especially how they are seen by employers. It then offers advice on choosing a degree course (Chapter 2). Because patterns of employment are changing faster than ever before, Chapter 3 discusses the trends likely to affect the employment of arts graduates. Finally, Chapter 4 describes the other skills which you should try to develop before starting your job search. (Employers of graduates are not just interested in academic qualifications.)

Section 2 looks at careers which could make direct use of your degree subject, and Section 3 at careers outside your subject. In summarizing each career, the goal is to describe the nature of the work, "warts and all," and to give you an indication of the training you will undertake, the opportunities for career progression, any personal qualities you will need, and sources of job vacancy information.

It would be impossible in one book to provide a full description of every career open to arts graduates. The aim here is to give enough information for you to decide which career you want to investigate further. Section 4 details some sources of additional advice and information.

Because the term "arts" covers such a wide range of subjects, you will find a brief description of the main arts disciplines below.

What Subjects Are Covered by Arts?

Arts subjects are sometimes called "the humanities," although this originally referred to the study of Greek and Latin. The range of arts subjects is very wide and can be confusing because similar names are used to describe courses which are very different from one another. As well, in Canada, Faculties of Arts often include Mathematics and Sciences in their list of subjects. But because *What You Can Do with a Science Degree* is the title of another volume in this series, this book will restrict itself to the following main subject areas.

Archaeology: This is the study of the people, lifestyles, and life of the past. There is a significant science component because of the techniques used for the identification, dating, and preservation of archaeological finds. Some courses specialize in Classical (Greek and Roman) archaeology, others in conservation or the science of archaeology.

Art and Design: Normally a single subject is studied, possibly with a specialty within it. Subjects range from three-dimensional design (such as interior design) to scientific illustration, fine art, and photographic studies.

Art History: Courses may be general or specialist. They deal with the history of painting, architecture, fashion, furniture, film, and photography, and cover periods ranging from antiquity to the present.

Classics: This covers the study of the history, philosophy, literature, and art of the ancient Greek and Roman world. Some, but not all, courses include studying Greek or Latin or both.

Communication and Media Studies: Typical course titles include Media, Culture and Society, Film, Video and Photographic Arts, Public Relations, and Journalism. Some of these — although they sound like it — are not vocational courses leading to careers in "the media." Rather, they deal with issues relating to the role of media in society.

Dance, Drama, and Performing Arts: Degree studies combine theory and practice, although the balance between the two varies. Most drama courses are weighted to the historical, social, and literary aspects of theatre. Dance and performing arts studies are more concerned with practical aspects.

English: Most courses are concerned with literature rather than language, but some balance the two. Courses include options to specialize.

Fashion Arts: These are design courses and can range from studying textiles or fashion alone or in combination, through to courses which include shoe, knitwear, and lingerie design. Many courses include the business side of the industry and some offer a language option.

History: Studies in history may be categorized by period (such as ancient, medieval, or modern), by type (such as political, economic, or social) and by place (such as Canada, the Near East, Europe). There is an almost infinite range of options.

Linguistics: This is the study of language, its structure and sounds, and how and why languages evolve. Most courses offer specialist options.

Modern Languages: Some courses emphasize studying the literature of a language or country, while others concentrate on developing practical skills. Most degrees cover two languages, and studying a third is sometimes an option. Languages are also a component of many courses in social science studies.

Music: University courses combine academic study with music-making in differing proportions. There is enormous variety in the types of music studied — from western classical to the music of the Far East, from electronic to pop. The Royal Conservatory of Music in Toronto also offers degree courses which are more vocationally orientated and so concentrate on performance, conducting, or composing.

Philosophy: This is the study of ideas, the discipline of thought, the nature of argument, and the search for ultimate truths. It includes the study of logic, ethics (moral philosophy), and metaphysics. There is usually a range of options.

Social Sciences: These include geography, economics, politics, psychology, and sociology, as well as other aspects of contemporary society and culture (e.g., women's and native studies).

Most of these subjects can be studied in combination with others. You will find more about this in Chapter 2.

1

WHY STUDY AN ARTS SUBJECT

ONE

THE VALUE OF STUDYING FACULTY OF ARTS PROGRAMS

There are two good reasons for taking an arts degree: because you are really interested in an arts subject for its own sake, and because much of the job market will be open to you once you have gained your degree. However, you will find that people have mixed views on the value of the arts.

Your broad [liberal arts] education will provide that most precious of commodities in today's labor market — flexibility.

Howard Figler, in his popular book,
The Complete Job Search Handbook

An arts degree isn't going to get you a real job, you know.

Anonymous liberal arts student, Queen's University

The arts degree does have an image problem. Quite bluntly, some people don't think arts subjects are very useful. They believe that a university education should prepare you for a specific type of job, and nothing more. Following their logic, you are expected to make a firm choice of career and then select the most appropriate degree course to qualify you for that career. Others see arts subjects as an easy option compared with science and technology disciplines.

These views are not well-founded and, as you will see below, do not stand up to scrutiny.

Should You Choose a Degree Course for Vocational Reasons?

About half of all vacancies for newly qualified graduates are open to those with a degree in any discipline, including arts. That being said, some careers *do* require specific degrees. For example, if you're certain that you want to enter a "closed" profession like medicine or architecture, then it's essential that you study for a specific vocational degree. You have no other choice because you cannot enter these careers without the appropriate qualifications. (Of course, you can study for an arts degree prior to applying to medical school, as long as you include certain prerequisite subjects in your arts program.) There are many more professions that have vocational degrees — such as accountancy, teaching, and journalism — but choosing these programs isn't essential. Instead, you could take a vocational postgraduate course after a general degree.

If you aren't sure what you would like to do and choose your degree because you like the subject, you won't be alone. According to a Canadian study[1] published in 1996, only 20.5% of students surveyed had a definite career plan beyond the first step — deciding to study a subject in which they are interested. Such a plan includes taking responsibility for themselves, evaluating career possibilities, and conducting vocational planning. The majority, however, seemed indifferent to additional educational and career planning. Most students don't know what career they want to follow until they're near the end of their university education, and not always then.

By the time you have completed a degree course you will have changed a lot. You will be more confident of your strengths and have a better understanding of your weaknesses. You may have discovered new interests, and will have a wider awareness of the opportunities open to you. Moreover, the world will have moved on and there will have been changes in the graduate employment market.

Unless you are absolutely sure of the career you want to pursue, it is best to defer any decisions until you are in your second year at university. By then, you will have a better idea about your interests and about the opportunities available, and you will still have time to prepare for your job search. You certainly do not have to choose a career in order to select a degree course.

Is Arts an Easy Option?

Many arts courses have high admission standards and are intellectually very demanding. Some — such as history, modern languages, and philosophy — will require you to work at least as hard as you would in any other area. In fact, since many arts courses are more popular than those in science and engineering, the competition for places is greater and you may need higher marks in your final year of secondary school in order to secure a place in a first-year program.

Do Employers Value Arts Degrees?

You probably assume the answer is no. And, certainly, few employers specify arts degrees for their graduate vacancies (although there are exceptions in areas such as teaching, art and design, and translating). So graduates with a science/technology degree have an advantage over arts graduates in the job market; they tend to find a job more easily and have a somewhat higher starting salary. *However*, the differences are not so great that these should be serious factors in choosing a degree subject.

Any degree course combines subject knowledge with skills that have virtually universal application. These skills, known as transferable skills, include:

- gathering and analyzing information
- problem-solving
- presenting arguments logically and persuasively
- communicating clearly, both orally and in writing
- computer literacy (including basic keyboard skills)
- social (human relations) skills

Outside the technical professions, employers are generally less concerned with the content knowledge of your degree than they are with the transferable skills you have acquired. In some cases, employers complain that graduates in disciplines outside the arts have poor communication skills, so they have difficulty in presenting arguments clearly and in mixing with colleagues. These graduates may have a wealth of technical knowledge, but often they can explain it only to other technical specialists.

Not surprisingly, then, employers in many different areas — for example, advertising, sales, banking, business management, government, and the Armed Forces — are putting even greater emphasis on transferable skills. This situation is likely to favour arts graduates. (Transferable skills are discussed more fully in Chapter 4.)

Working effectively with others has always been key in any career. Even those who work primarily on their own need to be able to relate to others at certain times.... Qualities such as leadership, effective communication, empathy, and cooperation will be even more important in the workplace of the future.... In order to work successfully in a team, you'll need strong communication skills so that you can explain to your team members exactly what you're doing and really hear what they're telling you.

Colin Campbell, Human Resources consultant[2]

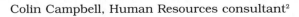

Will You Be Trapped by Your Degree Subject?

Many final-year undergraduates feel trapped by their subject. Some worry that their career choice will be restricted by the specialist nature of their degree subject. Others, studying subjects in which they have lost interest, worry that they will be trapped in a career related to their course.

Even in more stable times, career planning was never a once-only event. It is an ongoing process. As you grow and change, your goals and expectations change as well, and these changes must be taken into account when developing a career strategy.

Colin Campbell, Human Resources consultant

Your choice of degree subject need not limit you to careers linked to that discipline. In fact, many graduates enter careers which have nothing to do with the subjects they have studied. But this doesn't mean that their studies have been wasted. It is the skills and experience you acquire while studying for a degree that are often most important to employers. Remember, about half of all jobs for graduates are open to graduates of any discipline.

Key Points to Think About

You might like to discuss these points with family members, a guardian, or friends.

- Most students do not choose a career until near graduation.

- Only about 20% of students choose their degree based on a definite career plan.

- Most students worry about being typecast by their discipline.

- Most students gain new interests and discover new horizons during their studies.

- Some vocational degrees limit career options more than those which are non-vocational.

- Arts courses provide transferable skills essential to most employers.

- Over half of all graduate job vacancies are open to arts graduates.

TWO

WHY CHOOSE ARTS?

Obviously, you want to make the right decisions about your degree course. And you aren't likely to be short of advice, both from inside and outside of your family. What kinds of things do you need to take into account to make up your mind and feel confident about your decisions?

There are a number of things to think about when choosing a degree subject and then a particular university course. These include job prospects, your personal interests and aptitudes, your subjects and grades in secondary school (especially in your final year), the types of courses available, and where you would like to study.

Job Prospects

Many people believe that the purpose of a degree course is to train students for work related to the course subject, but this isn't always the case. Most graduates are recruited for their trained minds rather than their specialist knowledge. They know how to learn systematically, how to handle and interpret information, and how to analyze and solve problems. Employers also value the maturity, social skills, and self-confidence that can come from three or more years of university life. So, for most people, the value of studying for a degree is that it allows them to pursue an interest in a particular subject while developing skills that are valued by employers.

Nevertheless, when choosing your courses, keep in mind that not all arts subjects are given equal weight by employers. Consider the following examples.

Language Skills

Canadian employers are starting to expect a second language, particularly French. Obviously, most positions with the federal Public Service require that applicants have equal facility with English and French. Increasingly, advertisements for positions in the private sector outside Quebec will ask for fluency in French.

In a global economy, employers will be seeking managers and employees with the ability to speak the language of the country of business. In October 1996, *The Globe and Mail* reported that American Express, in cooperation with the Conference Board of Canada, identified five key emerging markets: Beijing, China; Seoul, South Korea; Mexico City, Mexico; Buenos Aires, Argentina; and Santiago, Chile.[3] The Vancouver-based Asia Pacific Foundation, which assists Canadian businesses on the other side of the Pacific, adds Thailand, Vietnam, and Indonesia as countries seeking Canadian expertise in energy, transportation, telecommunications, and environmental equipment and services. Business Travel International serves multinational clients through a network of 46 travel management companies in more than 60 countries.

As you can see, there will be good opportunities to use modern languages for businesses in and beyond Canada. However, if you're drawn to study languages because you want to work abroad, then you would be wise to combine them with another subject. Most overseas posts for those with a language-only degree are in translation, interpretation, and teaching English as a foreign language.

Companies doing business overseas, as well as overseas employers, will expect a vocational subject combined with one or more modern languages. Canadian universities offer a good range of suitable courses. Most arts subjects can be combined with modern languages in a joint major program, or in a major-minor program. In addition, there are a number of international business programs at the undergraduate and post-graduate levels. For example, Northern British Columbia University and Toronto's York University offer such programs, the latter with work-experience placements overseas.

Art, Performing Arts, and Design

Courses in art, design, music, drama, and dance may be seen as less rigorous than other subjects by employers outside the relevant areas. (Of course, to employers in related fields these courses may be essential qualifications.) If any of these subjects interests you, be aware of two facts. First, unemployment among newly qualified art and design graduates is about the same as that for most other disciplines. Recent surveys show that only about half were employed in jobs directly related to their program of study. These statistics suggest that there are few vacancies in careers directly related to music, drama, and dance, and most of these require further post-graduate study. This is not meant to discourage you from following one of these subjects if you have a passionate interest and the necessary talent. But be prepared for a very competitive job market and further study.

Personal Interests

The best and perhaps the only reason for choosing a particular degree course is that the subject fascinates you. As well as giving you intellectual satisfaction, your interest in the subject should help you to stay motivated in your studies.

You may have already done a computer or paper-and-pencil interest inventory test. If so, you were probably given a list of jobs compatible with your self-description. Treat this list with some caution; the tests cannot probe your answers. There are three reasons to be cautious:

(1) Your interest in a subject (or rejection of other subjects) could be based on false assumptions.

(2) Your experiences at school are not necessarily a reliable guide to what a particular subject will be like at university.

(3) Universities offer a marvellous range of courses in fascinating subjects you have probably never taken at school.

On the other hand, interest inventories do provide information about careers related to your interests, may help you decide between two conflicting alternatives, and are a guide to further investigation.

Finally, don't overlook your recreational activities; these may be an even better guide to interesting career areas. Often your leisure interests can transfer to an area of employment.

Aptitudes

Once you have assessed your interests, you need to take into account your abilities and your aptitudes — what you're good at, and what you could be good at if you receive the appropriate training. Most people tend to be better at the subjects they like than at those they dislike. However, don't underestimate your aptitudes. What you've done to date is not necessarily an indication of all you can do, or what you could be best at.

Your aptitudes also may have been assessed through one or more standardized aptitude tests. If you haven't taken this type of assessment and would like to, check with your school counsellor or a career counsellor at your local career centre.

Your Subjects and Grades

The subjects you have taken at school can give you an idea of the areas of study which interest you, and your grades can indicate whether you have an aptitude for them. Your choice of degree subject will be determined in part by your marks in your final year of secondary school. For example, 1996 admission requirements at the University of Waterloo Coop Accountancy Studies program were in the high 80s, while admission to Honours Arts required marks in the mid 70s. Both required English plus at least one other arts-related subject. Check with your school counsellor about subjects required for entrance and the likely marks you will need.

The Courses Available

You can study most high school subjects at a degree level, and there is a wide variety of others that may not have been available at your secondary school. The range is even larger than you might guess from looking through lists of courses; and degrees at different universities may have the same name but their content can differ greatly.

You should consult the *Spectrum* series (published by the Guidance Centre, University of Toronto), the *Directory of Canadian Universities* (published by AUCC Publications), provincial publications such as, in Ontario, *Info, The Guide to Ontario Universities for OAC Students*, published by the Ontario University Registrar's Association, and university faculty calendars. Various computer programs such as *Choices* and *Discover* are excellent resources for education and career information; they also help you relate your interests and aptitudes to appropriate programs of study. If you have access to the Internet, check out

- ⊃ CanWorkNet (http://canworknet.ingenia.com/canworknet)

- ⊃ SchoolNet (http://schoolnet2.carleton.ca)

- ⊃ Canadian Universities (http://watserv1.uwaterloo.ca/~credmond/univ.html)

- ⊃ Gateway to Opportunities (http://sbit01.sbit.edu.on.ca:8001/~careers/go/welcome.htm).

Once you have narrowed down your choices, you need to study the course calendars to find out in detail exactly what each university is offering. Many faculties and departments publish their own handbooks, which give a more detailed picture of the course content, teaching methods, entrance requirements, academic staff, and research interests.

The traditional degree course covers one subject (a single honours degree). However, there is an ever-growing choice of courses for which you can study two or more subjects. For example, you could take a two-subject course (a joint honours degree), combining economics with one of the following:

- computer science
- geography
- mathematics
- philosophy
- political science
- sociology
- statistics

There are combined honours courses which let you choose a number of modules from a seemingly infinite range of subjects. These courses have a variety of names, including combined studies, modular studies, independent studies, general arts, and humanities.

Here is one example. At the University of Toronto, to qualify for an Honours B.A., a student must:

- complete 20 courses;
- complete the requirements of a specialist program; or a two major program; or a major and a minor program; or three minor programs.

So it's possible to design your program based on two or three of the following:

- Aboriginal Studies
- Anthropology
- Classics
- Computer Science
- Drama
- East Asian Studies
- Economics
- English
- Environment
- European Studies
- Fine Art
- Finno-Ugric

- French
- German
- History
- Italian
- Latin
- Middle East and Islamic Studies
- Modern Languages and Literature
- Near Eastern Studies
- Political Science
- Psychology
- Slavic Languages and Literature
- South Asian Studies
- Geography
- Ancient Greek
- Ibero-American Studies
- Jewish Studies
- Linguistics
- Modern Greek
- Music
- Philosophy
- Portuguese
- Religion
- Sociology
- Spanish

There are also a number of mathematics and science courses that could be included in the above list.

Designing programs allows you to explore your interests, especially in the first year. But you would be wise to focus your studies from your second year onwards. If you end up with a degree made up of many unrelated subjects, potential employers may suspect that you lack focus or concentration.

Where to Study?

Universities differ not only in the subjects they offer and the content of their courses, but also in how they teach and assess you. Read the faculty calendars carefully; teaching quality varies a lot, and some courses have a better reputation with other schools (including graduate schools) and with employers than others. Another source of information is the annual university issue published by *Maclean's* magazine, which researches each Canadian university by surveying counsellors, students, and university faculty, and arrives at a rating for each school in a number of categories.

However, it's probably wise to do some research on your own. Visit the campus yourself. (After all, you wouldn't choose a home or community in which you want to spend four years or more without visiting the location!) Take advantage of campus visit programs that each school offers. Talk to faculty and students; check out the residences, the library, the activities offered to students, the availability of professors and teaching staff for individual assistance.

At the start of this chapter, you read that many people will probably be offering you advice. Try to make use of all of it that you can as you make your own decision. But remember, the final decision is up to you. Take ownership of your own life and career. Your degree choice is the first major step you take on that path.

One's lifework, I have learned, grows with the working and the living. Do it as if your life depended on it, and first thing you know, you'll have made a life out of it. A good life, too.

Theresa Helburn, author

Key Points to Think About

You might like to discuss these points with family members, a guardian, or friends.

- Most arts disciplines are valued by employers.
- Unemployment in most arts subjects is only slightly higher than in other fields.
- The best reason for choosing a particular subject is personal interest.

- Interests and aptitudes should be tested as a guide to career choice.

- Universities offer a far wider subject choice than secondary schools.

- Courses with the same name differ widely in content between universities.

- Combining courses is an increasingly popular option because of the flexibility it provides.

- Teaching standards may vary between university departments, so doing your own research is essential.

- You need good objective advice, but must then make your own choice of degree course.

- There is a wealth of resources — print, electronic, human — to draw upon to help you decide on a degree course or career path.

THREE

Western economies are undergoing a massive restructuring designed to increase competitiveness in world markets. This new "post-industrial revolution" is just as profound as the industrial revolution of the 18th and 19th centuries.

The growth industries are either those that create and manufacture products which make use of the latest science and technology or those which provide services to organizations and individuals. These services range from consultancy to insurance, hotels to health care, entertainment to retailing, advertising to public administration. The original industrial revolution was based on technical skills; the post-industrial revolution is based on information and knowledge.

How Are Jobs Changing?

As old industries die and new ones are born, there are many changes in the way people are employed.

Until about 1970, most people worked in "blue collar" jobs using manual skills. There were also large numbers of junior clerical staff doing routine and repetitive work. Managers and professional and technical workers were relatively few in number and most were not university graduates. University graduates were a tiny proportion of the workforce population and most often found employment in university teaching, research institutions, medicine, law, and the higher levels of the federal and provincial government. They were seen as an elite.

All this has changed. Many manual and clerical jobs have been replaced by machines. The use of increasingly complex machines and computers has created large numbers of jobs for specialists of various kinds. Most jobs now are "white collar," knowledge-based jobs, and the proportion is rising. More and more young people are entering higher education, and university graduates are an increasing proportion of the workforce.

As well, many existing jobs have become more complex and need greater intellectual skills. As a result, many careers which until quite recently were open to secondary school graduates — such as general accountancy, banking, journalism, and human resources — now require university graduates.

The way in which work is organized is also changing and this too is affecting university graduate careers.

How Are Graduates Affected?

The traditional graduate career was fairly predictable. You would probably have been taken on by one of a small number of big employers, having joined as a trainee on the assumption that you had a job for life. Your training program, lasting about two years, would have led to your first proper management post. Your career development would then have been by regular moves up the promotion ladder, in jobs of increasing seniority, which took you through the many ranks in the management pyramid.

However, employers have had to cut costs and become more efficient to meet growing competition at home and overseas. So they have stripped out whole layers of management, often leaving only four or five levels from the most junior positions through to the very top.

Changes such as these affect graduate careers in a number of ways:

⊃   There are fewer openings in big organizations.

⊃   There are new ways of working and fewer promotions.

⊃   There are fewer jobs for life.

⊃   Levels of education, training, and experience will determine income levels, but there are fewer management training programs.

Fewer Openings in Big Organizations

With far smaller management structure, the large traditional graduate recruiters will never again need the graduate numbers they did before. In the past, most large corporations actively recruited graduates on campus. Now, while career fairs are still a feature of career development activity on campus, many companies have moved to Just-In-Time Recruiting (JITR).[4] Much like just-in-time inventory control in most warehouses, companies recruit quickly to meet demand for contingency staffing. The implication here is that you should ensure that your résumé is listed on a number of Internet locations.

The New Ways of Working and Fewer Promotions

More often now, part-time work is replacing full-time employment. Many workers will be hired on a temporary or contractual basis. Work arrangements will be more flexible, with many people working out of their homes, telecommuting to work. If you do work full-time, it's likely that you will be part of a team, set up to develop new products, strategies, or challenges. As soon as that product or strategy is developed, you will be assigned to a new team that may require new skills.

With this type of arrangement, you will sometimes work on more than one job at a time. On some you might be the leader because the job needs your particular skills or experience; on others you would be a member of a team led by someone else. You will move through a series of multidimensional roles, rather than rigidly defined jobs. As you perform better and become more expert, your pay should improve, but promotion in the traditional sense — another rung on the ladder — will not automatically follow. The regular promotions of the past will be replaced by more flexible, but more unpredictable, career paths.

> *The new workplace bears little resemblance to one your parents and grandparents knew. Not only are the days of working for one organization for 40 years long gone, many of those organizations are gone as well.... No, there will not be the same type of security or reliance on an organization previous generations knew. But there will be a greater focus on self-managed careers, on quality of life issues and change, frequent change.*

Canadian Association of Career Educators and Employers[5]

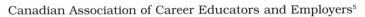

There will also be a developing need for specialists, but they will tend not to manage other staff. Many will be employed in consultancy roles requiring high levels of specialized knowledge. However, a growing proportion of graduate jobs will require a portfolio of transferable skills which can be applied in a variety of situations and roles. The knowledge content of these jobs will be less specialized.

Every career counsellor, placement specialist, and writer/researcher in the career planning field makes the same point: success will come to those with the appropriate mix of work-related and life skills. You should carefully consider the transferable skills discussed in Chapter 4 to assess which areas need to be further developed.

For arts graduates there is good news in this new flexibility. As employers outside science and technology need fewer graduates with specialist knowledge and more with general intellectual and work-related transferable skills, they are opening up more of their vacancies to graduates of any discipline.

Fewer Jobs for Life

Fewer graduates than ever before will be able to develop their entire careers in one organization. Employment contracts for a fixed length of time, or to complete a specific project, will become more common. Even in the professions, where your first job tends to be under a training contract, you can no longer assume that your employer will extend your contract into permanent employment once your training is completed. No longer will there be jobs for life. There will be more movement between employers, so you will have to be flexible in how you view your career. Think in terms of "portability" rather than "stability."

Fewer Management Training Programs

Since few graduates will be employed by one organization for life, employers cannot afford to invest in long training programs before they start to see a return. They now expect graduates to make an early contribution. Even in their first year, graduates are given real work which is important to the business. This means that employers expect greater maturity in their recruits, and are giving graduates responsibility earlier.

New Types of Jobs

Do these changes mean fewer graduate jobs? Although larger traditional graduate employers have fewer graduate trainee vacancies than in the past, this loss of opportunity is more than made up for by new posts. Many new graduate employers, mainly drawn from small- and medium-sized companies, are entering the market for the first time. Some want to strengthen their management team, some want technical specialists, while others recruit graduates into roles previously held by secondary school graduates.

Large employers, although recruiting fewer management trainees, are accepting growing numbers of graduates directly into posts for which they already have appropriate skills. This is more common with scientists and technologists than arts graduates. But large employers are also recruiting graduates into work formerly done by high school graduates. It is not that there are fewer graduate jobs, but that the nature of many jobs is changing. Employers now expect a higher level of education from a greater proportion of their employees.

Graduate Underemployment: A Real Risk?

Since graduates enter the workplace doing jobs previously undertaken by high school graduates, some people worry that graduates may end up under-employed in dead-end jobs. However, secondary school graduates often worked under close supervision. University graduates are expected to be self-starters who manage their own work. This means they are able to develop their job in ways that secondary school graduates couldn't, and put their own stamp on it.

In addition, as jobs become more complex, they increasingly need the skills which graduates can bring to them. Many careers which were mainly open to secondary school graduates have now become graduate entry jobs, and this trend will continue.

Some of the newer graduate employers have little experience in training and developing graduates or giving them early responsibility. (Others could, of course, go the other way and ask too much of young graduates too soon.) It will be up to you to prove your worth. Make the most of every learning opportunity. Accept responsibility and make something special of any job you are given, however mundane it may at first appear.

This is not to say that there are no dead-end jobs. When you are job-seeking, be selective. But if you make a mistake and enter the wrong job, do everything as well as you can and learn as much as possible from the experience before moving on.

What About Graduate Unemployment?

Employers and university career counsellors agree that if graduates take their job search really seriously as they approach graduation, they will almost certainly find a job, even during a severe recession. The keys to success are:

- ⊃ Develop your transferable skills. (See the next chapter.)

- ⊃ Make full use of your university's career centre services.

⊃ Start applying for jobs at the beginning of your final year — no later.

⊃ Take advantage of campus career fairs.

⊃ Monitor job advertising aimed at final-year under-graduates.

⊃ Target your applications carefully. (The scatter-gun approach rarely works.)

⊃ Apply only to organizations for whom you would really like to work.

⊃ Apply to small employers; they usually get fewer applications.

⊃ Make certain that your application is well presented. Use the Canadian Association of Career Educators and Employers (CACEE) formats for resumes and letters of application and the CACEE application form.

Also keep in mind the following findings from a study exploring the employment experience of liberal arts graduates.[6]

⊃ Graduates worked in a variety of positions, taking contract positions, part-time employment, and interim work.

⊃ Most experienced periods of unemployment.

⊃ Career planning and goal setting were important.

⊃ Graduates expressed the need to discover the connections between their education and areas of employment, to have a period of developing and testing out career aspirations before settling down to employment.

⊃ The primary job search strategy was networking.

⊃ Graduates needed to develop their own niche in which to market their skills and abilities.

⊃ The exact course content of their program of study did not seem to be significant.

Where Do Arts Graduates Go?

Tables 1 and 2 (published in 1996)[7] show the destinations of 1992 graduates, just as the recession was at its deepest point. As you read these statistics, keep these points in mind.

- The downsizing trend began in earnest in 1992.

- Many companies have moved to just-in-time recruiting.

- Many workers have been hired on a part-time or contract basis.

- The job market follows the economy — recession to boom to recession.

Table 1.   **Percentages (to nearest whole number) of Graduate Destinations from Arts Disciplines and All Subjects (*Job Futures*, 1996)**

Program	Continued Education	Stayed Home	Entered Labour Force	Worked Part-Time
Applied Arts	19	9	59	13
Music	37	3	52	8
Commerce Business Administration	12	2	75	11
English	32	5	54	9
French	39	7	44	10
History	40	4	47	9
Economics	27	2	68	3
Psychology	32	6	54	8
All Subjects	26	9	59	6

Table 2.   What Type of Work? Percentage (to nearest whole number) of Those Entering Full-Time by Arts Discipline (*Job Futures*, 1996)

Applied Arts	Percent (%)
☞ Creative Designers and Craftspersons	37
☞ Photographers, Graphics Arts Technicians, Technical Occupations in Motion Pictures, Broadcasting and the Performing Arts	14
☞ Creative and Performing Artists	12
☞ Retail Sales	14

Music	
☞ Teaching	56
☞ Creative and Performing Artist	11
☞ Child Care and Home Support Worker	8
☞ Clerical Occupations	6
☞ College Instructors	5

Commerce - Business Administration	
☞ Auditors, Accountants, Investment	23
☞ Finance and Insurance Clerks	15
☞ Administrative and Regulatory	10
☞ Administrative Service Managers	10
☞ Finance and Insurance Administrative	10

English	
☞ Teaching	32
☞ Writing, Translating, Public Relations	15
☞ Retail Sales	9
☞ Insurance and Real Estate	7
☞ Paralegals, Social Service	7

French	
☞ Teaching	59
☞ Child Care and Home Support	8
☞ Motor Vehicle and Transit Drivers	8
☞ Writing, Translating, Public Relations	7
☞ College Instructors	4

History	
☞ Teaching	32

☞   Child Care and Home Support   11
☞   Auditors, Accountants, Investment   9
☞   Recording, Scheduling, Distributing   7
☞   Paralegals, Social Service   7

Economics

☞   Auditors, Accountants, Investment   15
☞   Retail Sales   13
☞   Finance and Insurance Clerks   12
☞   Managers, Retail   11
☞   Insurance and Real Estate   10

Psychology

☞   Teaching   35
☞   Paralegals, Social Service   11
☞   Child Care and Home Support   11
☞   Psychologists, Social Workers   10
☞   Policy and Program Officers   6

Therefore, consider the numbers as a guide to help you with your decision. Where the numbers have not been encouraging and you decide to enter that field, you are assuming the risk that you will obtain the marks and skills to succeed in a very competitive job market. Be sure to check with your career counsellor, and the websites listed at the end of this book to help with your decision.

Notice that almost a quarter of all the graduates continued with further study or training. And over a third of History and French graduates did so, perhaps because they thought their subjects had less vocational value than applied arts and commerce, and believed a postgraduate qualification would improve their job prospects.

As you can see, many graduates from applied arts, commerce, and economics tend to enter work related to their program of study. Other arts graduates tend toward teaching, a career that in the waning years of the 20th century will have few openings because of government cut-backs. Careers in the broad area of business are the next most frequent choice, confirming again that entry level positions are available in business and industry for arts graduates with good transferable skills.

Graduate Starting Salaries

Finally, it is worth looking at the starting salaries paid to new graduates (Table 3). Salaries for bachelor degree graduates did rise somewhat from 1985 (about $25,000) to 1992 (about $31,000). However in the past few years, levels of compensation have stayed the same, or in some cases decreased, because of the recession and corporate downsizing.

The average salary for most arts graduates tends to be lower than the average for all bachelor degree graduates. This reflects the higher salaries generally paid to science and technical graduates. Also, a glance at previous tables will show that many students take low-paying part-time positions, or positions in child care, or the retail sales area, both of which pay at, or slightly above the minimum wage. Full-time positions in professional or managerial areas would pay closer to the average, or slightly above it.

Table 3. Statistics for new graduates salaries (*Job Futures,* 1996)

Course	Minimum Salary ($)	Average Salary ($)	Maximum Salary ($)
Applied Arts	11,300	25,700	45,900
Music	9,500	27,300	53,700
Commerce - Business Administration	16,900	31,600	56,600
English	7,700	25,100	48,900
French	13,000	30,000	46,900
History	7,200	26,500	53,200
Economics	13,100	31,500	59,700
Psychology	8,900	28,500	55,900

Key Points to Think About

You might like to discuss these points with family members, a guardian, or friends.

- Employment patterns are changing fundamentally.

- There will be fewer traditional graduate traineeships.

- There will be more non-traditional jobs for graduates.

- There will be few jobs for life and little job security.

- There will be fewer promotions in the average career path.

- Career progress will be achieved through flexibility and mobility.

- Underemployment in non-traditional graduate jobs is likely to be rare.

- Graduates have far lower unemployment rates than other workers.

- The search for a job should start early in the final academic year.

- Over 25% of graduates in most arts subjects undertake further study.

- Few arts graduates enter work related to their degree, except teaching.

FOUR

ADDING VALUE TO YOUR DEGREE

Until a few years ago, most employers recruited non-technical university graduates as management trainees destined for top jobs. If you had graduated then, you probably would have joined a training program lasting from one to two years. This would have involved going on courses, starting to study for a professional qualification, and doing project work in several departments.

This training rotation in various parts of the organization would have developed your work skills, given you an understanding of how the organization functioned as a whole, and helped you to identify what type of work suited you best. It was only after this long preparation that you would have started a real job and begun to work your way up the promotion ladder.

Evolving paradigms of business organizations pose a particular challenge to those making transitions in employment. The traditional pyramidal corporate structure — with its linear chains of command and communications and expectation of performing all necessary functions within the corporation — is already giving way to flatter organizational structures [characterized by:]

☞ *small batch production*

☞ *self-directed multiskilled teams*

☞ *workers required to use judgment and make decisions*

☞ *worker autonomy based on mastery of high-level skills*

☞ *few management layers*

☞ *emphasis on continuous training: the "learning" enterprise*

☞ *involvement in decision-making on investment and work organization.*

Canadian Labour Force Development Board, 1994[8]

Because of the changes described in the last chapter, employers are looking for fewer "high flyers" than before. On the other hand, they are recruiting graduates into a far wider range of jobs. Employers expect graduates to develop their career by moving between various types of work of increasing complexity and responsibility. Although graduates still receive good training, they are also expected to do real work almost from the beginning; they must now earn their pay as soon as possible.

These changes mean that employers are altering their recruitment criteria. At one time it would have been enough to have a good degree, to be polite and well-groomed, and to show an interest in the job and a willingness to learn. These qualities are still valued, but they are no longer enough. Employers now look for evidence that you also have the skills (also known as competencies) that will help you make a quick and successful transition from education to employment.

Before looking at these skills in greater detail, you might want to consider how the way you work as a student differs from how you will work once you're employed.

Study and Work: The Differences

As a student you work to a set curriculum. The information you need, and guidance on the reliability of your sources, is often at hand. If you have an essay or project to do, you usually have plenty of time to complete it, so you can work at your own pace.

At work you will be in a far less certain world. Your activities won't be confined to a fixed curriculum because the environment in which your future employers must operate is always changing. The most successful businesses are those which are flexible and adapt faster to changing circumstance. Similarly, the most successful people in these organizations are those who are also flexible and adaptable.

Given problems to solve at work, you will seldom have all the information you need to arrive at "ideal answers" and you will rarely have enough time to evaluate all the data you have before you're due to offer a solution. You must use your judgment and produce the best answer you can in the time available. Often you will work on several problems at once.

At work, your answers will not be an end in themselves but the basis on which decisions involving people, money, and time will be made. Many decision will be irreversible — even if better solutions turn up later. You will have to live with your decisions and do your best to make them work.

You will almost certainly work in a team of people of different ages and disciplines, aiming at shared objectives. Because team members depend on one another to achieve results, you will need good interpersonal skills and must understand how your work fits in with that of your colleagues and the organization as a whole.

Developing Transferable Skills

The foundation of a continuous learning society and ability to continually upgrade the performance of the labour force depends largely upon basic skills. Society, primarily educators, must ensure that new entrants into the workforce have

the basic skills required to progress in an environment of continuous learning.

Business Liaison Group of the Canadian Labour Force
Development Board

Transferable skills are skills that may be learned in one setting or situation and applied to a wide range of settings or situations. In recent years, a great deal of emphasis has been placed on learning and developing transferable skills. For example, the Conference Board of Canada — an organization whose member companies include many of the most prominent employers in the country — has outlined what it considers to be the critical skills required of the Canadian workforce in its *Employability Skills Profile*. (See page 36 and compare it to the transferable skills outlined below.)

Similar skills lists have appeared throughout North America. All have in common a recognition of the importance of transferable skills such as the following:

- communication skills

- problem solving skills

- numeracy skills (basic arithmetic and statistics)

- computer literacy skills

- business awareness skills

- personal self-management skills

- setting work priorities and time management skills

- adaptability skills

- teamwork skills

- leadership skills

Employability Skills Profile: The Critical Skills Required of the Canadian Workforce

Academic Skills

Those skills which provide the basic foundation to get, keep, and progress on a job and to achieve the best results.

Canadian employers need a person who can:

Communicate

- Understand and speak the languages in which business is conducted
- Listen to understand and learn
- Read, comprehend, and use written materials, including graphs, charts, and displays
- Write effectively in the languages in which business is conducted

Think

- Think critically and act logically to evaluate situations, solve problems, and make decisions
- Understand and solve problems involving mathematics and use the results
- Use technology, instruments, tools, and information systems effectively
- Access and apply specialized knowledge from various fields (e.g, skilled trades, technology, physical sciences, arts, and social sciences)

Learn

- Continue to learn for life

Personal Management Skills

The combination of skills, attitudes, and behaviours required to get, keep, and progress on a job and to achieve the best results

Canadian employers need a person who can demonstrate:

Positive Attitudes and Behaviours

- Self-esteem and confidence
- Honesty, integrity, and personal ethics
- A positive attitude toward learning, growth, and personal health
- Initiative, energy, and persistence to get the job done

Responsibility

- The ability to set goals and priorities in work and personal life
- The ability to plan and manage time, money, and other resources to achieve goals
- Accountability for actions taken

Adaptability

- A positive attitude toward change
- Recognition of and respect for people's diversity and individual differences
- The ability to identify and suggest new ideas to get the job done — creatively

Teamwork Skills

Those skills needed to work with others on a job and to achieve the best results

Canadian employers need a person who can:

Work with Others

- Understand and contribute to the organization's goals
- Understand and work within the culture of the group
- Plan and make decisions with others and support the outcomes
- Respect the thoughts and opinions of others in the group
- Exercise "give and take" to achieve group results
- Seek a team approach as appropriate
- Lead when appropriate, mobilizing the group for high performance

The Conference Board of Canada

These skills can not only help you to win your first job and to move easily from education to employment; they will be useful later in moving from one type of work to another. They are valuable in any career — whether it's in a profession, industry, commerce, public service, the Armed Forces, or the voluntary sector. (Note that the voluntary sector isn't the same as doing volunteer work; volunteer work is unpaid, but many organizations that use volunteers also employ staff in a variety of functions.)

Many transferable skills will also be useful in your private life. Because they have broad application, they are sometimes referred to as "life skills." It's well worth developing them while you are a student.

Employers won't expect you to join them from full-time education with these skills fully developed. What they will look for is evidence that you have gained a basic grounding in at least some of them. You could acquire some transferable skills through your academic work at school and university, through recreational activities (including volunteer work), through paid employment during weekends, holidays, and work-placement, and through special training courses.

Communication Skills

Whatever subjects you choose to specialize in, you should still do all you can to develop your ability to communicate. Occasionally, you'll have to explain your work, however specialized, to non-specialists and people of other disciplines. Try to develop a writing style in which you can present information and ideas logically, clearly, succinctly, and, where necessary, argue a case persuasively. Apart from jobs in publishing and advertising, most writing at work involves form-filling, letters, and memoranda (brief notes either giving instructions, passing on information, asking questions, or answering queries).

Clarity and brevity are more important than "literary" style. Many people who have written up experiments in science find this a good training for structuring essays and reports. Acting as secretary to a club or society — producing agendas, writing minutes of meetings, and writing letters — is also valuable practice.

Obviously, a knowledgeable use of grammar, spelling, and punctuation is important. No employer will want you to offend educated colleagues, customers, or suppliers (or distract them from the message) by the incorrect use of English, or any other language.

There's less skill and more plain hard work to writing than anyone except a writer thinks.

Mabel Seeley

Listen to people trying to pass on information, instructions, and ideas. Note what they do well, and what they do poorly. Use them as examples and warnings. At school and university you have plenty of opportunity to do this.

Effective communication skills include oral communication, as well as written communication. Practise your oral communication skills in discussion, debates, answering questions, organizing student events, and general conversation. Again, aim for clarity and brevity. You can also learn a lot from chairing meetings for a club or society: making announcements, introducing items on the agenda, leading discussions, summarizing the points made, trying to get a consensus view, and introducing and thanking guest speakers.

The more frequently you hear yourself say, "You know what I mean," the more you need to work at your communication skills. A simple and effective method, but easy to forget, is to get into the habit of pausing for a second or two to set your thoughts in order before you speak. The old advice, "think before you speak," can't be bettered. And if you have to make a presentation, open a debate, or attend an interview, carefully plan the outline of your remarks in advance.

When communicating, always try to consider your impact on other people. Employers in all fields, not just commercial firms, focus their activities on the customer. They will welcome proof of your awareness of others, or, better still, actual experience of customer service. Part-time or holiday experience serving people in a shop, cafe, hotel, or other service industry is extremely valuable. Learn how to make people feel welcome, ask questions to find out what they want, answer queries, persuade them that you can satisfy their needs, and handle complaints. When you are a customer, observe how staff treat you and communicate with you. Note what they do that you particularly like and dislike.

Problem Solving Skills

As a student, much of your work involves deciding on a solution to a set problem from many possibilities. This is a systematic process in which you draw on your knowledge and experience and organize this into possible solutions. This is the process of reasoning. It's a creative process that can be used equally well in student or working life to deal with theoretical and practical problems. Try to think carefully about the way in which you tackle work or other activities.

Numeracy Skills

These skills, also sometimes called computation skills, involve using numbers. Most graduate jobs (and certainly all aspects of life) involve working with numbers at times. But you don't need to be a math whiz to perform well in the working world. The math skills most employers want involve mainly simple arithmetic and common sense.

You should be able to add, subtract, multiply, divide, and work out percentages fairly quickly and with consistent accuracy — with and without a calculator. These are the most common calculations you will meet at work.

Statistical information is used by all kinds of employers and in almost every type of graduate work from time to time. You should be able to interpret information involving numbers, whether in the form of statistical tables, graphs, or charts.

Statistics can be misleading. They are rarely used to tell direct lies, but sometimes they are used to mask the truth. Mark Twain cynically warned, "There are three kinds of lies: lies, damned lies, and statistics." Consider these two examples from fictitious ads.

"Nine out of ten dentists prefer Brand X toothpaste."

This doesn't necessarily mean that nine out of ten (90%) of all dentists prefer Brand X. It could simply mean that nine out of the ten dentists who were asked prefer it.

"The earnings of our sales staff average over $35,000."

This could mean that three senior people with good sales territories are earning $100,000 a year, but another 17 people only earn $25,000 a year.

Statistics, used properly, are valuable and reliable. If you see them quoted to support an argument — especially by advertisers, salespeople, and politicians — look out for any possible loopholes. This will help your numeracy, improve your powers of judgment, and make you a more effective shopper and voter.

Computer Literacy Skills

The main uses of computers at work, outside of science and engineering, are for the electronic filing and accessing of information (databases), for entering and manipulating numbers such as financial data (spreadsheets), and for keyboarding and storing the written word (word processing). The use of desktop publishing and graphics packages is also increasing, and designers are now making extensive use of CAD (computer-aided design).

You'll probably use computers during your university courses, and certainly will have access to them. University facilities range from PCs through to powerful mainframes or supercomputers. (The University of Waterloo in Ontario, for example, has some of the best computer equipment in the world.) As well as practising your computer skills, you can tap into networks linking academic databases, giving you worldwide access to vast libraries of electronically stored information.

Computer literacy has become a new basic academic skill . . . . The skill of accessing electronic

information is as important as knowing how to sign out a library book. Even more important, when so much [information] is available, is being able to focus on what is relevant and what can be ignored.

Gary Hall, educator and author

Business Awareness Skills

If you're choosing arts because you think it's a way to escape the world of commercial values, you'll almost certainly be disappointed. It isn't only that industry and commerce are by far the biggest employers of arts graduates. Whatever field of work you enter, it will be affected one way or another by business factors. You'll have "customers" with needs to satisfy, whether they pay or not. In an employment agency, the customers are the people seeking work. In an art gallery, they are the viewing public, in a school the students, and in a hospital the patients.

It costs money to run any sort of enterprise and employ people. This money must be raised somehow, whether by selling goods or a service, raising taxes, or soliciting charitable donations. Income and expenditures must be budgeted and accounted for. All the laws about property, employing people, health and safety, insurance, consumer rights, and much more must be observed.

Get some practical work experience. Weekend and holiday work doesn't just help your finances (especially while you're at university), but provides experience that graduate recruiters value highly. Take any available opportunities to visit employers or go work-shadowing (observing someone in their daily working routine). If there's a family business, learn what you can from it. Take one or more of the cooperative education programs at your school.

When you're at work, even in a mundane job, you can learn a lot by watching, listening, and asking the right questions. Reflect on why your work is organized as it is and how it fits into the overall scheme of the business. What skills do you find are most important in your job? What would be the consequence for the business of different kinds of mistakes? How could they be rectified? Observe how managers succeed, or fail, to get the willing support of their employees or team.

The graduate recruiters you meet eventually are going to be very interested in how much you consciously learned from your work experiences!

Once at university, check with your career centre for details of career fairs, work-shadowing opportunities, vacation employment, and transferable skills workshops.

Personal Self-Management Skills

The premise of self-management is that you are in charge of yourself. You choose the way you think, act, and feel. Employers are looking for people with high self-esteem and confidence. Such people have faith in their talents and resources, and tend to more easily respect and accept others. They appear self-assured and poised, particularly in social situations. Their self-confidence tends to earn them the respect of others, and — equally important — can serve to motivate others.

Also important is the ability to cope with stress, maintain a balanced perspective, have a sense of humour, and know how to relax and free your mind from worries.

Setting Work Priorities and Time Management Skills

As a student, you're used to completing work, such as essays, by a set date. Working to deadlines is normal at work. At times, you may have several assignments at once, each with its own deadline. There may also be less urgent tasks that don't have strick time limits. Prioritizing involves deciding the relative importance of the tasks you have, and the order in which they should be carried out. Time management concerns using the limited time you have as effectively as you can to meet your deadlines.

You'll need to develop the ability to sort out in your own mind the advantages and disadvantages of each decision and to take action after considering alternatives and consequences. People with good goal-setting and time management skills can think in the future tense and act in the here and now. They know what they want to accomplish and are able to set in place a realistic plan to help them to be successful.

Graduate recruiters often test these skills, and others, at a second interview with a written "in-tray exercise." This simulates the typical pile of papers that might face you at work. You have to decide your priorities, maybe delegating some items and then carrying out the other tasks. These may include writing memos and letters.

Adaptability Skills

Much has been written over the past decade about the rapidity of change in the world of work and the need to be flexible. Employers are looking for people who have a positive attitude to change — who see change as a challenge, rather than a source of fear or anxiety. In most cases, the need is to be proactive, to prepare for possible scenarios, and to make plans to deal with changes.

A key component of this skill is the ability to respect people's diversity and individual differences. This is important not only in Canada's pluralistic society, but also in an increasingly global economy, where you will be working or negotiating with business contacts in other countries.

Teamwork Skills

Most work situations involve collaborating with people working in multidisciplinary teams. In a team, your personal objectives take second place to those of the group. You must see how your work fits in with that of your colleagues and of the organization as a whole. You also need good interpersonal skills. You must combine the ability to argue your point of view persuasively with the willingness to listen and learn from others, and to make compromises when necessary.

Taking part in team sports and other group pursuits is good preparation. Weekend and holiday jobs that involve working with others are also valuable. So, too, are such activities as scouting or guiding, and personal development courses such as those run by Outward Bound and other outdoor development training centres.

Leadership Skills

You read earlier that work groups today are frequently formed, dissolved, and regrouped to suit the projects at hand. As a result, the leadership of a team may move from one person to another as the project changes. In these situations, graduates can expect to find themselves moving in and out of leadership roles without any change in their formal status. The most effective leader, then, particularly in today's flexible organization, is likely to be the one people turn to when they need guidance and support. This type of leader gets the willing effort of others, motivates them to do their best, and earns the team's respect — usually through a combination of personal example, knowledge, enthusiasm, tact, decisiveness, tenacity, modesty, and, above all, integrity. Rank and status are largely irrelevant.

When the best leader's work is done, the people say, 'we did it ourselves.'

Lau-Tzu, philosopher

Get as much experience as you can working within a team, just as a member. You won't be able to lead effectively until you understand how teams work together. Your future employers will welcome any experience you have had as a sports team captain, on school council, or in a similar leadership role.

Employers also value any experience in running student or club events. If it includes coordinating the work of volunteer helpers and working within a budget and to a strict timetable, so much the better. But remember that serving on school or university committees and holding office are valued only if you take an active role. (Employers and admissions staff in universities are well aware that some students join societies and committees purely so they can list them on resumes and application forms.)

According to Stephen Covey, an author of several books dealing with leadership, principle-centred leaders share the following characteristics.[9]

⊃   They are continually learning.

⊃   They are service-oriented.

⊃   They radiate positive energy.

⊃   They believe in other people.

⊃   They lead balanced lives.

⊃   They see life as an adventure.

⊃   They are synergistic (that is, they thrive on bringing different people and talents together to find new solutions).

⊃   They exercise for self-renewal.

Skills and talents such as these are not only desirable to employers. They are also valid and valuable attributes for life in general.

Key Points to Think About

You might like to discuss these points with family members, a guardian, or friends.

🎓   Graduate recruiters give very high priority to transferable skills.

🎓   Skills gained through practical work experience are especially valued.

🎓   Activities that improve the following are to be encouraged:

- team working
- leadership
- clear and accurate use of oral and written English
- problem solving
- business awareness
- basic arithmetic
- interpretation of statistics
- computer applications
- self-management and self-awareness

2

CAREERS USING YOUR DEGREE SUBJECT

This section looks at careers in which you could make substantial use of your specialist knowledge. Some subjects are grouped together in one chapter because they offer similar career opportunities. Specifically:

⊃   Art history is covered in Chapter 8, Careers Using History

⊃   Some social science courses such as speech therapy are included in Careers Using Languages and Linguistics (Chapter 9) because they include language studies.

⊃   Linguistics has a section of its own in Chapter 9.

Whatever your area of interest, you might find it helpful to look at some of the other chapters in this section. They may offer options that you haven't considered.

Keep in mind that there are many more arts graduates than there are vacancies in work related to a particular discipline. Fortunately, other careers are open to you. Even when you can't use the specific knowledge you have learned, you will probably find that transferable skills acquired through higher study are invaluable. These careers are covered in Section 3.

FIVE

TEACHING YOUR SUBJECT

It is almost impossible to exaggerate the importance of education. Not only is our economy based more and more on knowledge-based activities, but many global problems (including poverty and disease) will only be solved through the application of knowledge.

But the wise know that we often need to hear most of that to which we are least inclined, and even to learn to employ, in certain circumstances, that which is capable, if employed amiss, of being a danger to us.

Matthew Arnold, poet and philosopher

If education is vitally important, then so is teaching. It seems odd, therefore, that the teaching profession doesn't have a very good image. But undervaluing teachers is nothing new. The following opinion has been famous (but unfair) for 90 years.

He who can, does. He who cannot, teaches.

G.B. Shaw, playwright

You're probably aware that there is some unhappiness in the teaching profession. Many teachers complain of being over-stressed, over-worked, and of not having enough time or resources to do their job properly. At present, they are also having to adapt to a succession of changes in the educational system — changes with which they do not always agree. If this sounds a bit negative, it's worth remembering that in most professions you will find people having to cope with continual change and who would like fewer time pressures, better resources, and less stress. These issues are not exclusive to the teaching profession.

On the positive side, teaching is a career in which you can help young people to develop their full potential. This can be both challenging and rewarding. Teaching offers variety and the opportunity to be creative and original. Prospects for promotion are good. And the financial rewards can be excellent in the long term, although starting salaries tend to be lower than in other graduate careers.

Although teachers can work with all ages from infants upwards, university graduates teaching the subjects they studied at degree level usually work in secondary schools, continuing education, or post-secondary education.

In Canada, because education is a provincial responsibility, requirements to enter the teaching profession vary. A typical route in many areas of the country is to complete a B.A., and then apply to a Faculty of Education for a one- or two-year program. Some universities, such as York University in Toronto, offer four- or five-year concurrent programs where you can earn both a B.A. and a B.Ed. Other schools, such as the University of Manitoba, offer four-year B.Ed. programs.

Your Work as a Teacher

Whether you teach in a school, college, or university, there are many common elements in the work you would do. Your aim is to help all your students to reach their full potential. This means not only developing their existing abilities, but also looking at their aptitudes and their aspirations.

Before you can teach anything to anyone, you must build a good relationship with the student and find ways to stimulate interest in your subject. You will quickly find out that what enthuses some people doesn't work with others. You will be teaching individuals, each with a different personality and range of aptitudes. You must find ways to reach every person in your class. You must also be able to keep order, sometimes having to cope with disruptive students.

For every person wishing to teach there are 30 not wanting to be taught.

W.C. Sellar and R.J. Yeatman, authors

When you are working with students, whether elementary or secondary, you will use a variety of teaching methods such as leading and facilitating discussions, giving demonstrations, conducting experiments, organizing individual and group projects, and going on field trips.

Good teachers make the best of a pupil's means; great teachers foresee a pupil's ends.

Maria Callas, opera singer

Away from your class, you will spend many hours preparing lessons, marking student work, and writing reports. You may spend time advising students on personal problems, either informally or as their counsellor or mentor. You will have administrative duties and will have to attend departmental, curricular, and other meetings. Much of this will be done outside normal school hours. Many teachers also get involved in extracurricular activities with students. These range from sports, drama, and concerts to overseas trips. Although such activities are not a compulsory part of their job, most teachers realize that these activities are important and give their time willingly.

Students are normally working toward formal qualifications, so your teaching must cover a set curriculum (although there is usually some room for flexibility). You also will have to draw up a program of studies, ensuring that your students have a balanced program that will enable them to study everything necessary in the time available.

Some people think that once a teacher has prepared a course of study, it can be repeated year after year without change. This is not so. Good teachers are always looking for better ways to cover the curriculum and to incorporate new ideas and knowledge. And there is an almost constant stream of change, beyond the teacher's control, which affects what is taught. The changes range from updates in curriculum guidelines to education initiatives from government (such as introducing new diploma requirements). One of the biggest challenges in teaching today is adapting to all the changes.

The Qualities You Need

To form good relationships with your students and maintain order you must combine sensitivity to others with patience, good listening skills, tact, fairness, and self-confidence. A sense of humour helps; being able to laugh at yourself is especially useful.

> *The skills you have learned in school are practical and necessary through life. You must know and practise "life skills" such as communication, problem-solving and decision-making in order to teach them.... Students will continue to need suitable role models and will look to their teachers to help them develop a whole range of skills that will enable them to become well adjusted adult members of society.*

Ontario Teachers' Federation[10]

You also need an enthusiasm for your subject, and must be able to organize information and ideas logically and then communicate them clearly. You must fire the imagination of your students and encourage them to take an active part in their own learning. Just presenting information and talking about it is not enough.

Teachers teach by example. As a teacher, you will be expected to guide your students to choose appropriate ways of thinking and acting, and you will be expected to set an example through your actions.

Ontario Teachers' Federation

To plan a balanced course of study, prepare lessons, set and mark assignments, and keep to your schedule, you need to be well organized and good at managing your time.

You spend much of the day on your feet. You may also have to walk long distances between classes, often carrying heavy loads of books, papers, and equipment. The work itself can be stressful. To maintain your enthusiasm you need plenty of energy and stamina — physical, mental, and emotional.

Teaching in Secondary Schools

Teens usually start secondary school at 13 or 14 years of age. By law, they must remain until they are 16, but most choose to stay on until they are 18 or 19. Most attend local, publicly financed secondary schools which cater to all levels of ability. There are also a number of private schools, recognized by provincial education authorities, which do not depend on municipal taxes but rather on tuition paid by students' families. Such schools tend to be smaller with smaller class sizes as well. However, salaries tend to be lower than those for teachers in publicly financed schools.

Teachers in secondary schools usually specialize in one or two subjects and work with students of all ages and abilities within the school. As well as the kind of teaching duties already described, you may have to act as a student mentor, assist with student portfolio development, prepare student reports, and organize work experience for your students. You will also come into contact with parents, social workers, school trustees, and many other people in the community. In some private schools, you may have to live in and help to care of your students outside school hours.

Entry Qualifications

In each province, you either follow your degree with a year or two at a faculty of education, or take one of the concurrent or B.Ed. programs offered at many universities. As part of these programs, you gain teaching expertise in two or three secondary subjects.

Successful completion of the practice-teaching and academic phases of the education program qualifies you for a temporary teaching qualification. This is usually valid for one or two years. It becomes permanent after you've successfully completed a probationary period in your first position.

British Columbia and Ontario have a College of Teachers, which defines what teachers should know and be able to do at each stage of their professional careers and sets standards for graduation from accredited teacher education programs. All teachers in these two provinces must be registered with the College. In all provinces, you will also be required to join the appropriate teaching federation (your professional association or union). The Canadian Teachers' Federation is an umbrella group of these associations.

Career Development

Once you're a qualified teacher, opportunities for career development are good both within the classroom and in school administration. A couple of years in teaching is also a good preparation for further post-graduate training as a school counsellor or educational psychologist.

Finding Vacancies

Most hiring authorities recruit at faculties of education. Ensure that you keep in contact with your career centre to stay informed of potential openings. Advertisements are also placed regularly in most major newspapers.

Provincial teaching federations produce careers literature. Contact the federation in your provincial capital.

✍ Further Information

Contact the teaching federation or the Ministry or Department of Education in your province.

National associations include:

**Canadian Teachers'
Federation**
110 Argyle Avenue
Ottawa, ON, K2P 1B4

**Canadian Educational
Association**
#8-200, 252 Bloor St. W.
Toronto, ON, M5S 1T8

Teaching in Colleges

Across Canada, there are thousands of community colleges, private vocational schools, and specialized schools such as agricultural colleges, schools of horticulture, and art colleges. These schools offer vocational-related programs with options in arts courses such as English, history, and psychology. However, the focus is typically on specific careers such as travel and tourism or early childhood education. Most courses are linked to the needs of local employers with whom lecturers have to maintain strong links.

Students can be 18 years of age and recent secondary school graduates. But with the current trend to return to school, students are more likely to be adults in their mid-30s or older, seeking a mid-career shift and retraining.

An instructor's duties are similar to those of a secondary school teacher, especially when teaching academic subjects. However, with vocational subjects there is likely to be a stronger emphasis on practical work. Working hours and holidays are similar to those of teachers in secondary schools, except that instructors may have to work evening sessions. While there is no formal training program for teachers at this level, they are usually hired only after a number of years of successful work experience in an occupation directly related to the courses they want to teach. Job security is poor, and promotion possibilities are limited.

Vacancies are usually advertised in major Canadian newspapers.

✍ Further Information

Contact:

Association of Canadian
Community Colleges
1223 Michael Street
Gloucester, ON, K1J 7T2

Teaching at Universities

Teaching may be to either undergraduate or postgraduate students. Much of the teaching is through lectures which may be attended by more than 100 students. Lectures may be supplemented by seminars with smaller groups of students and face-to-face tutorials with individuals. (Seminars and tutorials involve interaction between teacher and students, with the students contributing their ideas and knowledge for discussion.) Depending on the subject, lecturers also supervise sessions of practical work, lead field trips, and arrange work projects and placements.

Teaching at this level involves a lot of research and preparation. University teaching has to be at the forefront of knowledge, so it is vital that lecturers keep fully up-to-date with developments around the world in their specialist field. They must read extensively, and may attend seminars and conferences in other universities, sometimes overseas.

It also takes a great deal of time to set and mark assignments and examinations, carry out continuous assessment, and set up and monitor work projects and placements. Many lecturers also act as personal tutors to students, advising them on their studies, career aspirations, and personal problems. They often have a considerable administrative workload as well, which may include helping with student admissions, serving on committees, and acting as external examiners for other institutions.

Teaching methods on degree courses are starting to change. There is more emphasis on helping students to take responsibility for their own learning and on developing transferable skills. Lecturers must give greater attention than before to the needs of individual students and help them to plan their own learning programs.

Universities are concerned not only with education but also with the advancement of knowledge. Since much of the money supporting universities comes from research grants from government, industry, commerce, and other external sources, research is an important element in a lecturer's work. However, the balance between teaching and research varies between posts and departments, and usually by seniority.

Although the academic (and teaching) year is only 30 weeks, staff do much of their research, administration, and preparation during vacations. Many also work toward higher academic and professional qualifications, such as a Ph.D. In practice, many of them work hours at least as long as people in industry and commerce.

Entry Qualifications

Competition for teaching positions in higher education is fierce, and more so in the arts than in science or technology. You must have a higher degree, such as an M.A., to start as a graduate assistant, but eventually you will need a Ph.D. to be considered for assistant professor positions and eventually tenure. You don't need to have teaching qualifications; however, teaching a vocational subject, such as art and design, may require work experience in the field.

Career Development

Many instructors have little job security, often working on short-term contracts of one, two, or three years. These contracts have to be renewed if instructors are to keep their job. Promotion opportunities can be good but competition is intense. At present, career progress depends far more on academic reputation than teaching ability. Publication of original research in academic journals and books, a Ph.D., and administrative skills are often important prerequisites for advancement. Those who become recognized as experts often earn extra money, and add to their reputations, through outside work. This can include consultancy, writing, broadcasting, and speaking at conferences.

✍ Further Information

Contact:

**The Association of
Universities and
Colleges of Canada**
151 Slater Street
Ottawa, ON, K1P 5N1

SIX

CAREERS USING ENGLISH

All employers value the ability to use English accurately and persuasively, in speech and in writing. However, there are several careers where the skilful use of English is the main qualification: publishing (especially editorial work), journalism, public relations, and copy writing. This chapter looks at each of these options. Table 4 provides a snapshot of the number of people employed in each major area and areas of employment. In all areas, employment prospects to the year 2000 are improving.

Another career which can make great use of your oral communication skills is sales. You will find a section on sales in Chapter 17.

Table 4. Employment Patterns in Occupations Related to the Study of English (*Job Futures*, 1996 — percentages rounded to the nearest whole number)

A. Writing, Translating, and Public Relations Professionals	Percent (%)
74,000 workers employed	
Where They Work	
Printing and Publishing	17
Federal Administration	8
Radio and TV Communication	7

Provincial and Territory Administration	6
Education	6
Other Business Services	11
Other Service Industries	15

B. Writers

17,000 workers were employed
Where They Work

Advertising Services	7
Printing and Publishing	7
Radio and TV Communication	6
Federal Adminstration	5
Education	4
Other Business Services	6
Other Service Industries	40

C. Editors

7,000 workers employed
Where They Work

Printing and Publishing	53
Radio and TV Communications	8
Education	5
Federal Adminstration	5
Provincial and Territorial Administration	2
Other Business Services	3
Other Service Industries	8

D. Professional Occupations in Public Relations and Communications

25,000 workers employed
Where They Work

Federal Adminstration	10
Provincial and Territorial Administration	10
Education	9
Advertising Services	5
Other Business Services	11
Other Health and Social Services	8
Other Service Industries	8

Book Publishing

Publishing companies in Canada range from big international businesses to small or specialist publishers. Many small publishers rely on government assistance in order to compete with international firms and to continue to publish works by Canadian authors.

The main functions in publishing are:

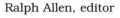

- design and production
- marketing (including sales, public relations, and publicity)
- distribution
- contracts and rights
- adminstration (including accounts and computing)
- editorial

This section concentrates on the editorial function, since it's the area where your English degree is likely to be most relevant. However, some of the other functions offer a good way to start in the publishing industry and so are looked at briefly.

An editor is a referee between the writer and the reader.

Ralph Allen, editor

Acquisition Editors

The manuscripts of unpublished books are often sent to publishers by literary agents acting on behalf of authors. The agents use their experience to match manuscripts to publishers so that a thriller is not sent to a publisher specializing in cook books, or a reference book to a fiction house. Authors also send in unsolicited manuscripts themselves, but less than one in fifty of these is published. Acquisition editors decide which manuscripts to accept or reject.

Many acquisitions editors, particularly in the technical or educational fields, specifically order or "commission" books to be written. It is the role of acquisitions editors to know what will sell in their market and to secure manuscripts accordingly. They need to be widely read and to have an instinct for what readers want or need. Once a need for a book on a particular subject has been identified, the acquisition editor will contract an author (or group of authors) to write it. Another editor will then oversee the production of the book from editing through to typesetting (now often replaced by computer setting at the publishers). A production controller will liaise with the typesetter, and oversee the printing and binding.

Copy Editors

Supporting the work of acquisition editors are copy editors. (Text is called "copy.") Their function is to read the manuscript to check the clarity and effectiveness of the language. They will try to eliminate repetitive statements and contradictions and to pick out any errors of spelling, grammar, and punctuation. Extensive revisions are sometimes needed. All these must be discussed and agreed with the author. Writing is lonely, difficult, and often frustrating and authors sometimes vent their frustrations on their editors. Editors must be good with people if they are to get the best out of their writers.

The writer's job is to write while the editor's job is to worry.

Gregory Clark, journalist

Once edited, copy goes to design and production to be turned into a printed book. Illustrations may be chosen or commissioned, involving discussion between the author, artist, and editor. Note that computers are used by all publishers, in almost every department, including editorial. Many authors now submit manuscripts on floppy disk or via e-mail, and edited text may be sent to the typesetter by computer. An editor will, therefore, often work on-screen.

Other Publishing Functions

Experience of different functions makes good preparation for an editorial career. Jobs in marketing or rights are especially useful. Working in these areas will develop an awareness of what is required of a book if it is going to sell. You will also be in contact with authors.

Marketing: This area covers all the activities necessary to promote and sell books. Marketing staff produce advertising, press releases, book lists, and other materials. They may also run special events such as lecture tours and arrange appearances by authors on TV and radio talk shows to promote their latest book. Sales staff sell the books to the book trade, to specialist library suppliers, or direct to customers such as schools or colleges. Marketing employs more people than editorial and production combined.

Contracts and Rights: In large publishing companies, the staff in this area handle the legal side of publishing. They will cover the initial agreements and contracts with authors and any issues arising from further development of a book, such as translation or the sale of film or serial rights. In smaller companies, the publisher or acquisitions editor often handles these matters.

Entry Qualifications

It is very hard to go directly into editorial work because there are so many applicants for each opening. You will need a good knowledge of English grammar, punctuation, and the precise meaning of words. You will also need to have a meticulous eye for detail and be well organized. A flair for creativity is also helpful. You must be good with people, including others in the publishing team as well as authors. You will need to be adaptable and willing to take on other mundane jobs, such as photocopying manuscripts. A second language is required in some international publishing houses. As in any highly competitive job market, postgraduate qualifications can be helpful — in this instance, a higher degree or a diploma in publishing.

Your career may start in copy editing. Alternatively, many graduates join a publishing house in any job they can get and then apply for an editorial vacancy when one arises. Another option is to join a small publisher, where people take on a range of general duties including some editorial work.

Training and Career Development

Simon Fraser University in Vancouver offers programs in publishing, editing, and technical writing. Montreal's Concordia University has English-language editing courses. And many community colleges across Canada offer courses such as book and magazine publishing and desktop publishing. Check with the schools in your area since these courses are only offered in response to demand and may not be offered every year.

Workshops and seminars are offered by some professional groups. The Book Publishers' Professional Association presents seminars in Toronto. And from time to time, the Canadian Book Publishers' Council gives seminars.

Further Information

Contact:

**Editors' Association
of Canada**
35 Spadina Road,
Toronto, ON, M5R 2S9

**Canadian Book
Publishers' Council**
250 Merton Street, Suite 203
Toronto, ON, M4S 1B1

Journalism

"   *Literature is the art of writing something that will be read twice; journalism what will be grasped at once.*

Cyril Connolly

Journalists collect and disseminate information, keeping the public informed about the news and current affairs. Work is available in three main areas: broadcasting, news agencies, and the press.

Broadcasting

Television has become the main method of delivering information to the public. This fact (combined with the rapid advent of news on the Internet, particularly by CNN) means that the best-paid jobs will be in television journalism. In Canada, the "big" networks (CBC, BBS, and Canwest-Global) tend to dominate in national and international news. Local stations tend to focus on local news. Radio is another source of employment, particularly with the recent development of all-news radio stations. Journalists write, and often present, news and current affairs programs.

News Agencies

News agencies feed news to other media. In Canada, many major newspapers contribute to the Canadian Press, the agency that develops Canadian (and international) news stories for Canada's newspapers. Other newspapers are associated with the Southam Press group. The work of news agencies is especially useful in those situations where other media representatives may not be present. This might include war zones where journalists from specific countries have been excluded for political reasons.

The National Press

In Canada there are 104 daily newspapers as well as hundreds of weekly newspapers, magazines, and trade and technical periodicals (over 125 published by 29 members of the Canadian Business Press).

Many new publications are born each month, while others die. In news agency and broadcasting work, speed is essential; audiences expect news to be constantly updated.

Newspapers cannot compete with radio and TV for speed, so they offer more detailed news and analysis. Journalists can develop as specialist reporters or "correspondents." National papers have journalists who specialize in one subject. On other papers, and in news agencies, they usually mix general reporting with one or more specialties. The main specialist areas are:

- agriculture
- business
- education
- entertainment
- fashion
- finance
- food and drink
- home interests
- political
- real estate
- science and technology
- social trends
- sport
- travel
- womens' issues

Entry Qualifications

Technically, your degree is your qualification to enter journalism. However, competition for jobs is tough, and a postgraduate qualification in journalism will give you an advantage. You must be able to write factual, concise, and clear English. The emphasis in journalism is on accuracy, clarity, brevity, and speed. Curiosity, an interest in current affairs, and a good general knowledge are essential. You must combine tact and sensitivity with assertiveness; you will have to interview people of all kinds, some of whom will not want to talk to you. Having physical and mental stamina is important because the job can involve a lot of travel and irregular hours. Reporters in newspapers, radio, and TV often work evenings and weekends; shift work is common on daily newspapers and in broadcasting.

Keyboarding skills are essential. To be a radio or television journalist you also need a good voice. When submitting a job application, you may have to complete an audition tape as well as an application form. To enter periodical publishing, it is also helpful if you have a good knowledge of the subject covered by the magazine you want to join.

Experience on a student or community publication is valuable. It is also useful to have had a brief work experience placement on a newspaper. Try writing to some local newspaper editors asking if you can join their team of reporters as an unpaid observer for a few days.

Training

Journalists must have completed a community college diploma course in journalism or equivalent, or an appropriate degree course, preferably in journalism. Graduate programs in journalism are offered at Ottawa's Carleton University and the University of Western Ontario in London.

Almost every journalist starts as a trainee reporter, usually on a regional daily or local weekly newspaper. Trainee reporters cover everything — local council meetings and court cases, fires and floods, accidents, political demonstrations, sport events, and interviews with visiting celebrities.

Career Development

To begin with, be aware that few openings exist, especially on newspapers. Community papers, however, may provide greater opportunities.

If you do land a position with a newspaper, there is no set career structure. You may aspire to head specialist parts of the paper such as Lifestyles. You may become a news editor, allocating stories to individual reporters and attending editorial conferences. You may become a sub-editor, working on stories fed in by reporters, often rewriting opening paragraphs, cutting for length, and giving stories an angle. You would also write the headlines.

If you want to reach senior positions (such as assistant editor and editor) where you have control over the content of a whole publication, you will need to have been a sub-editor and probably have headed a number of specialist sections.

If you aspire to a career in broadcast journalism, again there is no set career structure. Most reporters start with local TV stations, or in a specialty area such as weather broadcasting. Movement along a career path will depend both on your qualifications and broadcast ratings. Previous training through courses like Radio and Television Broadcasting at schools such as Toronto's Ryerson Polytechnic University may be helpful in developing your career.

✍ Further Information

Contact:

**The Canadian Association
of Journalists**
Carleton University
St. Patrick's Building
Ottawa, ON, K1S 5B6

**Canadian Community
Newspapers Association**
90 Eglinton Avenue East
Toronto, ON, M4P 2Y3

**Canadian Daily Newspaper
Association**
890 Yonge Street, Suite 1100
Toronto, ON, M4W 3P4

Public Relations

The aim of public relations is to manage the reputation and image of an organization or, sometimes, an individual. The job focuses on developing and maintaining good relationships with everyone whose support and good will are essential to the client's success. These may include customers and potential customers, suppliers, shareholders, trading partners, employees and potential employees, the stock market, community leaders, public interest groups, and government at all levels.

Public relations specialists are used by all kinds of people and organizations: commercial and industrial firms, federal, provincial and local government, celebrities, charities, politicians, public services, trade and professional groups, and various kinds of community action groups. Some organizations have their own public relations (or public affairs) departments. There are also agencies which act on behalf of a number of clients.

Public relations (PR) staff provide factual stories about their client or organization, and its products where appropriate. The information has to be carefully targeted. For example, customers will be interested in new product launches, shareholders and brokers want news of the financial health of the business, and so on. Most of the information is issued through press releases, press conferences, brochures, annual reports, and in-house magazines. Your work will bring you into close contact with journalists. Feature articles may be placed in the media. You might even "ghost-write" speeches and articles for the organizations' executives.

An important aspect of PR work is crisis management. When something goes wrong, or when an organization does something which might be unpopular, PR people have to put the best possible light on it and minimize any damage to the organization's reputation. Sometimes this can be planned in advance, such as when an organization fires employees, raises its prices, or builds a factory in a sensitive area. On other occasions, problems are totally unexpected, such as the accidental release of a pollutant into the environment or the arrest of a senior executive.

The aim of PR is to project an "image" of the organization. This can extend to the design of a "house style" for the company stationery, the decorations on company vehicles, product packaging, and so on. Some agencies specialize in this area of design.

Other agencies specialize in producing annual reports, brochures, and videos and films. These are often called "corporate communications" consultancies.

As you can see, PR work covers a lot of ground. The range of your duties will depend on where you work. In-house departments vary in the scope of their activities; they may divide their work between internal staff and external experts. Some agencies specialize in one area of PR work, such as corporate communications. Others handle all aspects of PR. However, typically, your work will include going to client briefings and other meetings, making presentations, attending press conferences, and writing material for public or press information.

Entry Qualifications

While there are no formal requirements for entry to this profession, a number a new entrants transfer from journalism. In addition, several community colleges now offer diploma programs in public relations. An MBA is highly desirable in some positions.

You will need to be articulate and able to write clearly and succinctly. Assertiveness, but not aggression, is essential. You will need a lot of self-confidence to handle tough questions from a hostile journalist, to give a speech, to cope with a dissatisfied customer, or to talk to a visiting celebrity. Obviously you have to remain calm under pressure. Computer literacy is a must.

Career Development

Job titles vary widely. You may work your way up in a large consultancy from account executive through senior account executive to a partnership. In government, you will be known as an information officer. For more information about the public service, see Chapter 13.

✍ Further Information

Contact:

**The Canadian Public
Relations Society**
#720, 220 Laurier Avenue West
Ottawa, ON, K1P 5Z9

Advertising Copywriting

There is no function in advertising, with the exception of copywriting, which will make specific use of your English skills. However, graduates of any discipline are employed as account executives. This is discussed more fully in chapter 17.

Copywriters are employed in advertising agencies to create advertising, TV and radio commercials, and other promotional materials for clients. Some are also used by corporate communications companies to write brochures and annual reports.

Many advertising agency copywriters have become well-known authors. They include Dorothy L. Sayers, Aldous Huxley, Salman Rushdie, Jack Rosenthal, Fay Weldon, Len Deighton, and James Herbert.

It is easier to write ten passably effective sonnets than one effective advertisement.

Aldous Huxley, author

Although sometimes seen as a form of journalism, even by some PR companies which use journalists on copywriting tasks, copywriting is very different. The "Copy Guidelines," issued to writers by Trotman and Co., a corporate communications company, say, "Good copywriting is the most disciplined form of writing excepting poetry. It is concerned with clarity of thought and clarity of expression. Every word and phrase must serve a clear purpose and be exactly right. The structure must aid, not hinder, comprehension. The idiom must be appropriate to the target audience and should also reflect the 'corporate personality' of the client."

Copywriting positions are extremely hard to find. This is because identifying an individual's talent is difficult until it has been tested on the job. However, good copywriters are rare so, once established, the best can ask their own price. To write good copy, you must understand the characteristics of the product and what will motivate your audience to buy it. You need imagination to find new ways of saying things that have been said scores of times before and to catch and hold the public's interest. And you should be aware of prevailing fashions in order to keep your ideas one step ahead of the trend.

You must be able to work well with other people, especially clients, creative directors, and designers. Much of your copy will be dissected by others, changed, and often rejected. You need the temperament to accept such conditions without anger or frustration.

Copywriters for TV commercials tend to be specialists who can think in visual terms and work closely with a producer. Brochure writers, too, are often specialists. However, many copywriters ply their trade in a variety of fields.

Entry Qualifications

Copywriting does not have any formal qualifications, although it helps to have a degree. You will need to be fluent in English, imaginative, and a disciplined writer. You must understand people and their motivations, and have an interest in helping businesses to achieve commercial success. You will need to be a good team worker, able to work to tight deadlines, with a high tolerance for frustration

Many entrants to copywriting will have some related work experience, possibly in journalism, sales, or marketing. Otherwise you will probably need some form of vocational training. Community colleges offer two- or three-year programs in advertising. A broad university education with courses in the humanities, social sciences, and business may be helpful. There are also specialized programs in creative writing, journalism, or communication studies at the college or university level.

Long before you apply for any copywriting positions, you will need to study the advertisements and commercials around you. Read and view them critically. Who are they addressing? What is the key message? What motives are they appealing to? How could the advertisements be improved? Write your own versions. Prepare a portfolio of advertisements you have written to show creative directors at interviews. Above all, when applying for a job as a copywriter, remember that your résumé and letter of application are themselves advertisements aimed at your target audience.

Career Development

Advertising agencies do not have trainee entry schemes for copywriters. You learn on the job. Your progress will depend on the success of the campaigns you work on. This will be reflected in your salary and your reputation in the industry. Career development is often achieved by moving between agencies.

✍ Further Information

Contact:

Institute of Canadian Advertising
30 Soudan Avenue, 2nd Floor
Toronto, ON, M4S 1V6

SEVEN

CAREERS USING ARCHAEOLOGY

There is an inescapable and persistent element of excitement in the search for the origins of humanity.... The key to our future lies in a true understanding of what sort of animal we are.

Richard E. Leakey and Roger Lewin

What image do you have of the archaeologist? Do you see Indiana Jones pursuing ancient treasures in competition with hordes of villains? Or perhaps, more mundanely, do you see someone supervising a crowd of volunteers excavating ruins with trowels and soft paint brushes, or a lone expert poring over bits of broken pottery and other artifacts in the back room of a museum?

Archaeology does have moments of high drama, comparable to the fictional adventures of Indiana Jones. In 1922, an archaeologist, Howard Carter, was excavating in the Valley of the Kings in Egypt. A staircase of 16 steps was uncovered in the sand leading down to a sloping rubble-filled rock tunnel. At the end was a blocked doorway. With three companions beside him, Carter pried out some of the stones and inserted a candle through the hole. What he saw is best described in his own words.

"At first I could see nothing, the hot air from the chamber causing the candle to flicker, but presently, as my eyes grew accustomed to the light, details of the room within emerged slowly from the mist, strange animals, statues and gold — everywhere the glint of gold. For the moment — an eternity it must have seemed to the others standing by — I was struck dumb with amazement, and when Lord Carnarvon, unable to stand the suspense any longer, enquired anxiously, 'Can you see anything?' it was all I could do to get out the words, 'Yes, wonderful things.'"

He had found the tomb of the child-Pharaoh Tutankhamun — four chambers, hewn from rock, containing a treasure of unimagined magnificence.

Although such dramatic finds are relatively rare, archaeology is all about discovery. Archaeology is the investigation of the human past through physical remains. These can range from buried cities to microscopic organisms. Archaeology is the chief source of information about much of our history, especially about those times before written records were kept. Everything we know about the beginning of agriculture, the origin of towns, the discovery of metals, and the history of life on our plant comes from physical remains.

Archaeology is growing in popularity as a degree subject. This has two consequences. First, to be accepted for a degree course you will need good marks on secondary school university preparation courses such as history, art history, English, geography, mathematics, chemistry, and physics. Check with your counsellor for specific requirements at the universities you are considering. Second, when you graduate, you will find there are many more archaeology graduates than there are relevant jobs. In fact, most people graduating in archaeology have to follow another career. For example, the Career Centre at Erindale College, University of Toronto, suggests that anthropology graduates (the area in which you will find undergraduate archaeology courses) most often find employment in research, business and industry, human services, and government.[11]

This should not necessarily discourage you from studying archaeology. It combines practical and theoretical skills, gives you practice in the collection and analysis of data, and provides team-work experience when carrying out field projects. All of these skills could be attractive to employers in other areas, especially in industry and commerce. However, this chapter will concentrate on employment opportunities as an archaeologist.

Working as an Archaeologist

Archaeology involves far more than digging up artifacts on historic sites. The work of the archaeologist may start with trying to locate a site. Some are discovered by accident (perhaps in the course of development work, such as building a road). On other occasions, archaeologists may suspect the existence of buried remains of historic importance. Locating such a site precisely may entail careful research such as the study of aerial photographs and the use of remote sensing methods. Plotting and analyzing these can involve computer-based techniques. Geophysical procedures, adapted from oil and mineral prospecting, can also reveal much of the layout of the hidden remains before digging begins.

Once digging starts, the position of every object found has to be precisely plotted in three dimensions. The positions of an object, both on the site and in relation to other finds, often reveals more than the object itself. (This is why archaeologists get so upset with amateurs using metal detectors to locate and dig up finds.)

All sites are built up from an accumulation of sediments. These may be the result of either the decay of buildings and other human-made remains, or the development of soils and vegetation over the site. The study of these sediments can yield vital clues to the history of the site. For example, the study of pollen grains can reveal changes in the vegetation. This in turn gives evidence for changes in the climate of the area.

Many delicate artifacts are preserved in the soil or under water, and start to decay as soon as they are exposed to the air. Conservation — preserving and caring for objects so that they survive after excavation — is a vital part of archaeological work. Finds have to be catalogued, photographed, drawn (drawings often reveal details not seen in photographs), and examined. Artifacts are studied, physically and chemically, to find out how they were made and to identify the origin of the raw materials. They are also dated, using a range of radiocarbon and other techniques. As you can see, archaeology spans the arts and sciences. Conservation and the examination of artifacts are usually carried out in laboratories by those who have studied science-based archaeology.

All aspects of the project must be written up (and perhaps published) in order to give other scholars access to the work. Most archaeologists work in universities or museums and their way of life is similar to that of teachers of other professions.

Participation in field excavation work is often required. In Canada, this can involve excavating Native village sites. Heritage Canada helps Canadians identify, protect, and enhance their natural, cultural, and built environment and heritage. Archaeologists can be involved in some of these projects. Outside of Canada, there are archaeological and excavation sites in virtually every country in the world and archaeologists can be involved in any area related to periods of historical interest.

The Canadian Archaeological Association is the professional association in Canada. Each province has its own archaeological society.

Entry Qualifications

Although archaeology is an arts subject, it links with many disciplines, including physics, chemistry, biology, geology, technology, the medical sciences, mathematics, geography, history, art, social science, and religion. You can take either a B.A. or a B.Sc. degree in archaeology, the B.Sc. concentrating on physical archaeology.

To work as a professional archaeologist, you will normally need a master's degree in archaeology. It is helpful to have experience of fieldwork. (Most degree courses include some field projects.) Indeed, it's a good idea either to join an archaeology association before you start your degree, and to take part in digs or other fieldwork, or to do volunteer work in a museum. University admission counsellors will seek evidence of your interest in the subject, so this could also help you win a place for a postgraduate course.

There are some specialist aspects to archaeology — such as conservation, heritage management, and studies dealing with specific historical period — where a postgraduate qualification will be required. You will also find computer skills useful, since computers are used increasingly to store and analyze data. Some archaeologists also use computer-aided design (CAD) in reconstruction work, devising three-dimensional images of sites or objects from incomplete data. And increasingly, there will be Internet, CD-ROM, and virtual reality versions of archaeological sites and information.

To work on excavations, you need to be in good shape. Working on digs in all kinds of weather can be tough. Because you are trying to build up a picture of the past from thousands of tiny bits of evidence, you must be painstakingly methodical and thorough. Patience and determination are essential. (Howard Carter had five years of fruitless digging in the Valley of the Kings before the steps leading Tutankhamun's tomb emerged from the sand.)

You should be a good team worker and have leadership potential. You will have to collaborate with people from other disciplines, especially scientists, and you may have to supervise teams working on sites. You will also need to communicate clearly and lucidly, orally and in writing. Some archaeologists specialize in underwater sites, working on sunken ships or in places which have become flooded or submerged. To work on these excavations you would, of course, need additional skills.

Career Development

In Canada, there are limited positions available. Field archaeologists usually need extensive experience and funding before becoming a site supervisor. The few positions available are in universities and museums and at Canadian historic sites.

✍ Further Information

Contact:

**Canadian Archaeological
Association**
Box 127, 3170 Tillcum Road
Victoria, BC, V9A 7H7

**Canadian Museum of
Civilization**
Hull, PQ, J8X 4H2

EIGHT

CAREERS USING HISTORY

 Let us make haste to write down the stories and traditions of the people before they are forgotten.

Henri-Raymond Casgrain, editor

The main vocational value of studying history is that is provides good training in gathering, sorting and analyzing information and ideas, and in explaining things in clear written and spoken English. In many fields, historians are valued for their intellectual discipline and skills, not for their specialist knowledge. However, in addition to teaching history, there are a few careers in which you can use your knowledge. This chapter looks at working in museums, art galleries, and archives. There may also be some opportunities in archaeology, particularly if you have a relevant postgraduate qualification.

Museum and Art Gallery Work

The work of museums and galleries is very similar and often overlaps. Museums collect, document, preserve, exhibit, interpret, and store materials of historical, scientific, and cultural interest. Art galleries do the same for paintings and other works of art. For the purposes of this chapter, both are referred to as museums.

In Canada, there are hundreds of museums that are oper-
ated by a number of jurisdictions. For example:

⊃   National museums such as the National Gallery of
Canada and the Canadian Museum of Civilization.

⊃   Provincial museums such as the Royal Ontario
Museum, the British Columbia Provincial Museum,
and the Manitoba Museum of Man and Nature.

⊃   University museums (whose jurisdiction often
overlaps with provincial museums) such as the
University of British Columbia Museum of
Anthropology, the McCord Museum of Canadian
History at Montreal's McGill University, and Memorial
University of Newfoundland Art Gallery.

⊃   Local museums such as the McMichael Gallery in
Kleinburg, Ontario and the Beaverbrook Gallery in
Fredericton, New Brunswick.

Three main occupational groups in these settings are
archivists, conservators, and curators.

Archivists

Archivists acquire, research, and stock historical documents,
photographs, maps, and other materials. They ensure the
preservation and storage of these materials and develop clas-
sification systems so that users can gain access to them.
Archivists require a master's degree in archival studies, library science, or history.

Conservators

Conservators restore and conserve paintings, photographs,
sculptures, furniture, pottery, and other works of art and
antiquity. They provide consultation to museums and art galleries and supervise conservation technicians. Conservators
require a master's degree in art conservation.

Curators

Curators recommend the acquisition of paintings, pho- tographs, sculptures, documents, and other museum and gallery artifacts. They research the origin and history of arti- facts, develop the storyline and theme of displays and exhibitions, and supervise curatorial assistants and other museum technicians. Curators must have a bachelor's or master's degree in museology, art history, or in a field re- lated to their area of work.

Museum Educator

One other area of employment that is related to both teaching and public relations is that of museum educator. Educators develop communication strategies, design and organize work- shops, and prepare and deliver educational and publicity programs to increase awareness of museums and galleries.

Career Development

In Canada, only about 3000 workers are employed as archivists, conservators, and curators. With government cut- backs, the employment opportunities are likely to decrease, so competition for available positions will be fierce. Since vol- unteers are often used in museums and galleries, experience with volunteering would be an asset. You must have intellec- tual curiosity and enjoy knowledge for its own sake.

Once you find employment you can aspire to a management position. Typical job titles are archive director, art gallery manager, curator director, and historic sites administrator. Managers and directors plan, organize and direct activities, promote public relations, prepare and administer budgets, and recruit staff. Again, the number of openings will be few.

A variety of career development programs are offered by uni- versities, colleges, and associations in the following areas:

- ⊃ archival studies
- ⊃ art conservation

- art gallery administration
- arts administration
- cultural resources management
- fine arts exhibition curatorship
- historical resources intern program
- museology
- museum methods and procedures
- public history
- voluntary sector and arts management

Several conservation internships are available, all, with the exception of curriculum, restricted to professionals in the field:

- curriculum internships
- specialized techniques internship
- professional development internships
- conservation research internships
- mobile conservation laboratory internships

For these programs, you should contact the Canadian Museums Association for the most recent revision of *Museum Studies in Canada.*

You are most likely to make progress in your career by moving from one museum to another, taking care of larger collections or possibly developing as a specialist. In the largest museums there are opportunities to progress internally. Your career may lead to senior management posts in which you will be concerned with running the whole museum. This is increasingly seen as a job distinct from curatorship. Although some large museums have appointed directors from outside the world of museums, most senior post-holders begin their career as curators.

✍ Further Information

Contact:

Canadian Museums Association
280 Metcalf Street, Suite 400
Ottawa, ON, K2P 1R7

Association for Preservation Technology
PO Box 2487, Station D
Ottawa, ON, K1P 5W6

Canadian Conservation Institute
1030 Innes Road
Ottawa, ON, K1A 0M8

Heritage Canada Foundation
PO Box 1358, Station B
Ottawa, ON, K1P 5R4

International Institute for Conservation
PO Box 9195
Ottawa, ON, K1G 3T9

Association of Canadian Archivists
PO Box 2595, Station D
Ottawa, ON, K1P 5W6

Canadian Council of Archives
314 Wellington Street West, Suite 3020
Ottawa, ON, K1A 0N3

NINE

CAREERS USING LANGUAGES AND LINGUISTICS

Our great advantage, over other nations, is our tradition of diversity, which was born of the historic necessity of English- and French-speaking Canadians working together and which has blossomed into a basic respect for the multitude of cultures, which make up Canada.

Joe Clark, former Prime Minister of Canada

With the growth of the global economy, having another language would appear to open up many job opportunities in other countries. In fact, in many parts of the world, you would be considered illiterate if you did not speak at least one foreign language fluently. But saying to an employer that you speak another language is often no more useful on its own than saying you speak English. So it's not usually enough to take a modern language degree by itself to enter university graduate work.

There are four exceptions to this:

⊃ teaching languages (see Chapter 5)

⊃ teaching English as a Second Language (ESL)

⊃ interpreting

⊃ translating

If you want to work with a language outside these areas (and opportunities outside teaching languages are very few), you are strongly advised to complement it with other vocational skills. Fortunately, you can study most modern languages with a wide range of options.

There are many other occupations in which another language is an asset or even a requirement, but it isn't the main skill and may not even be part of your day-to-day work. They include, for instance, broadcasting, the diplomatic service, librarianship, law, banking, insurance, travel and tourism, and so one. Your language skills will enhance your prospects in any of these careers, but are secondary to the other skills of the job.

If you are studying linguistics, either on its own or as part of your modern languages degree, you may also be able to train as a speech and language therapist. There is a section on this at the end of the chapter.

Teaching English as a Second Language

Teaching English as a Second Language (ESL) involves teaching people from other countries to speak and write in English, although the emphasis often tends to be on the spoken word. It helps to be fluent in the language of your students, but this isn't necessary. Your students can be school-age children enroled in local schools, or adults enroled in adult day or continuing education classes run by local education authorities or community groups. ESL is one of the few subjects where job opportunities may exist in larger numbers than in other teaching areas.

Opportunities also exist to teach English outside Canada, mainly in Asia. Currently both Japan and South Korea are actively recruiting Canadian English teachers. But some opportunities exist in many other countries.

Entry Qualifications

Requirements to teach ESL vary widely. If you are employed by a school board, you would require at least a bachelor's degree, a teaching certificate, and specialist training as an

ESL teacher. However, community groups often employ graduates who simply have a bachelor's degree, usually in English. Various levels of government also sponsor language training for immigrants, and requirements for teachers will also vary.

Teaching overseas will also have different requirements. Japan, for example, usually advertises for qualified teachers. South Korea, on the other hand, advertises simply for university graduates.

Interpreting

There are two forms of interpretation: consecutive and simultaneous. Consecutive interpreters listen to a speech, either in part or whole, and then relay it to the audience. This may mean taking notes as a reminder of what was said. Consecutive interpretation is slow, because the audience must listen to the original, then the translation.

Simultaneous interpretation involves translating what you hear immediately to your audience as the speaker continues to talk. You may do this on a one-to-one basis, known as "whispering" because you whisper your interpretation into your client's ear. More frequently, simultaneous work involves sitting in a sound-proof booth and listening to the speaker through headphones. You speak your interpretation into a microphone which feeds your voice to the headphones of your audience. Simultaneous interpretation is generally considered more stressful work because there is virtually no thinking time. To ease the pressure, two interpreters often work together, alternating in sessions lasting perhaps a half-hour. However, this is not always the case. Interpreters can sometimes work three hours or more without a break.

In either form of interpretation, you must have a superb knowledge of both languages. There are many words and sayings in any language which cannot be translated directly into another, so you must be able to give far more than just a literal translation.

The only full-time work for interpreters is in "conference interpreting," and this is a very small profession. However, in Canada, there is a constant demand at various levels of government for simultaneous translation of English to French or French to English. A new and growing area is the translation and interpretation of Native languages. For example, Northern College in Ontario offers a certificate program in Cree Interpreter/Translator.

Most conference interpreters work for conference organizers or governments in Canada. Outside Canada, many work for international bodies such as the United Nations or NATO; as an interpreter, you may be required to travel all over the world, to translate at all the conferences and meetings attended by the representatives of such bodies. There are also self-employed freelance interpreters and those who are employed by specialist communications agencies. Both these groups tend to do a range of interpreting and translation work in addition to conference work. They, too, will be expected to travel in pursuit of their work. This may be attractive at first, but the novelty eventually wears off. The life is physically and mentally demanding.

Businesses also need interpreters — for example, during trade fairs — when receiving delegations from abroad and in negotiating overseas contracts. In this case you will be translating — into and out of your own language. In most cases this is part-time work, although some companies are large enough to require full-time interpreters. If you can speak one of the languages used by new immigrants to Canada — such as Hindi, Mandarin, or Urdu — you may find work, usually self-employed or on a part-time basis, helping local authority departments, the courts, or community groups.

Translating

Translating requires a good knowledge of languages. You must be able to write idiomatically, as well as lucidly and succinctly. The work is usually of two types: literary or technical and commercial.

Literary Translation

This covers novels, poetry, plays, biographies, and similar material. Almost all literary translators are self-employed, but few can make a living from it exclusively. This work is generally very challenging, because you must catch the "spirit" of the text, not just the literal meaning. In effect, you are producing a paraphrase of the original rather than a translation.

The only tribute a French translator can pay Shakespeare is not to translate him.

Max Beerbohm, author and playwright

For example, here are two versions of the opening verse of the Rubaiyat of Omar Khayyam, both translated by Edward Fitzgerald:

"Awake! For Morning in the Bowl of Night
Has flung the Stone that puts the Stars to Flight:
And Lo! the Hunter of the East has caught
The Sultan's Turret in a Noose of Light."

"Wake! For the Sun behind yon Eastern height
Has chased the Session of the Stars from Night;
And, to the field of Heav'n ascending strikes
The Sultan's Turret with a Shaft of Light."

Notice the range of variations that may be offered for a single text.

Technical and Commercial Translation

This work is more straightforward and offers the best prospects. However, you will probably need detailed knowledge of a specialized field such as law, medicine, science, or engineering. Accuracy is the most important aspect of this work. Most is done on a freelance basis, although some translators are full-time employees. Work can range from translations of books, to scientific papers and legal contracts, to operating manuals for appliances.

Entry Qualifications

Translators usually require a bachelors's degree in translation with specialization at the graduate level. A college diploma in interpretation is the minimum requirement for interpreters.

Training and Career Development

You may require a certified translators diploma from the Canadian Translators and Interpreters Council. In addition there are specialist courses at the university level. For example, York University's Glendon College offers a B.A. in translation.

Most interpreters and translators start in other careers where they can use their languages and do freelance interpreting and translation on the side. As their skills improve, they may continue to work freelance or they may try to enter one of the organizations recruiting full-time staff. However, such opportunities are few and far between. Although there is no formal career development, earning for those who are successful can be relatively high. But for most people in translation and interpreting work, the life is an uncertain one.

Table 5 gives you a general idea of where most graduates in translation and linguistics find employment in their degree.

Table 5.   Occupation Destinations for Master's Degree Graduates in Linguistics, Translations, and Interpretation (*Job Futures*, 1996 — percentages rounded off to the nearest whole number)

Writing, Translating, and Public Relations	53
Secondary and Elementary Teachers	17
University Professors and Assistants	11
Library, Correspondence, and Related Information Clerks	4
Managers in Art, Culture, Recreation and Sport	3

Using Linguistics in Your Career

Linguistics is the scientific study of language. It involves the study of sounds and how they are made, grammatical constructions, and how meaning is conveyed. You may study linguistics as a subject in its own right, or as a specialist paper forming part of a modern languages degree. There are few occupations where you can use the subject directly, although linguistic theories are applied in various careers including teaching, social work, and computer programming. For example, the software industry aims to produce programs which will translate from one language to another. This calls for people who can analyze the structure of languages and design appropriate software. However, the career which will probably make most direct use of specialist knowledge is speech and language therapy.

Speech-Language Pathologists/Therapists

In Canada, professionals in speech and language may train as speech-language pathologists, speech therapists, or speech and hearing clinicians. These professionals diagnose, evaluate, and treat speech, language, and voice disorders. They are employed in hospitals, community health agencies, and educational institutions, and may work in private practice.

Many of the clients are children who may be very slow in learning to talk, find it difficult to articulate, or have a stammer or hearing difficulties. Many are physically or mentally challenged or emotionally disturbed. Working with adults may involve helping people who have lost the ability to speak through illness or accident. Someone whose brain has been damaged through an accident or stroke may have to re-learn how to speak and use language. People who have had their larynx (voice box) removed need to develop an alternative method of sound production. Although some people are treated in groups, most get individual treatment. Pathologists, therapists, and clinicians also attend case conferences and must work closely with physicians, social workers, psychologists, teachers and other professionals.

If you want to work in this profession, you will need to understand people of all ages and temperaments and be able to win their confidence. You must be able to communicate clearly. You need almost infinite patience because treatment can often be long and difficult. You will also need to be well-organized because your work is largely unsupervised and you have to arrange your own schedules.

Entry Qualifications

Speech-language pathologists usually require a master's degree. The University of Waterloo offers a bachelor's program in speech communication. Certification with the Canadian Audiology and Speech-Language Pathology Association may be required. A provincial licence is required for speech-language pathologists in New Brunswick, Quebec, and Manitoba.

✍ Further Information

Contact:

Canadian Translators and Interpreters Council (member of the International Federation of Translators)
1 Nicolas Street, Suite 1402
Ottawa, ON, K1N 7B7

International Association of Conference Interpreters
62 Park Avenue
Ottawa, ON, K2P 1B2

Canadian Association of Speech-Language Pathologists and Audiologists
130 Albert Street, Suite 2006
Ottawa, ON, K1P 5G4

Canadian Council of Teachers of English Language Arts
340 Education
University of Manitoba
Winnipeg, MB, R3J 2N2

TEN

CAREERS USING ART AND DESIGN

When I am finishing a picture I hold some God-made object up to it — a rock, a flower, the branch of a tree or my hand — as a kind of final test. If the painting stands up beside a thing man cannot make, the painting is authentic. If there's a clash between the two, it is bad art.

Marc Chagall, artist

Working as an Artist

Very few artists can make a living from selling original paintings or sculpture. In Canada, about 7000 painters, sculptors, and related artists currently list art as their primary job, while about 11,000 list it as their secondary job. However, their reported income is low, only about $14,000, with 55% of that coming from cultural income.[12]

Great talent is rarely enough. Your art must also appeal to at least some of your contemporaries or it may not sell for years. Vincent van Gogh sold only one painting in his lifetime — to his friend Paul Gauguin.

There are rare commissions for murals and sculptures for commercial and public buildings and spaces. Most go to well-established artists. There are also a few private commissions, often for portraits of people or animals. Commercial galleries accept some works to sell on commission, rarely buying them outright. Galleries display only what they believe will sell. (And painters usually have to pay for good-quality framing before their works are put on display.) However, on the positive side, if you do develop a reputation or a following, you can make good income through numbered prints. Commercial galleries often bid highly to obtain prints from artists like Robert Bateman, Trisha Romance, or Kathy Hagerman.

To sum up, it is extremely difficult to make your entire living from selling your work. You must be prepared to supplement your income in some other way.

Some artists work in the community as an artist in residence or as a community arts officer (promoting artistic activities). Such posts are often of limited duration. For example, arts centres may offer residencies lasting one or two years.

Many artists need to teach full-time (part-time posts are very scarce), which means getting a postgraduate teaching qualification (see Chapter 5). Some artists work, usually part-time, as art therapists in homes for the mentally handicapped and in psychiatric hospitals. They help withdrawn patients to express themselves through painting and other forms of art. This helps to relieve patients' tensions and can provide psychiatrists with valuable clues to patients' problems from the work produced. To do this sort of work you will need to undertake special postgraduate training. The Faculty of Education, University of British Columbia, for example, has been conducting research into the use of Jungian art counselling with children.

Design

Art... begins with the world we construct, not with the world we see. It starts with the imagination, and then works towards ordinary experience: that is, it tries to make itself as convincing and recognizable as it can.

Northrop Frye, educator

Artists working in design have more career opportunities, although there is still a lot of competition, especially in such popular areas as fashion design and set design. In Canada, about 2,600 people are employed in design full-time, another 4,300 on a part-time basis. Designers earn an average of about $28,500 (*Canadian Social Trends*, Summer, 1996).

Designers must harness their artistic skills and creativity within tight constraints. They must be aware not only of the appearance of what they produce, but how well it functions, the ease and cost of production, and any other factors which may be important.

Designers work can be categorized into two broad categories: two-dimensional and three-dimensional.

Two-Dimensional Design

Two-dimensional design is concerned with visual communication using flat surfaces, and includes graphic and textile design. As a two-dimensional designer you may work on graphic design, which includes typography (choosing and designing the layout of lettering), illustration (including photography) and the design of company symbols (logos). You may be employed by a design agency or as part of an in-house team. Organizations requiring design work on a frequent basis often have their own commercial artists and designers. You could work freelance but this is only advisable after some experience in employment. Areas in which graphic designers and commercial artists are employed include the following.

Advertising: Designing posters, advertisements for newspapers and magazines, TV commercials, product packaging, and display cards.

Book Publishing: Designing dust jackets and covers, typography, illustration (including technical illustration and photography); designing book catalogues and promotional material.

Periodical Publishing: Designing covers, typography, page layouts, and choosing illustrations and photographs.

Industry and Commerce: All types of graphic design for advertising, packaging, sales catalogues and other promotional literature.

TV, Film and Video: Designing opening titles, credits, animation sequences and other graphics.

Image Consultancy: Designing logos and corporate designs for big organizations (this covers everything from the stationery to colour schemes for shops, offices, and company vehicles).

Textile Manufacturing: Designing fabrics (using patterns, colours, weaves, fibre mixtures) for garments, bedding, carpets, and soft furnishings.

Three-Dimensional Design

Three-dimensional design involves the design of solid shapes — from cars to jewellery, CD players to ceramics, stage sets to furniture. You will work in one of four main areas: craft, interior, product, and fashion design.

Craft Work: This work involves designing and producing both decorative and functional items such as jewellery, silverware, furniture, ceramics, and glassware (including stained glass). You might work in craft workshops, designing individual, handmade, or unique objects. Alternatively, you could work in craft manufacture, producing designs or prototypes for similar objects for mass production.

Interior Design: Interior design is concerned with the use, furnishing, and decoration of interior spaces. Interior designers must be aware of how people use space. For example, when designing an exhibition in a museum or gallery, the designer must take into account the flow of people past the exhibits, and the views they will get. They must also be aware of any safety or security aspects in the design, especially in public or commercial interiors.

Interior design work falls into the five main categories:

- ⊃ Consultancy: Designing interiors for ships, aircraft, hotels and other industrial, commercial and domestic buildings; also managing contracts to ensure that the work is done on time and as specified.

⊃   Theatre, TV, or film: Designing sets can involve historical research into details of architecture and furnishings.

⊃   Exhibition organizers: Designing displays, usually in collaboration with graphic designers and advertising or marketing specialists.

⊃   Museums: Designing gallery layout and special exhibitions.

⊃   Retail stores: Designing window and "point of sale" displays.

Product Design: Product design is concerned with manufactured goods such as cars, food mixers, furniture, cookers, CD players, light fixtures, ballpoint pens, machine tools, and thousands of other products. This involves close collaboration with design engineers, production engineers, and other technical specialists, as well as with marketing people who understand customer likes and dislikes. Designers in this field have to know a lot about the characteristics of materials (both in manufacturing and when the product is being used) and production methods.

Fashion Design: Fashion design includes everything from haute couture to garments and shoes for mass production. Areas of employment include the following.

⊃   Haute couture: Fashion houses which design exclusive "model" garments. Only one or two copies of each design are made, almost entirely by hand.

⊃   Wholesale couture: Similar to haute couture, but several copies of each original are made for sale through selected retail outlets.

⊃   Wholesale manufacturing: Design clothes for mass production. Most designers specialize, for example, in children's garments, men's suits, knitwear, contour fashion (swimwear, lingerie and foundation garments), and shoes. Designs may follow trends set by the haute couturiers or could be based on "classic" lines. The clothes produced will range from inexpensive, seasonally changing fashion items to longer-lasting quality goods.

⊃ Film, TV, and theatre costume design: Can involve historical research as well as design. You may be required to adapt previous costumes as well as design completely new items.

Entry Qualifications

No formal qualification is needed to enter art or design, only great talent. Even so, you would be wise to get a degree in art and design. It is hard to find employment in this field with a degree, and even more difficult without. Courses vary in their secondary school graduation requirements. Admission officers will expect evidence of artistic talent in a portfolio of your work.

If you intend to become an artist you may be wise to take a postgraduate teaching qualification so that you can supplement your earnings with teaching. Apart from an exceptional talent, you will need to be resilient and flexible, and a good manager of your money (as you may have to live on a shoestring for quite a long time before your talent is properly rewarded).

To be a designer your talent must be supplemented with an ability to work in a team and a willingness, at times, to compromise your artistic standards to meet the constraints of costs, simplicity of manufacture, and other factors. You will need an interest in production techniques and in solving technical problems. You must be interested in fashion trends in their widest sense. You have to understand why people buy some products and not others.

Training and Career Development

As an artist you are largely responsible for your own development. You may be wise to continue taking classes and to establish contact with fellow artists.

An art can only be learned in the workshop of those who are winning their bread by it.

Samuel Butler, author

In design, training is primarily on the job. Few employers will offer formal training at any stage, although some may pay for you to attend specialist courses when you're established in your career. You are likely to start as an assistant of some kind. (Job titles are no clue whatsoever to your status, experience or responsibility. In advertising, for example, almost every designer is called an Art Director.) As an assistant you may initially work mainly in a supporting role, involved in routine typography, producing working drawings for a product from a designer's rough sketch, designing simple components or researching materials for someone else's interior design proposals. Further progress will depend on your performance, not only in creative terms but also as a member of a team creating a product.

✍ Further Information

Contact:

Interior Designers of Canada
#506, 260 King St. E.
Toronto, ON, M5A 1K3

Canadian Art Therapy Association
216 St. Clair Ave. W.
Toronto, ON, M4V 1R2

Many universities offer Fine Arts and Design Programs. In addition, check into the programs offered at the following university level institutions:

The Ontario College of Art and Design
100 McCaul St.
Toronto, ON, M5T 1W1

Ryerson Polytechnic University
350 Victoria St.
Toronto, ON, M5B 2K3

The University College of the Cariboo
Box 3010
Kamloops, B.C., V2C 5N3

ELEVEN

CAREERS USING MUSIC, DRAMA, AND DANCE

There can be few of us who, after watching television or going to a theatre, concert hall, or movie, have not dreamed of becoming a performer. The urge is the same whether we want to act in Shakespeare or a television soap, play the concert piano or electric guitar, sing opera or pop, or dance in a ballet or the floor show of a cruise liner.

However, unless you have exceptional talent, together with a lot of luck, you're unlikely to find work as a professional performer. And if you do, you will probably earn a lot less than graduates elsewhere. There are few permanent jobs and many performers have to take whatever they are offered. Most face regular periods of unemployment and endure financial uncertainty all their working lives. For instance, three-quarters of professional actors and actresses are out of work at any one time. There are many hopefuls and few openings.

Nevertheless, if you have an overwhelming compulsion to perform, really believe in your talent, and are prepared to accept insecurity and living on a shoestring, go for it. You will regret it all your life if you don't.

In Canada, nearly 22,000 people are employed as actors, dancers, or musicians (*Canadian Social Trends*, Summer, 1996). Another 42,000 people are employed part-time. Earnings range from $16,000 for dancers to $31,000 for actors.

If you do try to become a performer, it is wise to insure against periods of unemployment. This means getting the best academic qualifications you can, together with some transferable work skills, so that you can get temporary or part-time work.

When considering a career using music, drama, or dance, you need to be aware of the limitations of degrees in these fields. University degree courses may include a large element of performance, but they are not usually intended as a substitute for the kind of performance courses (including degrees) offered by the specialist music, drama, and dance academies. However, a university degree can equip you for careers in production, stage management, direction, and arts administration and management. You can also teach music, drama, or dance in primary and secondary schools if you obtain a postgraduate teaching qualification (see Chapter 5).

This chapter covers both performance work and other career options in which you could use music, drama, or dance. Where appropriate, there's information on alternative training for performers, so that you can see whether or not a degree will be the best route for you to follow.

Studying Music

University programs in music are offered in two or more categories. The University of Toronto, for example, offers a Bachelor of Music (with concentrations in Composition, History and Culture, and Music Education or Theory), a Bachelor of Music (Performance), and an Artists Diploma in Music. St. Francis Xavier University in Antigonish, Nova Scotia offers Bachelor of Arts degrees in classical and jazz music.

Entry Qualifications

To enter a degree course, you will normally need an advanced secondary school graduation diploma, and Royal Conservatory of Music (or equivalent) credentials at the grade 2 theory and grade 8 practice or higher. An audition is always required.

Music creates order out of chaos; for rhythm imposes unanimity upon the divergent, melody im-

*poses continuity upon the disjointed, and harmony
imposes compatibility upon the incongruous.*

Yehudi Menuhin, musician

Performing Music

Performance can be divided into two categories, classical and
popular music, although there is some overlap between the
two areas.

Classical Music

Most classical musicians play in orchestras, ensembles, or
chamber groups. A minority also work as soloists. Some symphony orchestras, opera houses, and smaller groups employ
musicians on a full-time salaried basis. Others use freelancers
who also play for other groups and work as "session musicians"
recording music for film, radio and television, commercials and
jingles, and backing tracks for recordings. Singers, similarly,
may be salaried members of a professional choir, but most
work freelance. There are opportunities in opera, oratorio, solo
recitals, and various types of concert work, including light music and cabaret. In Canada, there are 100 music companies,
including 12 opera companies. These would be the main employers for those with considerable talent.

Hours can be long and unsocial. Performances are usually
given in evenings and on weekends. Most musicians also
travel long distances, either to performances or while tour-
ing in Canada, the U.S., or outside North America. There are
lengthy rehearsals and long hours of private practice if you
are to retain, let alone improve, your skills. Many freelance
musicians also supplement their income by part-time private teaching.

Entry Qualifications

If you aspire to becoming a concert soloist, you will continue
to take lessons and to train. It is extremely hard to build up
a solo career as either an instrumentalist or a singer. (It's

equally tough becoming a conductor and most are experienced performers. There are postgraduate courses in conducting, but these will not guarantee you a job. It's a highly competitive field.)

Popular Music

Professional musicians also play popular music, ranging from pop and rock, through country and western and folk, to dance music and musicals. Some combine playing an instrument with singing. Like classical musicians, popular musicians spend their time rehearsing, performing, and practising. Many work in both popular and classical music. Some performers, mainly in pop, rock, and country and western, compose, write, and perform their own material. Popular musicians often have to project a flamboyant personality on stage and in video recordings, and sometimes give performances which combine theatre with music.

Music is your own experience, your thoughts, your wisdom. If you don't live it, it won't come out of your horn.

Charlie Parker, musician

Music Therapy

Music has been found to help the physically and mentally challenged in many different ways. This has led to the appointment of music therapists working in both education and the health services. The act of making and listening to music can help people to relax, provide them with mental stimulus, and give them an emotional outlet.

Music therapy programs are offered at Waterloo, Ontario's Wilfrid Laurier University, University of Windsor, and Open University in British Columbia. Windsor takes secondary school graduates directly into its program. Wilfrid Laurier and Open University require the successful completion of two years of a university music degree program.

Music and the Media

There are opportunities for radio and television producers specializing in music programs. However, specialized training courses are found at the college level, so Arts graduates may have to return to school to attend courses in sound engineering and studio management.

Drama

To be a professional actor, stage singer, or dancer, it's vital to have an "Equity card." This is the membership card of the Canadian Actors Equity Association (CAEA), the trade union of the profession. Equity limits the number of new entrants to the profession because at any one time around three-quarters of its members are unemployed.

To receive an equity card you must have performed in three stage productions within a 20-month period. Many professionals in the theatre, ballet, and opera are represented by CAEA.

The Association of Canadian Television and Radio Artists (ACTRA) covers work in radio, television, film, commercials, and writing for these media.

The National Theatre School of Canada is a highly reputable school located in Montreal. The school considers applicants between the ages of 18 and 25 after secondary school graduation. Areas of specialization are English Acting, French Acting, Technical Production, Design Production, and Playwriting (English and French).

It isn't easy to get into a good drama school like the National Theatre School. Your potential is assessed by interview and audition. Auditions vary, but you must perform for a selection panel.

There are five main areas of employment for actors:

⊃ theatre

⊃ radio

⊃ television

⊃ films

⊃ commercials

Acting is not being emotional, but being able to express emotions.

Kate Reid, actor

Theatre

The two main areas of theatre are repertory, the main learning ground for novice actors, and the commercial theatre. In Canada there are 226 theatre companies, including 52 for-profit companies and 14 summer theatre companies.

Commercial theatre companies are usually set up for one particular play or show, which normally runs for a fixed number of weeks or months. If the show is particularly successful, the run may be extended or transferred to another theatre. If the show fails, it closes early.

Realism doesn't mean copying art back into life. It means making life into art: not just accepting the facts of life but elevating them.

Sir Laurence Olivier, actor

Radio

Radio (primarily the CBC in Canada) uses actors in plays, poetry readings, dramatized features, serial readings, comedy, and other programs. Most work, apart from serial, is on a single-performance basis. Unlike theatre, you don't have to learn your lines but work from a script instead. On the other hand, you have only your voice for creating characters.

Television

Actors are usually employed to work on single-performance programs, although there are opportunities in series of various lengths. Television directors, like film directors, record programs in a series of short takes. These rarely last more than a minute or two. Actors usually rehearse each take on the set and then record it at once. There is a lot of waiting time on the set while equipment is prepared and technical problems are sorted out, so patience is a must.

Film

Toronto is the third-largest film-making centre in North America where 95% of Canada's $1 billion film industry is located. More than 500 films have been shot in Toronto in the past decade, generating 20,000 jobs in one especially good year. There are many opportunities for "extras" although the number of good jobs are limited.

Commercials

This can be a useful way to boost your income, but the work is almost never regular. Work invariably comes through casting agencies. TV commercials are well-paid, radio less so. If you're in a fairly high-profile TV campaign, you must not accept work for a competing product. If you do, you're likely to lose the chance to do any future commercial work.

Dance

Think of the magic of that foot, comparatively small, upon which your whole weight rests. It's a miracle, and the dance ... is a celebration of that miracle.

Martha Graham, dancer

If you are considering a career in dance, you face a choice of whether to take a dance degree, a dance and drama degree, or to attend a specialist dance academy. In making this decision, you should be aware of the limitations of a dance or drama degree, especially as preparation for performance. While you will dance with most dance degree courses, degree studies in the subject do not offer the extent of specialist performance training provided by the dance academies. Dance degree graduates most often enter arts administration and management, teaching, the health and leisure industry, or a completely unrelated career. Here's what you will need for a performance career as well as other options for using your dancing skills.

Performance

There are two main types of dancers: ballet or modern stage. Ballet dancers may specialize in classical or contemporary ballet. (Canada supports five ballet companies.) Modern stage dancers cover a variety of styles. They work in light entertainment of all kinds including musicals and other stage shows, cabaret, films, and television. There are 54 dance companies operating in Canada, including 19 contemporary and jazz dance companies.

You will have no employment prospects as a ballet dancer, and few in modern stage dance, unless you attend a specialist school such as the National Ballet School.

Ballet Training: To become a ballet dancer, you should ideally start serious training with a professional teacher, or at a specialist school such as the National Ballet School, the Royal Winnipeg Ballet, and Les Grands Ballet Canadiens. This means that you must have been taking basic classes from an early age. Otherwise, you won't have attained a sufficient level of competency to start specialist training. For information about dance schools and companies in Canada, contact the Dance in Canada Association.

Modern Dance Training: To become a modern stage dancer you don't have to be quite as dedicated or as firmly disciplined as a ballet dancer. However, you should have started serious training by the time you were 14. Later, you would be wise to train at one of the professional schools. You should choose a course which includes voice production, stagecraft, drama, and singing.

Other Options for Dancers

Remember that any active dance career is usually quite short. Most dancers retire from performing at around the age of 40. Many, particularly those from classical ballet, later develop osteo-arthritis (inflammation of the joints) and osteoporosis (a loss of bone density leading to easily fractured bones). So think about alternative careers, even if you intend to spend part of your life as a performer.

Choreography: Some dancers progress to choreography — creating and arranging dance. You can do this either after spending time as a performer and relying on your years of experience, or after undertaking specialist training, usually at workshops sponsored by the major dance companies.

Teaching Dance: If you have professional training or a dance degree, you could consider teaching dance. There are certainly more openings in teaching than in performance. You might teach privately, in recreational classes, or in a professional dance school. You could also teach dance as part of physical education in schools.

Fitness Coaching: You could consider using your dance skills by coaching at a health or leisure centre. For instance, some fitness coaching uses dance in mobility or aerobic exercise. You will probably have to follow additional courses, in either health and leisure management or physical training.

A Career in Stage Management

Stage managers and their assistants are responsible to the director for the smooth running of rehearsals and performance. They ensure that artists are in the right place at the right time, and are responsible for stage safety. They obtain props and organize lighting, sound effects, microphones, prompting, and set changes. Stage managers often work in the theatre all day, and stay until the lights go out after the evening performance. The equivalent job in television is a floor manager and in film, an assistant director. A career in stage management may provide opportunities to move into directing or producing.

There are about 9,000 directors, producers, and choreographers employed full-time in Canada, with about 13,000 employed part-time. In addition, there are about 14,000 other administrators, managers and supervisors employed with another 17,000 employed part-time.

Directing and Producing

I feel you have to be able to make a movie the way a writer writes a novel, changing, adapting, erasing a paragraph, putting in something that comes along.

Don Owen, director

The director is responsible for turning a script into a theatrical, film, television, or radio production. Working with the producer and, where appropriate, the writer, the director is responsible for casting and is in charge of the performers, designers, and technicians. The main work is in interpreting the script, working with the artists, and rehearsing until the production is ready. Directors (apart from some in television companies) are usually employed by the production.

In the theatre the director is God, but unfortunately the actors are atheists.

Zarko Petan, producer

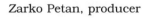

Producers are responsible for choosing a play or commissioning a script, hiring a director and performers, financial budgeting, and for the overall shape or treatment of the production. For stage work this may also involve renting a theatre, raising money for the production, and hiring the technical staff.

Social Director

One option in which you could use your talent as a performer, alongside other skills, is to work as a social director, perhaps at a holiday resort or on a cruise ship. This work involves keeping your guests or passengers happy with a range of entertainment from games nights to stage shows. As a social director you will perform a range of duties including socializing with the guests, producing shows, and taking part in performances. There may be opportunities to progress to management positions, running the entertainment program for a leisure operation.

Arts Administration

Arts administrators perform a similar function to producers working in the theatre. They organize events such as concerts and plays, usually in a publicly owned stadium or building. The responsibilities include:

- planning seasonal programs
- organizing individual events
- booking venues
- hiring performers
- publicity
- handling ticket sales
- negotiating grants from public funds and commercial sponsorship
- day-to-day adminstration

Employers are often local authorities working alone or together with private industry. Alternatively, you might work directly for a theatre or theatre company. The exact nature of your job depends largely on the size of the organization for which you work. For example, in a large theatre company you might specialize in marketing; at a small local theatre, you would be responsible for administrative support.

Entry Qualifications

Several universities offer programs in Art Administration. Scarborough College, University of Toronto, for example, offers a four-year cooperative education program with admission requirements similar to the Faculty of Arts.

✍ Further Information

Contact:

**Academy of Canadian
Cinema and Television**
158 Pearl St.
Toronto, ON, M5H 1L3

**Alliance of Canadian
Cinema, Television
and Radio Artists**
2239 Yonge St.
Toronto, ON, M4S 2B5

**Association of Canadian
Film Craftspeople (Ind.)**
#105, 65 Heward Ave.
Toronto, ON, M4M 2T5

**Canadian Association
for Music Therapy
Wilfrid Laurier University**
Waterloo, ON, N2L 3C5

**Canadian Association
of Professional Dance,**
RR#1
Kinburn, ON, K0A 2H0

**Canadian Conference of
the Arts**
189 Laurier Ave. W.
Ottawa, ON, K1N 6P1

**Canadian Film and
Television Production
Association**
#404, 663 Yonge St.
Toronto, ON M4Y 2A4

**Canadian Opera
Company**
227 Front St. E.
Toronto, ON, M5R 2B1

**Council for Business and
the Arts in Canada**
#1507, 401 Bay St.
Toronto, ON, M5H 2Y4

**Canadian Actors
Equity Association**
260 Richmond St., 2nd Floor
Toronto, ON, M5A 1P4

**Dance in Canada
Association**
322 King St. W.
Toronto, ON, M5V 1J2

Directors' Guild of Canada
#401, 387 Bloor St. E.
Toronto, ON, M4W 1H7

**International Theatre
Institute, Acadia University**
Wolfville, NS, B0P 1X0

**Les Ballets Jazz
de Montreal**
3450 rue St. Urbain
Montreal, PQ, H2X 2N5

Les Grand Ballet Canadiens,
4816 rue Rivard
Montreal, PQ, H2J 2N6

National Ballet of Canada
157 King St. E.
Toronto, ON, M5C 1G9

**Organization of Canadian
Symphony Musicians**
#6, 445 rue Gerard-Morrisset
Quebec, PQ, G1S 4V5

TWELVE

CAREERS USING POLITICAL SCIENCE, PSYCHOLOGY, AND SOCIOLOGY

Social sciences in most universities cover courses such as geography, economics, political science, psychology, and sociology. Since geography is often placed in a Bachelor of Science program, it will be covered in a companion volume, *What You Can Do With a Science Degree.*

Political science is the study of government and political institutions and processes. As such, it is a program that is good preparation for careers in many areas, including government service, teaching, and journalism. (You'll find out more about opportunities in the first two of these in chapters that follow; journalism was discussed in Chapter 6.) Traditionally, political science has been concerned with theoretical matters, such as the nature of the state, sovereignty, and government. Today, however, greater emphasis is placed on human associations, such as the behaviour of interest groups, and the decision-making process.

Many students of political science go on to graduate school in order to specialize in one of the following areas: political theory, philosophy, and methodology; public administration; international organizations, politics, and law; foreign governments; government and policies of Canada and the United States; and constitutional and administrative law.

Economics is the study of the most efficient use of scarce resources (such as land, labour, and capital) in producing goods and services to satisfy numerous different and competing demands. A program in economics leads well to careers in government and in business, discussed later in this book.

What if you're interested in psychology or sociology? As we noted in Chapter 3, more than 32% of psychology graduates continue their education. This trend is also true of graduates in social work and sociology. Many positions available to graduates in these three areas require a post-graduate degree, a teaching certificate, or further training for entry to a career in business or industry. (Notice, in Table 2 on page 28, that only 10% of psychology graduates work as psychologists and social workers.)

While good opportunities exist in social services for graduates with above average grades, remember that most such positions are government funded, and governments at the provincial and federal levels have eliminated or reduced a number of social programs in recent years. Thus, competition for available positions is particularly heavy at this time.

Psychologists

Registered psychologists must have a post-graduate degree at the master's level, at least, and preferably a doctorate degree. In 1994, 10,000 psychologists were working in Canada. They are employed in government agencies, clinics, correctional facilities, health care institutions, and social service and welfare agencies. Some go into private practice. Psychologists may diagnose cognitive, emotional, or behavioural disorders, counsel clients, provide therapy, and conduct research. Today, many psychology graduates find employment in business, particularly in human resources divisions.

Social Workers

Since social work has as its aim the alleviation of social problems, it's not surprising that those who become social workers tend to like working with people. Social work may utilize casework, group work, and community organization. Casework involves close cooperation with individuals or families who are under mental, physical, or social handicaps.

Group work involves group education and recreational activities. Community organization involves the identification of community problems and the coordination of local welfare services, both public and private, in solving them. A social worker's training may include psychology, sociology, law, medicine, and criminology. He or she might specialize in family service, child welfare, or medical, psychiatric, or correctional social work.

Social workers are employed in hospitals, school boards, and social service agencies. They may interview clients individually or in groups (such as families) to assess their needs and determine the types of services they require. They plan programs of assistance, including referrals to agencies that provide financial help, legal aid, housing, medical treatment, and other services. Some social workers also devise and deliver programs aimed at developing clients' coping and other life skills.

Careers Using Sociology

Sociology is the systematic study of collective human behaviour, as seen in cultures, societies, communities, and subgroups. The field shares its subject matter with anthropology (which focusses on small, relatively isolated societies) and social psychology (where the emphasis is on the study of group behaviour). The main focus in contemporary sociology is on the study of social structures and institutions, and on the causes and effects of social change. Some current areas of inquiry are the family, work, urban life, politics, and religion.

Over 23% of graduates in sociology enter teaching, while another 16% become psychologists, social workers, and other counsellors. Another 11% become child care and home support workers. With specialties in women's or native studies, other opportunities are available.

Career Development

Most graduates in psychology, social work, and sociology will need to complete post-graduate programs to obtain good positions or to move into management in their chosen field.

Master's programs in these areas are offered at universities in every province. Because of the number of undergraduate students in these programs, and because of the shortage of good positions, competition for entry to post-graduate programs is fierce. High marks are required. However, as in every area, if you aspire to work in one of these fields and demonstrate your interest and skills clearly in positive ways, your chances for success are good (even if a few of your grades are not so high). Summer jobs and volunteer work for community, health, or social agencies can count heavily on your résumé.

✍ Further Information

Contact:

Canadian Association of Social Workers
402 - 383 Parkdale Avenue
Ottawa, ON, K1Y 4R4

Canadian Psychological Association
205 - 151 Slater Street
Ottawa, ON, K1P 5H3

3

CAREERS OUTSIDE YOUR DEGREE SUBJECT

There are several good reasons why you may opt for a career that doesn't make use of your degree discipline.

You may have taken your interest in your subject as far as you wish, and prefer to widen your horizons. You might even have lost interest in your subject and want to escape from it. On the other hand, you may find it impossible to find related work, either because your subject is non-vocational or because there aren't enough jobs in your field. Remember, the supply of arts graduates far outstrips the supply of related jobs.

Fortunately, about half of all jobs for graduates are open to any discipline. The following chapters describe the main areas of graduate employment which aren't tied to specific academic subjects. The employers covered in this section recruit graduates for the transferable skills they develop while studying for a degree (such as analyzing information, problem solving, and communication), not for their specialist knowledge. For some of these careers, particularly in financial services and some areas of management, you will be expected to study for a recognized professional qualification during your early years at work. Although this can be equivalent to taking another degree, it's usually an excellent career investment.

THIRTEEN

CAREERS IN PUBLIC SERVICE

Public service in Canada employs university graduates at the federal, provincial/territorial, and local government level. This chapter looks at all three career areas.

Government is the primary potential employer for graduates who have majored in political science at university. (Others areas for political science graduates would include business and finance, and communications. These career possibilities are covered in other chapters.)

Public Service Commission of Canada

The Public Service Commission is responsible for a huge range of services affecting almost every area of our lives. There are 40 government departments and agencies which employ a total of over 200,000 people. The departments and agencies include the following. (Examples of some of their key functions are listed where they may not be obvious.)

- ⊃ Agriculture and Agri-Food Canada
- ⊃ Atomic Energy of Canada
- ⊃ Business Development Bank of Canada (assists small business with start-up funds)

- Canada Deposit Insurance Corporation (protects investors' deposits in banks and insurance companies)
- Canada Labour Relations Board
- Canada Mortgage and Housing Corporation
- Canadian Centre for Occupational Health and Safety
- Canadian Coast Guard (patrols Canada's ocean and lake borders)
- Canadian Heritage
- Canadian International Development Agency
- Canadian Radio-Television and Telecommunication Commission (sets rules and regulations governing the operation of radio and TV stations and networks)
- Canadian Security Intelligence Service
- Citizenship and Immigration Canada
- Civil Aviation Tribunal (sets rules and regulations affecting airlines)
- Commissioner of Official Languages
- Correctional Service of Canada
- Defence Construction Canada
- Department of Justice Canada
- Environment Canada
- Export Development Corporation
- Federal Court of Canada
- Financial Institutions (sets rules and regulations for banks and other financial institutions)
- Fisheries and Oceans (controls the quality and quantity of seafood)
- Foreign Affairs and International Trade (covers diplomatic service, trade)
- Health Canada (administers medicare)

- Human Resources Development Canada (new name for Canada Employment Commission)
- Immigration and Refugee Board
- Indian and Northern Affairs Canada
- Industry Canada (established to promote the growth and development of business and industry in Canada)
- National Defence
- National Film Board
- National Research Council
- Natural Resources Canada
- Parks Canada
- Privacy Commissioner of Canada
- Public Works and Government Services Canada (builds and maintains government buildings and property)
- Revenue Canada (collects taxes and other government income)
- Statistics Canada (provides figures on the economy, social trends, immigration, employment)
- Transport Canada
- Transportation Safety Board of Canada (establishes and reviews safety rules and procedures for public transport)
- Treasury Board Secretariat
- Veterans Affairs Canada

The Treasury Board is responsible for the management framework for human resources. It develops, applies, and evaluates personnel policies, systems, and methods, and establishes wages and conditions of employment. The Public Service Commission administers the Public Service

Employment Act and sets standards for hiring and appointments. It shares with the Treasury Board training, human resource planning, and the career development of the executive group.

Most government departments recruit through Public Service Commission offices located in major cities across Canada, on university campuses, and through Human Resource Development Canada offices. Some departments and agencies, such as Transport Canada, recruit directly. Transport Canada operates the Transport Canada Training Institute, which provides training for air traffic controllers, flight service specialists, electronic technicians and engineers, and meteorological technicians. They will advertise directly in major newspapers. Vacancies offered through the Public Service Commission are also advertised on the Internet (..//www.psc-cfg.gc.ca/recruit/psrhome.htm).

Employment Positions

Most areas in the public service offer positions in up to seven levels of responsibility.

Level 1. In most occupational groups, this is considered a training or junior level where your work would be closely supervised. For example, most customs inspectors would be at this level.

Level 2. Once initial training is completed, you would move to Level 2. For example, a counsellor at Human Resources Canada might be at this level.

Level 3. This is similar to Level 2, a full working level, but includes regional managers for a federal department. At this level you might manage part of the financial compensation program in a Veterans Affairs Canada office.

Level 4. This is considered the entrance level for middle management. For example, you might be the manager of a District Taxation Office.

Level 5. At this level you are involved in management and policy planning. An example would be the superintendent of a national park.

Level 6. This is similar to Level 5, but with additional responsibility. For example, you might be the chief of financial audit with responsibility for establishing priorities, policies, and procedures for the financial audit program.

Level 7. This is a senior management position at the executive level. Most positions would involve you in policy development.

Entry Qualifications

The Public Service Commission recruits once a year for university graduates who are bilingual (English and French), and who achieve satisfactory scores on entrance examinations (one or more of the General Competency Test, The Written Communication Test, and/or the Foreign Service Knowledge Test). The Public Service Commission is also committed to employment equity and encourages applications from women, the disabled, visible minorities, and native Canadians.

Junior positions of interest to Faculty of Arts graduates could include the following:

- actuarial science
- auditing
- economics
- sociology
- statistics
- education (Indian and Northern Affairs schools, teaching a second language to civil servants)
- historical research
- psychology
- social work/welfare
- university teaching (at Royal Military College, Kingston, Ontario)
- administrative services
- commerce

- financial adminstration

- foreign service

- information services (similar to public relations)

- organization and methods

- personnel administration

- program administration

- purchasing and supply

- translator

- social science support

- chaplains

- corrections

The selection process usually involves a three-part process. The first step is the writing of any of the three examinations noted above that may be required. The second step is a screening process involving an interview with an interview team; a group simulation exercise may be required during this stage. Step three is the selection phase. For example, if you have applied for the foreign service you would undergo a medical examination and a security clearance.

Remember that governments at all levels are cutting back in numbers of employees. Not all areas will be open every year. For example in 1996, the Public Service Commission offered positions in the following:

- Foreign Service (Foreign Affairs and International Trade, Citizenship and Immigration)

- Development Officer (Canadian International Development Agency)

- Auditor/Audit Officer (Revenue Canada)

- Financial Officers (Treasury Board Secretariat)

- Statisticians (Statistics Canada)

ᗡ   Accelerated Economist (Public Service Commission Training Program)

ᗡ   Economists (Finance Canada, Industry Canada)

ᗡ   Information System Specialists (Statistics Canada)

ᗡ   Management Trainee (Public Service Commission)

✍ Further Information

Contact the student placement centre on your university campus, or the Public Service Commission office located in one of the following cities:

Eastern Canada:
Halifax, Moncton
St. John's, Charlottetown

Central Canada:
Winnipeg, Regina

Quebec:
Montreal, Quebec City

Western Canada:
Victoria, Vancouver, Edmonton
Whitehorse, Yellowknife

Ontario:
Ottawa, Toronto

Provincial/Territory Government Service

In Canada, each province and territory has specific responsibilities under the Constitution Act of 1982. You will find that each government is organized in a similar way to the federal government, with departments and agencies established to administer government services that are provincial and territorial responsibility. In most provinces, you will find some, or all, of the following departments.

ᗡ   Agriculture

ᗡ   Attorney-General

ᗡ   Citizenship

ᗡ   Culture and Recreation

ᗡ   Community and Social Service

ᗡ   Consumer Relations

⊃ Economic Development

⊃ Education

⊃ Energy

⊃ Environment

⊃ Finance

⊃ Health

⊃ Intergovernmental Affairs

⊃ Labour

⊃ Management Board

⊃ Municipal Affairs and Housing

⊃ Native Affairs

⊃ Natural Resources

⊃ Northern Development

⊃ Ombudsman

⊃ Solicitor-General and Correctional Services

⊃ Tourism

⊃ Transportation

⊃ Workers Compensation

Finding Vacancies

Recruitment and hiring procedures are similar to those of the federal government. Positions are advertised on university campuses, in major newspapers, and through provincial government offices. Check with your local member of the provincial parliament for the civil service office in your area.

The number of positions open will be even fewer than the federal government over the next few years. However, there will still be a need for administrators, social workers, financial graduates, teachers in provincial schools, and correctional personnel for the provincial jails. So if you have an interest in government positions, check out the possibilities before you by-pass this opportunity.

Municipal Government

Local government is concerned with providing services to the community. In career terms, it is a group of hundreds of employers across Canada. Like the provincial and federal governments, municipalities offer a wide range of programs and services. These include some or all of the following:

- community services
- conservation authority
- electricity
- finance, assessment, and taxes
- fire
- health
- housing, buildings, inspections
- human resources
- library
- licensing commissions
- parks, culture, and recreation
- planning
- police
- street cleaning and snow removal
- tourist attractions
- transportation and transit
- water - sewage
- works
- zoos

In recent years, most areas have been served by two or more levels of local government: town or city councils and regional authorities. The regions have provided the large-scale strategic services such as education and roads. Town authorities have looked after such areas as housing and waste management.

As you will realize from looking at the list of services, there is a huge range of career opportunities available. A number of these are professional careers. Many can be followed both inside and outside local government. These include accountancy and finance, archive work, librarianship, museum work, and public relations. For others, such as the police, local government is one of the employers.

Local government also employs many people in administrative roles, such as managers who hold senior department posts. They provide support to council committees and sub-committees, advise councillors, and research and prepare reports, sometimes involving the compilation and analysis of statistical information. A degree is increasingly required for these positions. Training is primarily on the job, although you will be encouraged to undertake further study and to qualify for membership in professional groups (for example, the Personnel Association of Ontario, or the Certified General Accountants).

Because each authority is an individual employer, conditions of employment and training programs differ between regions or towns. Salaries also vary according to the size and type of authority. However, local authorities generally have a good reputation for their conditions of employment and commitment to the training and development of their people. They often provide day-release or part-time study for job-related qualifications. They also actively encourage staff to qualify for membership in a relevant professional body.

Promotion opportunities at senior level may be restricted within a single authority. Career advancement is commonly made by moving from one local authority to another. Although this involves applying to openly advised posts, preference is usually given to people who already work in local government and so have relevant experience.

Finding Vacancies

Vacancies are advertised in local newspapers or on campus. You should visit the personnel department in the town or region in which you would like to work. At any given time, entrance positions may be open as a result of internal promotions.

FOURTEEN

The major uniformed professions are the Armed Forces, the police, and fire, ambulance, security, and prison services. Although they cover a range of very different activities, these professions (and the people who work in them) have certain features in common:

- ⊃ They provide a public service, and often undertake tasks which most people would not want to do.

- ⊃ The work can sometimes be dangerous.

- ⊃ There are more rules and regulations than most civilians are governed by.

- ⊃ They are highly disciplined and must exercise self-discipline.

- ⊃ They work unsocial hours.

The nature of the work, the shared risks, the discipline, and the irregular hours tend to separate members of the uniformed services from the general population. Each service has a strong esprit de corps.

Police, firefighters, ambulance, and security services do not have specific university graduate entry requirements, but various police forces do encourage applications from university graduates. Since university graduation may not be an advantage to entering firefighting, the paramedic field, or security work, this chapter will concentrate on careers in the armed forces, the police, and correctional services.

Armed Forces Careers

The Canadian Armed Forces is an integrated force made up of 20 branches, including traditional land, sea, and air branches.

The main purpose of the Canadian Armed Forces is to defend our country and to help allies to whom we are bound by treaty. In recent years, the Canadian Armed Forces have been involved in peace-keeping missions (such as in Bosnia) and disaster relief (for example, helping residents of Quebec cope with severe floods in 1996). However, armed conflicts do arise, and Canadian troops can be called on to participate in United Nations efforts to end hostilities. You can, therefore, be expected to risk your life and to take on responsibility for ordering and leading troops under your command into battle at any time. Even peace-keeping missions can expose you to dangerous situations as you try to intercede between two groups or countries at war. Canadian troops in Bosnia did sustain a number of casualties. And while the government of Canada kept Canadian troops out of combat during the Gulf War, the possibility of action was always present.

The Armed Forces offer a huge range of career opportunities for specialists. For example, because modern defence and warfare systems use sophisticated technology, some roles require graduate engineers. The Armed Forces also require qualified professionals such as lawyers, doctors, and dentists. There are also plenty of openings for arts graduate as officers. The following are the major positions that could be of interest to students considering an arts degree, or currently enroled in one.

Careers

➲ Branch: Administration — Graduates can become
     Personnel Administration Officers who provide
     leadership, professional direction, and administrative

services in the two main areas: personnel administration and personnel services. Officers require a degree from a recognized university with majors in business administration, commerce, psychology, political science, or administrative law.

⊃ Branch: Air Operations — This branch offers career opportunities in navigation, air traffic control, air weapons control, and piloting. All officers in this branch must attend the Aircrew Selection Centre, take specialized aptitude testing, and demonstrate proficiency in mathematics and physics.

⊃ Branch: Armour — One career, as a Combat Arms Officer — Armour, is available in this branch. Officers command and lead armoured units on the modern battlefield. They must be successful in an interview with the Combat Arms Officer Selection Board.

⊃ Branch: Artillery — As with the armour branch, one career, as a Combat Arms Officer — Artillery, is a possibility. Officers command artillery units, advise infantry and armour commanders on the most effective use of artillery resources, and coordinate all fire support resources during land and air operations. They are also chosen through a Combat Arms Officer Selection Board.

⊃ Branch: Chaplain — Chaplains provide religious ministry and pastoral care for military personnel and their dependents. Just as for civilian clergy, chaplains require an arts degree or equivalent, a full course in theology, and must have been ordained. Two years of pastoral experience is required for Protestant chaplains.

⊃ Branch: Infantry — Graduates can apply for positions as Combat Arms Officers — Infantry. Officers command soldiers in land operations, and coordinate the support of artillery, tanks, mortars, and fighter aircraft. They also must be successful at a Combat Arms Officer Selection Board.

⊃   Branch: Intelligence — Intelligence officers collect and
    process strategic and tactical information. They
    require a university degree.

⊃   Branch: Legal — Military legal officers act as
    prosecutors or defence attorneys at military court
    martials, and provide advice about military law.
    Officers must be lawyers and a member of a
    provincial law society.

⊃   Branch: Logistics — Logistics officers support troops
    in the areas of supply, transport, finance, and food
    services. They must have a degree from a recognized
    university (business administration, commerce, or
    economics preferred), or be a member of a recognized
    professional association, or be a graduate of a
    suitable course from an institute of technology. Food
    Services Officer applicants must hold a degree or
    diploma with emphasis on nutrition and/or food
    services administration.

⊃   Branch: Medical — Graduates from an arts faculty
    can enter the Armed Forces as a social work officer.
    Officers provide social services to serving members
    and their dependants. They must hold a minimum of
    a Bachelor's degree in Social Work and be eligible for
    membership in the appropriate provincial association
    of professional social workers.

⊃   Branch: Naval Operations — Graduates can enter as
    a Maritime Surface and Sub-Surface Officer. They are
    responsible for the operation and control of ships and
    submarines of the Canadian Armed Forces. To enter,
    they must be successful at the Naval Officer Selection
    Board.

⊃   Branch: Personnel Selection — Personnel Selection
    Officers use interviews, psychological testing, and
    other sources of information to assist Canadian Forces
    authorities in the employment of Canadian Armed
    Forces personnel. They must hold a Master's degree in
    psychology from a recognized university or be a
    member of the Canadian Psychological Association.

⊃   Branch: Public Affairs — Public Affairs officers
     provide the Canadian public with information about
     the Canadian Forces and the Department of National
     Defence. Officers are selected from officers already
     serving in the Armed Forces.

⊃   Branch: Security — Security officers ensure physical,
     personal, and computer security, enforce the Code of
     Service Discipline, and safeguard the Armed Forces
     from espionage, subversion and sabotage, and
     terrorism. Preference is given to applicants who hold
     a degree in a computer science or a social science
     related to law enforcement.

Entry Qualifications for the Armed Forces

As you can see, an arts degree is acceptable for most of the
careers listed above, although in some cases you would need
mathematics and physics courses in your degree program.
And for the Canadian Coast Guard, you would need secondary school math and science courses.

As well as your degree, personal qualities are important.
Armed Forces officers are good problem solvers and have plenty
of common sense. They can think on their feet and make quick
decisions. They can express themselves easily and clearly. They
are physically fit and have plenty of stamina. Most importantly,
perhaps, they have leadership potential and can motivate and
encourage others by their personal example.

Officer Selection

Recruitment takes place through selection boards. These combine written and psychological tests and interviews by a
selection board of Armed Forces officers. Two entry routes exist.

1.   The Regular Officer Training Plan (ROTP) applies to se-
      lected secondary school students who wish to obtain
      a bachelors degree at either Royal Military College or
      a civilian university, subsidized by the Canadian
      Armed Forces. Commitment after graduation is usu-
      ally three to five years.

2. The Direct Entry Officer (DEO) program applies to those who hold a university degree or technologist diploma. Enlistment is for a period of three to five years after completion of basic and officer training.

Applications

Contact the Canadian Armed Forces recruiting office in the city nearest you. If you're still in secondary school, consult your guidance counsellor. Canadian Armed Forces recruiters try to visit every secondary school in their recruitment area. Your counsellor can put you in touch with your local office.

Canadian Coast Guard Careers

The Canadian Coast Guard patrols Canada's ocean and lake border areas. While related to the Armed Forces, it is a separate force. One career that may be open to arts graduates is as a Navigation Officer. Officers must be graduates of the Canadian Coast Guard Officer Training Plan. To enter the plan, they must have completed university preparatory courses in Math, Physics, French, English and Chemistry and be a secondary school graduate.

The Police

The Royal Canadian Mounted Police is the national police force. It's also employed as the provincial police force in eight of the ten provinces and in the territories. The RCMP have a strength of 15,600 officers. Ontario (4,630 officers) and Quebec (4,400 officers) have established provincial police forces. Most large cities, towns, and regions have their own police forces. There are about 56,000 people working as police officers across Canada.

Police officers perform some or all of the following duties:

➲ patrol assigned areas to maintain public safety and order and to enforce laws and regulations;

➲ investigate crimes and accidents, secure evidence, interview witnesses, compile notes and reports and provide testimony in courts of law;

⊃   arrest criminal suspects;

⊃   provide emergency assistance to victims of accidents, crimes, and natural disasters;

⊃   participate in crime prevention, public information, and safety programs;

⊃   may supervise and coordinate the work of other police officers.

Promotion is through the ranks, with sergeants supervising the work of police constables. Inspectors divide their time between operational and management roles. As you progress through the senior ranks, you take on managerial roles of increasing importance. The more senior you become, the more you will be involved in liaising with the leaders of the community you serve.

The major sectors of the RCMP are:

⊃   drug enforcement

⊃   economic crime directorate

⊃   traffic law enforcement

⊃   Interpol (two RCMP officers are permanently stationed with Interpol headquarters in Lyon, France)

⊃   protective policing directorate

⊃   aboriginal policing program

⊃   police dog services

⊃   marine services

⊃   land transport

⊃   air services

⊃   identification services

⊃   forensic laboratory

⊃   forensic identification support services

⊃   Canadian Police Information Centre

⊃   equitation and Musical Ride

- Canadian Police College
- federal policing
- telecommunications
- counterfeiting
- technical security services
- detachment (front-line policing)
- contract policing
- computer crime
- Music of the Mounties

The provincial and municipal police forces are involved in a wide range of duties including:

- traffic patrol
- processing of criminal charges
- crime prevention measures
- promoting positive policing
- community relations
- preparing court documents
- testimony in court

Entry Qualifications

Every candidate applies for entry to a specific force. Most police forces encourage university graduates to apply. In assessing candidates, the Ontario Provincial Police, for example, assigns points for your education, interview, and physical and psychological tests. Maximum points are given for university graduation.

The selection process is rigorous in all police forces. To use the RCMP as an example, basic requirements are age 19, grade 12 minimum education, valid driver's licence, fluency in English or French or both, Canadian citizenship, physical and mental fitness, being of good character, and willingness to serve anywhere in Canada.

Applicants must write the RCMP Recruit Selection Test. The score will determine if they are selected for an interview. If selected, they must complete the following steps in order:

- initial medical and completion of applicant package
- Physical Abilities Requirement Evaluation (PARE) Certificate
- personal interview
- background investigation
- final medical and final PARE
- First Aid, C.P.R., and Firearms Acquisition certificates
- minimum typing speed of 18 words per minute

Successful applicants are then sent on a six-month training program in Regina, Saskatchewan.

Correctional Services

There are two broad areas of work in correctional services: correctional service officers and probation officers. (The latter is not really a uniformed service but is included here because of the profession's relationship to correctional service officers and because the requirement is for a university degree in arts.)

Correctional Service Officers

Employed by federal, provincial, and municipal governments, people in this occupation guard prisoners and maintain order in correctional institutions and other places of detention. They can be asked to escort prisoners in transit and during temporary leaves.

The main requirement is at least secondary school graduation, but increasingly a community college diploma is required. University graduates may have to take the technical program at their local community college before being considered for employment. In some jurisdictions, correctional service officers must meet certain standard of height, weight, hearing, and age. Officers are expected to be able to think and act quickly, get along well with others, and have keen powers of observation.

Probation Officers

Probation officers are officers of the court who prepare background reports on offenders and supervise adults and young offenders who have been released into community supervision. They investigate backgrounds of offenders at the request of a judge; perform community assessments to ensure lodging, care, and support (and perhaps a job) for offenders; supervise people who have been paroled; may be called on to provide specialized services such as enlisting community support for release programs, making referrals to community services, or even developing community services.

Probation officers require a university degree, preferably in the social sciences, and they must have good oral and written communications skills. Candidates with a knowledge of criminology, criminal justice, and law and administration will have an advantage in securing a position.

✍ Further Information

Contact:

Canadian Police Association
141 Catherine St.
Ottawa, ON, K2P 1C3

Royal Canadian Mounted Police
120 Vanier Parkway
Ottawa, ON, K1A 0R2

Uniform Recruitment Unit, Ontario Provincial Police
777 Memorial Avenue
Orillia, ON, L3V 7V3

Quebec Provincial Police Commission
10 Craig Street East
Montreal, PQ, H2Y 1A8

Registrar, Coast Guard College
PO Box 3000
Sydney, NS, B1P 6K7

Royal Military College of Canada
Kingston, ON, K7K 5L0

Director of Recruiting National Defence Headquarters
Ottawa, ON, K1A 0K2

Correctional Services Canada
340 Laurier Ave. W.
Ottawa, ON, K1A 0P9

FIFTEEN

CAREERS IN MANAGEMENT

The popular idea of a typical graduate career, outside science and technology, is that you join a large well-known company — like IBM or the Canadian Imperial Bank of Commerce — as a management trainee and then progress steadily up the many rungs of the promotional ladder to a top management position. But what does a manger do and what is management about? This chapter looks at the basic role of management in business and describes some of the management functions in which you could seek employment.

What Is Management?

Although most people are familiar with the word "manager," very few can clearly define what a manager is or say what a manager actually does. To some a manager is someone at the top — the "boss" — remote in some large plush office. To others managers are those who direct the work of other people, doing their job by getting other people to do theirs. In industry and commerce there are probably as many definitions of management as there are businesses, and there is no general agreement on what qualities make a good manager. The problem is that there are many kinds of management jobs, and they are carried out in many different ways.

It is the responsibility of a management team to run the business and to safeguard its future. This involves developing products or services which will satisfy the customer and ensuring that these are available to customers when and where they are needed and at the right price. Because most businesses operate in very competitive markets, the management team must constantly seek improvements by developing new and improved products and finding better ways for making them and putting them in the hands of the customer. No business can stand still and survive.

The principles are the same whatever your business. For example, you could be a forestry company growing timber or a quarrying group producing crushed stone for railway ballast and road surfacing. You could be manufacturing jewellery or jet aircraft, books or baby clothes, cars or confectionary. Or you could be providing accommodation and meals through a hotel chain, selling food and goods through supermarkets, providing transport through shipping or bus companies, selling houses through real estate agencies, or providing entertainment in theatres and concert halls.

Different Management Functions

Running any business, especially the sort of large and complex business that recruits graduates, involves a wide range of specialist management functions. Although each of the functions listed below is a specialist activity, and will have specialist manager, they are all interdependent and form part of an organic whole. The managers of each area must collaborate as one team to run the business successfully.

Product Development

This concerns the development of new or improved products. If you're in business to make such things as space satellites, packaged foods, pharmaceuticals, computers, or toiletries, you will have teams of scientists and technologists. If your products are items such as fabrics, china, furniture, clothing, or jewellery, then these will be created by designers. The development team must liaise with marketing personnel (to design products which satisfy customer demands) and with production personnel (to ensure that the designs are realistic in practical terms).

Marketing

The role of the marketing team is central to the business. Marketing people work closely with other functions, especially product development and sales. They identify markets for both existing and new products and may suggest ideas for products which need to be developed. The marketing team will either conduct or commission market research. They work with specialists to create an identity or image for the product through carefully thought-out brand names, packaging, advertising, and other promotional campaigns. They watch what their competitors are doing and monitor the performance of products in terms of sales, customer satisfaction, and profitability.

Sales

Selling is about persuading people to buy your products. Salespeople call on potential and existing customers. They identify customer needs through discussion and then show how the company's product can satisfy that customer's needs better than those of its competitors. The sales department is often the customer's primary point of contact with the company; salespeople must deal with queries and resolve any problems that customers may have through incorrect or late deliveries, product faults or other mistakes. Salespeople may work closely with marketing staff, following up leads for new business or passing on customer feedback about the products. You will find more information about different forms of selling jobs in Chapter 17.

Production Management

Products are made in many ways. These include computer-controlled production lines for making items such as cards,

CDs and chocolates, and processing plants such as oil and chemical refineries. There are assembly lines in which people build up parts into finished products such as clocks and video recorders, assemble mass-produced garments, or sort fruit and vegetables for freezing or canning. Other products may be made to order — buildings, television films, wedding cakes, and ships. Production managers ensure production lines operate efficiently in accordance with just-in-time business philosophies.

Buying

All organizations need to buy goods and materials to go about their business. Manufacturers need to buy raw materials and components to make their products. Buying is not just a matter of negotiating a good price, but also of securing consistent quality and guaranteed delivery times. Reliability of supply is essential; no employer wants machines or people idle when there are orders waiting to be filled. Some materials can be in scarce supply, and buyers may have to seek out suppliers worldwide.

Retailers buy goods for re-sale, either direct from manufacturers or from wholesalers. Retail buyers are concerned with establishing customer buying trends and finding the products to satisfy them. There is a lot of forward planning. For example, retail perfumery buyers look for Christmas goods in the spring. In service industries, buyers are responsible for acquiring all those supplies necessary for their business to operate; for instance, in hotels they might buy everything from buildings to bedding to food and furniture.

Warehousing and Distribution

After goods are made or purchased they must be stored until needed. As soon as they are required they must be distributed in such a way that they reach the customer on time and in perfect condition. Customers may be located anywhere in the world. Reliability is essential. Controlling costs by careful route planning and using appropriately sized vehicles for each delivery is also important. Managers in this function ensure all these tasks and concerns are looked after properly.

Accounting and Finance

Every business has to keep full details of all its financial transactions and have them audited each year. These include invoices sent to customers and received from suppliers, payments received and sent out, wages, rents, rates, taxes (such as the GST), and fees for professional services.

To control the money going in and out of a business, and to make sure more isn't spent than comes in, each department works within a budget. Managers in each department need to know, monthly or even more often, how they are doing against their budgets through a system of management accounting.

Many businesses finance growth by borrowing money to build new premises, buy more or better equipment, take on more staff, and so on. Those which import or export goods often need to buy and sell foreign currency.

There are many openings for graduates in the financial management of business. These are discussed in more detail in Chapter 16.

Management Services

Most organizations now use computers for their financial records, market statistics, sales data, production planning, stock control, customer information, personnel records, and many other purposes. Management services personnel analyze the information needs of each department, and design and run integrated management systems.

Human Resource Management

A business needs to recruit, train, and develop staff for every function. It also has to look after everyone's health, safety and welfare, make sure that people are paid fairly, deal with all aspects of equal opportunities, negotiate with trade unions, possibly provide cafeterias and other facilities, and much more. Human resource managers, particularly in large organizations, may specialize in such areas as recruitment or training.

It is this interdependence of functions which determines the way in which managers work. Everyone has to start in one function, but none of us, however specialized our role, can work in isolation. We are part of a multidisciplinary team working towards shared objectives and we must be constantly ware of how our own function interacts with those of our colleagues and with the organization as a whole. We must work together, not just with our peers, but with colleagues at all levels.

Graduate recruitment brochure

What Do Managers Do?

In traditionally organized companies, managers head a department (or part of a department) and lead a team of people. This is often known as "line management." Managers are normally assessed on the performance of their team. The line manager reports to senior managers who plan, coordinate, and supervise the activities of all the specialist departments so that they work together as a single organization. This level is usually known as "general management."

Managers will no longer act as commanders of troops but as coaches, coordinators, partners, facilitators, feedback generators, skills builders, progress monitors, outcome evaluators, and information sources. They'll become responsive to the needs of individual employees and of teams of employees.

Colin Campbell, author

However, since many organizations now employ fewer managers than before and are organizing their work in new ways, more work is carried out by project teams. These teams are put together on the basis of the skills and knowledge needed, and stay together only for the duration of a specific job. In this type of work you move from one project to another. On some you may lead the team because you have the relevant skills or experience, on others you will be managed by someone else. If you're pursuing a management career the biggest difference is that, in a project management structure, you may not have responsibility for a permanent team of staff.

Whichever system of working is in place, the majority of managers are primarily concerned with operational management. This involves implementing policy decisions and organizing resources so that the activities of the business run smoothly and profitably. (Setting strategy and making policy decisions tend to be the responsibility of the more senior managers who have the necessary overview of the organization.) As an operational manager you will typically:

- plan the work of the department or section
- attend planning and other meetings
- prepare budgets and get them vetted
- set team and individual targets
- ensure you have the resources your department needs
- monitor team and individual performance, making sure that targets are met
- monitor the quality of the work done by members of your staff
- keep records and monitor them against targets and budgets
- report to senior management
- train, supervise, and motivate your staff
- keep your staff informed about what is going on within the company
- constantly seek better ways of doing things
- solve problems when they arise
- liaise with managers in other departments, with suppliers, and with customers.

Are Managers the Same as Executives?

Although the words manager and executive are often used to mean the same thing, they are different. A manager is someone who leads a team of people. An executive is an expert who makes decisions which can affect the whole organization's future, and who must take responsibility for those decisions. Executives are supposed to have the specialist knowledge that makes them better qualified than anyone else to make the right decisions.

Most managers are executives, but not all. Supervisors in shops or on a factory floor are managers because they manage the work of others, but they are not executives with the expertise to make policy decisions. On the other hand, many non-managers are executives because of their expertise.

Most modern organizations need both managers and individual experts. An increasing proportion of graduate jobs are in expert roles. But unless you are a science or technology graduate, you are unlikely to find yourself in an executive role without experience in line management.

Although the words manager and executive are often used in confusing ways, don't worry about it. Most organizations use the language of management, including job titles, in different ways. Once you join an employer, you will soon get used to the internal language.

'When I use a word,' Humpty Dumpty said, in rather a scornful tone, 'it means just what I choose it to mean — neither more nor less.'

Lewis Carroll, author

What Qualities Do You Need?

If you like to concentrate on one thing at a time without interruption, then management probably isn't for you. You probably won't enjoy it either if you prefer to do things yourself rather than depend on others to do them. You need to be flexible, a good team worker, and able to motivate those around you to do things your way. Effective managers earn the willing respect and cooperation of their team. They do not rely on their rank to intimidate or control people.

You need to be reasonably self-confident, have good social skills, and be able to communicate clearly and persuasively. You must be able to earn the respect of others, including those over whom you have no direct authority. You will also have to collaborate with managers at all levels throughout the organization. In dealing with others, you must be able to argue your point of view persuasively and persistently, and yet be willing to listen and learn, and make compromises when appropriate.

In your early days you may be responsible for leading people who have many more years of specialist experience than you. You need to listen to your staff and show that you are willing to learn from them. You must know when to admit your own lack of expertise and ask for help. This is a sign of strength, not weakness.

The best managers employ good-calibre people and train and develop them so that they become as good or better than themselves at the job. This too takes self-confidence, knowing you have good people ready to step into your shoes. However, remember that managers are usually judged on the calibre of the people they develop (and they cannot easily be promoted unless someone is ready to be promoted into their place).

1. What ought to be done.
2. How should it be done.
3. Who should do it.
4. Has it been done.

Joseph Atkinson, publisher[13]

All managers need transferable skills. (See Chapter 4.) Some employers in their recruitment brochures and advertisements also ask that applicants be ambitious. It's worth looking at this in a bit more detail.

Ambition to some people is the competitive spirit which drives a person to get to the top. To others it is the pursuit of excellence. Many people, including some employers, think ambition is the same as competitiveness. Because businesses must compete with one another in the marketplace to survive and prosper, it is assumed that competition between individuals within a firm is also a good thing.

However, the functions of an organization interact with one another. So do the people employed by the company. An organization, like a sports team, is a group of individuals, each with a specific role and responsibilities. Can you imagine how well a team would do if all the players competed against one another as well as against their opponents?

This does not mean good team players are faceless cogs in a machine; there is still scope to show individual brilliance and the willingness to accept increasing levels of responsibility. In these organizations, management authority comes from recognized expertise and the ability to collaborate with others, not from one's rank in the hierarchy.

Entry Qualifications

There are two usual entry routes into a management career: traditional management training programs, usually run only by large organizations, and direct entry. A management training program is designed for those capable of progressing though line management to general management relatively quickly. In direct entry you are recruited into a specific function and trained on the job.

Be wary of the wording in graduate recruitment brochures. Some direct entry programs are also known as traineeship, so make sure you know exactly what it is that you are applying for. Management traineeships are only intended for those with the potential to reach the very top of general management. The majority of graduates will be recruited via the direct entry route.

For either route, any degree subject is usually acceptable, although business degrees or even M.B.A.s may be required, mainly because of increased competition. At a minimum, you will need an honours degree.

The most critical requirement is personal qualities. This generally means the transferable skills described in Chapter 4. Work experience (from weekend jobs, holiday work, helping in a family business, co-op work placements) is especially valued.

Second-language facility is also important, particularly in Canada's two official languages. And with business now being conducted anywhere in the world, competence in other languages, particularly those of the Pacific Rim, would be a definite asset.

Training and Career Development

Your initial training and career development will differ according to whether you are on a management training program or direct entry. However, in the long term both groups have similar opportunities to reach the top.

Traditional Management Training: This usually lasts about two years. The training program typically combines formal business education, skills training, and project work. You are likely to spend time in a number of functions to understand how the business works as a whole, and to find out which specialist area is best suited to your interests and aptitudes.

Once you move into a specialist area you may, depending on your function, be expected to combine your internal management training with study for membership of an appropriate professional institution. This is usually equivalent to studying for another degree.

Among the professional qualifications for which you might study are those of the Fellow Institute of Canadian Bankers, the Certified Management Accountant Society, or the Human Resources Professionals Association. You will normally get time to write examinations and your employer will usually reimburse tuition expenses; but study will be on your own time.

Although you will have undertaken project work and spent time helping managers in various departments, you won't take up a management post of your own until your formal training period is over. Even then, you will continue with any professional studies you may have started.

Your career development will then be up to you. As a trained manager, you can expect regular moves upward into jobs of increasing responsibility, and laterally through different functions.

Direct Entry: If you are a direct entrant you will have a few days of orientation to learn about the organization, the goods or services it provides, its systems, and so on. You will then start your job. Initially you will work under close supervision, being trained on the job. You're likely to go on courses from time to time. Some will cover general management skills such as making presentations, writing reports, preparing budgets, and understanding balance sheets. Others may deal with technical aspects of your job function.

Depending on your function, you will probably be able to study for a relevant professional qualification. However, you may have to take the initiative yourself. If you do, your employer is likely to give you a lot of support.

It's well worth getting a professional qualification if you can. It will not only enhance your prospects with your existing employer, but also give you a valuable qualification to help you get a new job if you decide to move.

Finding Vacancies

Even in your first year at university, you should visit your school's career centre. Many businesses offer summer internship or training programs. But certainly, by early in your final year, you should be talking with career counsellors and signing up for the various recruitment campaigns as they come to your campus.

Get a copy of *Career Options: The Graduate Recruitment Annual*. It lists the companies who are actively recruiting for graduates in the current year. As well, check the following publications at your career centre or local library:

- *Canadian Trade Index*

- *Scott's Industrial Directories*

- *Canadian Key Business Directory*

- *Community and Social Service Directory*

- *Canadian Advertising Rates and Data*

- *Dun and Bradstreet International*

⊃ *Financial Post* surveys (annual list of the top 500 companies)

⊃ *Fraser's Canadian Trade Directory*

⊃ *Directory of Associations in Canada*

✍ Further Information

Contact:

Institute of Chartered Secretaries and Administrators in Canada
#255, 55 St. Clair Ave. W.
Toronto, ON, M4V 2Y7

Institute of Certified Management Consultants of Canada
Heritage Building,
BCE Place, Box 835
181 Bay St.
Toronto, ON, M5J 2T3

Canadian Management Centre of AMA International
150 York St., 5th Floor
Toronto, ON, M5H 3S5

Canadian Institute of Certified Administrative Managers
#700, 2 Bloor St. W.
Toronto, ON, M4W 3R1

SIXTEEN

CAREERS IN FINANCIAL SERVICES

Particular skills and knowledge can be rendered obsolete very quickly.... What business values most is lateral thinking, curiosity, and breadth of knowledge.

Matthew Barrett, Chair of Bank of Montreal

About one in eight arts graduates goes into financial services. This is not as surprising as it sounds. Most people assume that anything to do with finance involves doing lots of math, but this is a fallacy. You do need to be numerate and to have an analytical mind to interpret data, but only in a few specialist areas, such as actuarial work, do you need a high level of mathematical skill. In most financial services, having good communication skills is far more important.

The main financial services functions, which will be looked at in turn, are accountancy, banking, credit unions and trust companies, insurance, stockbroking, and actuarial work.

Accountancy

Accountants are concerned with managing money. They prepare and analyze accounts and provide expert financial advice. The popular image of deskbound number-crunchers is false; accountants have to understand the whole business of the organizations they serve. Consequently, their responsibilities frequently take them out of the office. And the training for an accountancy qualification is excellent preparation for a general management career in almost any area of the economy. Accountancy training can also be a good foundation for people who want to start and run their own business. (See Chapter 17.)

Every organization is required by law to keep financial records of all items of income or expenditure. These records, which are often computerized, form the basis of the annual accounts. All but the very smallest limited companies must, by law, have these accounts audited — that is, checked that they are a true and fair view of the company's affairs. Only chartered accountants from outside the organization can carry out an audit.

There are three main areas in which accountants work:

⊃   business and industry

⊃   chartered accountant firms and private practice

⊃   public service

The emphasis on financial accounting, management accounting and auditing in your work will vary according to which field you join. There is specialist training for each.

Financial Accountants

These accountants are usually company employees who keep and analyze records of company income and expenditure, produce annual accounts for shareholders and Revenue Canada, interpret financial information, and borrow money. They also ensure that salaries and bills are paid, and that customers are invoiced and pay their bills on time. In Canada, most financial accountants belong to the Certified General Accountants (CGA) Association. There are 43,000 certified general accountants currently registered in Canada.

Management Accountants

If you become a management accountant you may examine policies and long-term plans, look at the costs and benefits of different business strategies, and present the findings to senior management. These accountants also help to prepare budgets and monitor the performance of departments against their budgets. The work involves spending time talking to colleagues throughout the company and providing them with advice. In effect, management accountants are internal consultants. They often move into the consultancy sections of public practice firms or into management consultancy. In Canada, their professional group is the Certified Management Accountant (CMA) Society. There are 24,000 management accountants in Canada.

Chartered Accountants

These accountants work in firms of partners. The core of their work consists of auditing company accounts and giving technical advice on taxation. They may also produce annual accounts on behalf of self-employed individuals and small businesses. Many larger chartered accountant firms also provide insolvency and consultancy services. Many partnerships have a network of regional offices.

Chartered accountants often carry out audits in clients' offices, and this may involve a lot of travel and time away from home. Apart from checking financial records, both manual and computerized, an audit usually involves interviewing staff at all levels to explain various aspects of the figures. Audits can last from a day or two to several months, depending on the size of the company. Although auditing once had the reputation of being boring, computers and new systems have removed a lot of the drudgery of routine checking. If you are prepared to look beyond the figures, at what lies behind them, auditing is a very good way of examining a variety of businesses from the inside and learning how they work.

Taxation work involves giving advice and negotiating tax assessment with Revenue Canada on behalf of various clients. Insolvency work involves dealing with the financial affairs of businesses which face bankruptcy or have already been declared bankrupt. This may include trying to save the business, selling it, or, failing all else, selling off the assets so that creditors can be paid.

Consultancy can involve advising organizations on any aspect of their business which will enable them to improve their efficiency and profitability.

In Canada, the professional group is the Institute of Chartered Accountants. There are 53,000 chartered accountants in Canada.

Entry Qualifications and Training

1. Chartered Accountant

    University graduation is the basic requirement, with a major in Commerce or Business Administration, although graduates from other programs can enter the profession. Applicants must present 45 semester hours in accountancy and related subjects. Students must secure employment in a chartered accountant office and write admission examinations for the School of Accountancy. Students then attend the Institute's School of Accountancy, a combination of self-study and full-time study prior to writing the Uniform Final Examination.

2. Certified General Accountant

    University graduation isn't a requirement for admission, but university graduates in business can qualify for advanced standing. Students are expected to be employed full-time while completing their studies through correspondence. Students can choose from a variety of courses to suit their career goals.

3. Certified Management Accountant

    University programs are available. For example, at the University of Waterloo programs are available in both Arts and Mathematics. Minimum requirements are the completion of a university program and two years of work experience.

✍ Further Information

Contact:

**Canadian Institute of
Chartered Accountants**
277 Wellington St. W.
Toronto, ON, M5V 3H2

**Certified General Accountants
Association of Canada**
#740 - 1176 West Georgia St.
Vancouver, BC, V6E 4A2

**The Society of Management
Accountants of Canada**
#850, 120 King St. W.
PO Box 176
Hamilton, ON, L8N 3C3

Banking

Canada's financial institutions can be grouped into three major types: institutions that take deposits or make loans, insurance companies and pension funds, and investment dealers and investment funds. In 1992, the federal government implemented a major overhaul of the laws governing financial institutions and narrowed the differences between certain types, particularly between banks and trust companies. The legislation also liberalized cross-ownership rules. Trust companies, for example, can now own an insurance corporation, and banks can own securities dealers.

Institutions that take deposits or make loans include the chartered banks, trust and mortgage loan companies, caisses populaires and credit unions, and government savings institutions such of the Ontario Savings Office and the Alberta Treasury Branches.

Chartered banks operate under the Bank Act. There are eight Canadian-owned banks with 8000 branches, and 54 foreign-owned banks with 271 branches. These banks handle retail or personal banking, taking deposits and making loans, clearing cheques, and selling a range of financial products to individuals and organizations.

The Federal Business Development Bank is a crown corporation created in 1974 to lend money or provide equity capital to Canadian companies.

Trust and mortgage loan companies operate under the Federal Loan Companies Act and the Trust Companies Act. Both must also be licenced in each province. Trust companies conduct two main types of business. The first is financial intermediation. Their main business is channelling savings into mortgages. They operate like banks, investing funds in exchange for trust deposits and investment certificates. The second is fiduciary (holding assets in trust). Trust companies are the only corporations in Canada with this power. They act as trustees for pension funds and corporate debt issues, and as registrars and transfer agents for corporate share issues.

Mortgage loan companies borrow money and re-lend it as mortgages. They accept deposits and issue debentures. (Debentures are like government bonds but are issued by corporations.)

Credit unions are provincially regulated cooperative associations serving particular memberships. There are 2600 chartered local credit unions and 13 central credit unions in Canada. Credit Union Central of Canada is the national organization that provides technical and financial support services to credit unions.

The Bank of Canada

The Bank of Canada supervises the Canadian banking system, prints money, and acts as banker to the federal government and to the other banks. Much of its work involves the collection, analysis, and interpretation of economic and financial data related both to the Canadian economy and to economic conditions outside Canada. The Bank of Canada is responsible for monetary policy, banking services, and government debt management.

Branch Management

Bank managers are responsible for running branches profitably. This involves leading a team which, among other things, opens and monitors bank accounts for individuals and businesses, deals with inquiries, assesses credit risks and provides loans, sells insurance, arranges mortgages, and offers financial advice. Branches are organized into districts. Branch managers can authorize loans only up to a fixed limit. Requests for loans above this limit are analyzed at district or head office level.

Entry Qualifications

Banks accept any degree, although preference is given to business-related courses of study. The Bank of Canada will consider any degree subject, but prefers graduates who have an economics or a related degree. Language skills, especially French/English, are an advantage.

You will also need commercial awareness, basic numeracy skills, and an analytical mind. You must be able to lead a team. Above all, because you are offering services to people at all levels up to the most senior of business professionals, you will need mature communications and social skills.

Training and Development

University graduates are placed on an accelerated training program of approximately one year, which prepares them for supervisory positions as accountants and a progression to administrative positions in two or three years. Three-year management training programs are available, and the banks all sponsor their career officers at the Fellow Institute of Canadian Bankers.

Progress depends on your performance. You may move up in management roles of increasing seniority or become a specialist in a particular area of banking such as international banking, investment management for institutional clients, and treasury (buying and selling foreign currency).

✍ Further Information

Contact:

Institute of Canadian Bankers
Box 348, Exchange Tower
#600, 2 First Canadian Place
Toronto, ON, M5X 1E1

Association of Canadian Financial Corporations
Sussex Centre, #401
50 Burnhamthorpe Rd. W.
Mississauga, ON, L4B 3C2

Trust Companies
Association
of Canada Inc.
#720, 50 O'Connor St.
Ottawa, ON, K1P 6L2

Association of Canadian
Financial Corporations
Sussex Centre, #401
50 Burnhamthorpe Rd. W.
Mississauga, ON, L4B 3C2

The Trust Institute,
Commerce Court West
PO Box 348, Suite 1830
Toronto, ON, M4L 1G2

Insurance

Insurance is a way of protecting people from losses arising from sickness, theft, fire, accident, and other misfortunes. Insurance is offered against the risk of specific incidents taking place. You don't insure a person, event, or object — you insure against something happening to that person, event, or object. The industry is based on the laws of probability, that is, the likelihood of certain events taking place or happening to people. The basic principle behind insurance is that many people regularly pay into a common fund, but only a few people will need to claim compensation for a mishap.

Insurance coverage can be provided for practically anything — from a second-hand car to a jumbo jet or from a paint factory to a painting by Leonardo da Vinci. At a more personal level you can insure against a cancelled holiday, having twins, losing a limb, or having your home burglarized.

In Canada, insurance is provided by 395 federally registered companies, governed by the Insurance Companies Act, and by 900 insurance companies and societies that are licenced provincially. There are 82 life and health federal and provincial companies as well as 73 branches of foreign companies and 60 fraternal benefit societies. There are 104 Canadian property and casulty insurance companies as well as 148 foreign companies. All investments in these companies are protected, as are bank deposits, by the Canadian Deposit Insurance Corporation.

There are also insurance brokers, independent specialists who advise on and negotiate insurance policies on behalf of their clients. Most brokers specialize in a particular area such as automobile, home, or marine insurance.

The four areas of insurance work which you, as an arts graduate, might consider are:

- ⊃ underwriting
- ⊃ insurance adjusting
- ⊃ claims examiner
- ⊃ sales

The Work of Underwriters

Underwriters calculate risks, decide what is insurable and, if so, on what terms. Some risks are simple to assess and are based on standard guidelines. Others, such as Prince Edward Island's mainland bridge or a space satellite are more complex. As an underwriter you might have to calculate the risk of an aircraft crashing, a factory being destroyed by fire, a film star becoming ill during filming, and many other types of mishap. Insurance is highly competitive, so if an underwriter sets the premium too high the company may lose business. If premiums are set too low, claims may exceed premiums.

The Work of Insurance Adjusters

Insurance adjusters investigate the circumstances surrounding insurance claims to determine their validity. They consult with clients, interview witnesses and medical personnel, and examine records and reports. They determine the amount of loss or damage and negotiate settlement of the claim. If you have ever been involved in an automobile accident, the first person, after the police, that you met with was the insurance adjuster.

The Work of Claims Examiners

Claims examiners work with the adjuster to calculate and authorize insurance claims. They examine reports and ensure that all payments are in accordance with company practices and procedures. They may have to consult lawyers or doctors to discuss claims.

The Work of Insurance Agents and Brokers

Insurance agents and brokers sell automobile, fire, health, life, property, and other types of insurance to clients. Their primary responsibility is to establish the client's insurance coverage, calculate premiums, and work out the method of payment.

Entry Qualifications

Any degree is acceptable. You need to be numerate, to have an analytical mind, and to combine assertiveness with tact. (You have to deal sensitively with people who have suffered various calamities.) You also must be a persuasive communicator, both orally and in writing.

Training and Career Development

In large insurance companies, you are likely to join a graduate training program which will combine on-the-job work experience in a variety of functions with part-time study.

Underwriters must complete an educational program through the Insurance Institute of Canada, leading to professional recognition as an Associate of the Insurance Institute of Canada or Fellow of the Insurance Institute of Canada.

Adjusters and examiners need several years of on-the-job training and completion of insurance industry courses and training programs. Independent adjusters require a provincial licence issued by the Superintendent of Insurance. Professional recognition is obtained through the Insurance Institute of Canada.

Insurance agents and brokers also have to be licensed by the Superintendent of Insurance and must complete courses leading to recognition as an Associate, or Fellow, of the Insurance Institute of Canada.

✍ Further Information

Contact:

**Canadian Institute of
Chartered Life Underwriters
& Chartered Financial
Consultants**
41 Lesmill Rd.,
Don Mills, ON, M3B 2T3

**The Insurance Institute
of Canada**
18 King St. E., 6th Floor
Toronto, ON, M5C 1C4

**Canadian Life & Health
Insurance Association**
#1700, 1 Queen St. E.
Toronto, ON, M5C 2X9

**Canadian Independent
Adjusters' Association**
1305 - 55 Queen St. E.
Toronto, ON, M5C 1R6

**Insurance Brokers
Association of Canada,**
#701, 181 University Ave.
Toronto, ON, M5H 3M7

Stockbroking and Investment Dealing

The Stock Exchange is a marketplace where industry, commerce, and the government can raise money by selling stocks and shares in companies or ventures to individuals and institutions. As part-owners of the business, these people hope to share in the financial success of the company. Many individuals buy stocks and shares, collectively known as securities. Many more have investments made on their behalf by the banks, trust companies, pension funds, and other who hold their money.

The future for traditional stockbrokers is uncertain. With computerized trading increasing, individuals or groups will be able to carry out their own trading, and banks are increasingly offering no-frills services. Career opportunities will be with pension funds, mutual fund organizations, and in derivative trading.

Main employment possibilities will be for financial and investment analysts, securities sales agents, and traders. Analysts collect financial and investment information and provide investment advice and recommendations to clients, senior company officials, pension fund managers, and securities agents. Analysts require a university degree in commerce, business administration, or economics. The Chartered Financial Analyst (CFA) designation, available through the Institute of Chartered Financial Analysts in the United States, may be required.

Securities sales agents buy and sell stocks, bonds, treasury bills, mutual funds, and other securities for investors, pension fund managers, and companies. Traders buy and sell stocks, bonds, commodity futures, foreign currencies, and other securities at stock exchanges on behalf of investment dealers. They develop trading strategies by reviewing investment information and monitoring market conditions. Both must complete the Canadian Securities Course and the Registered Representative Manual Exam offered by the Canadian Securities Institute.

✍ Further Information

Contact:

Canadian Securities Institute
Suite 360,
33 Yonge Street
Toronto, ON, M5E 1G4

Investment Dealers' Association
Suite 350, 33 Yonge Street
Toronto, ON, M5E 1G4

Toronto Stock Exchange Information Centre
2 First Canadian Place
The Exchange Tower, PO Box 450
Toronto, ON, M5X 1J2

Vancouver Stock Exchange
Stock Exchange Tower
609 Granville St., P.O. Box 10333
Vancouver, BC, V7Y 1H1

Actuarial Work

Actuaries calculate risks, working out the odds of things happening. The theory of probability underlies much of this work, with the emphasis on probabilities related to living, dying, sickness, and health as well as all those risks against which individuals and organizations insure. This differs from the work of underwriters who are concerned with specific cases of insurance risk, although they will use actuarial data in their work.

About 70 per cent of actuaries work for insurance companies. Some actuaries work as consultants to individuals, labour unions, employers, or pension fund administrators. Other are employed by government or work as university professors.

Working in Life Insurance

In life insurance companies, actuaries calculate the theoretical life expectancy of those buying life insurance. This varies by age, sex (on average women live longer), occupation, state of health, and other factors. The actuary can then calculate rates to be charged as premiums and, as these are paid, check that the assets cover any claims that will arise. Actuaries do similar calculations for pension plans run by life assurance companies, trying to ensure that the premiums paid while people are working provide sufficient funds to cover their pensions from retirement until death.

Working in General Insurance

Actuaries in general insurance companies calculate the odds against homes being burglarized or cars stolen. These odds differ by geographical area. They will also calculate the odds for being involved in car accidents according to the type of car being driven, and the age and occupation of the driver.

The profession is relatively small but highly influential. It's essentially a desk job, although those working in consultancy spend a lot of time visiting clients. The work has a high mathematical content drawing on probability theory, compound interest calculations, and a range of statistical techniques including mathematical modelling on computers. However, since the results of any calculations have to be explained to non-specialists, actuaries must also communicate clearly both orally and in writing.

Entry Qualifications and Training

Most entrants to the profession have a degree in mathematics. Actuarial degree programs are offered at Montreal's

Concordia University, the University of Waterloo, and the University of Western Ontario in London. After university you obtain a position to work under an actuary and complete the course offered by the Canadian Institute of Actuaries.

✍ Further Information

Contact:

Canadian Institute of Actuaries
#1040, 360 Albert St.
Ottawa, ON, K1R 7X7

SEVENTEEN

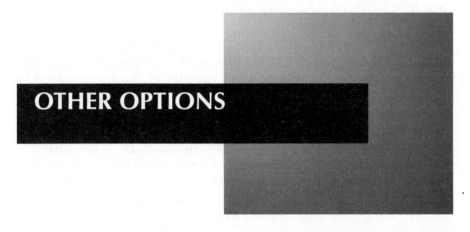

OTHER OPTIONS

Even in a book of this size it's impossible to describe adequately every career open to an arts graduate. This book has sought to describe some of the mainstream choices. There are many more options, and some of the most fruitful ones are briefly described in this chapter. However, if nothing in this book appeals to you, there are still plenty of other careers to consider. Do some research — and don't just look at the obvious.

Advertising Agencies

As well as copywriting (Chapter 6), you could consider working in advertising as an account executive or in a media department.

Working as an Account Executive

An account executive looks after a group of clients and is in almost daily contact with them. As an account executive, you are the link between the agency and the client. You must get the best possible work, on behalf of your client, from your colleagues in other departments — copywriters, art directors, media executives, researchers, and administrators.

Being an account executive has a glamorous image and many people are attracted by the travel and entertainment that this work entails. However, the novelty of rising at dawn to catch an early train or plane and getting home late in the evening soon wears thin, especially if you're doing it two or three times a week. Even lunching in expensive restaurants loses its glamour when, in mid-mouthful, you are asked to explain why the client's sales are falling, or why the production costs for a new television commercial have gone over-budget.

The account executive's job is to keep clients happy. If the agency loses a big client, the account executive responsible is often dismissed. It's a highly stressed job. David Ogilvie, who built Ogilvie & Mather into the world's fourth largest advertising agency, says the head of an agency "must be a good leader of frightened people." He also quotes a study which shows that the death rate from stress-related causes is 14 per cent higher among senior advertising executives than their counterparts in other white collar occupations. However, you will certainly be offered plenty of intellectual and management challenges. Being an account executive is also a route to top management in advertising.

Working in a Media Department

In a media department you are responsible for recommending the best medium, or mix of media, for a particular advertisement or advertising campaign. You have to weigh the respective merits of different newspapers, periodicals, radio and television stations, poster sites, and so on in terms of their potential to reach your target audience. You will draw on circulation figures, readership surveys, and other statistical sources. You need an analytical mind and the ability to put statistical data in lay terms. You also buy time or space from media owners. Advertising rates can be open to discussion, so you should also have a taste for negotiation.

Graduates are often found on the other side, selling advertising space or time on behalf of media owners. Much of this is done via the telephone direct to advertisers. However, with large advertisers and agencies the selling may be conducted face-to-face. Media sales can occasionally offer a route into other areas of publishing (Chapter 6). You will find more on selling below.

✍ Further Information

Contact:

**Association of Canadian
Advertisers, Inc.**
#803, 180 Bloor St. W.
Toronto, ON, M5S 2V6

**Canadian Association of
Marketing Research
Organizations**
#409, 1 Eva Rd.
Etobicoke, ON, M9C 4Z5

Retailing

Retailing used to have a poor image among graduates. This wasn't helped by experiences of Saturday jobs, filling the shelves in one's local supermarket. This gives a totally false impression of the jobs which graduates do in retailing. The larger retailing operations now offer very interesting challenges in a variety of areas such as finance, quality assurance, marketing, buying, and merchandising. (Some of these functions were described in Chapter 15.) The more successful retailers run very sophisticated operations using the latest systems and technology. The main openings are in store management

About 333,000 people are employed as managers in retail trade. Most vacancies for store managers are in supermarkets, chain stores, and department stores. If you're interested in job possibilities with a retailer, choose one with a good training program, a reputation for success, and good staff relations. The average salary is about $38,000.

Retailing is likely to offer a number of interesting opportunities in the next five to ten years. While opportunities in the field are expected to remain stable, there are increasing numbers of new retailers entering the Canadian market. In most mid-size to large communities, you will find new retailers such as Winners, Home Depot, and Future Shop. All are actively recruiting managers and assistant managers.

Unlike most careers, you can sample what different retailers are like by visiting their stores. Watch how they deal with customers, and talk to people working there. If you are really keen, ask to meet some management staff.

✍ Further information

Contact:

Retail Council of Canada
#600, 210 Dundas St. W.
Toronto, ON, M4G 2E8

**Retail Merchants Association
of Canada**
1780 Birchmount Rd.
Scarborough, ON, M1P 2H8

Sales

Most of us enjoy persuading others to accept our point of view. Whether this involves a subtle academic point or a decision on how to spend the evening, we tend to be pleased if we convince others to see or do things our way. The art of persuasion is not just a useful social skill. It is also invaluable in any career. Most jobs involve team working. You need to be persuasive if you are to:

⊃   obtain the help of colleagues over whom you have no authority;

⊃   convince people working under you to give you their willing effort;

⊃   win the support of your boss or manager for any initiatives you want to take;

⊃   get good service from your suppliers;

⊃   persuade customers to buy from you.

Many areas of selling require a keen analytical mind. Yet mention selling to people and they see a glib extrovert pressuring the unwilling into buying the unwanted. In the past, there was some truth to this stereotype; businesses were geared to production and their sales staff had to sell whatever the company chose to make.

> *Tell your story to the public — what you have and what you propose to sell. Promise them not only bargains but that every article will be found just what it is guaranteed to be.*

Timothy Eaton

Now, most businesses have a better understanding of customers' needs. They are market-led, creating products and services for which they have identified a clear need. Also, customers have become more knowledgable. They are better aware of the choices open to them and have higher expectations of both the products and the quality of service that they get from suppliers.

Because winning and looking after customers are central to the survival of every business, selling is a key function. Selling ranges from trading in market stalls through to negotiating the sale of aircraft to governments and airlines. However, graduate sales careers rarely involve selling direct to the public; the only major exceptions are the sale of financial services.

There are two types of selling, canvassing and servicing, although both are often combined in one job. Canvassing is approaching potential customers for the first time to win an initial order. Servicing is following up earlier sales and obtaining new orders from existing customers.

The principles of selling are similar whatever the product. You first have to identify a customer's needs through questions and discussion. (You cannot sell anything until the customer recognizes a need.) You then have to describe, briefly and persuasively, how your product would satisfy that need better than competing products, and provide convincing evidence to support your claims. If the customer raises objections, and most will, you must know how to overcome them without entering an argument.

Win the argument and lose the sale.

Old sales proverb

You will need to negotiate prices and delivery dates. You will have to liaise with your own production and delivery department in order to meet the delivery schedules. And you will have to make follow-up calls to ensure that the customer is satisfied, to answer any queries or resolve any complaints, and to ask for more orders.

Selling can be either face-to-face field sales or by telephone (or increasingly on the Internet). If you are selling on the telephone, you may be making 20-30 calls a day. Working in field sales, you may be calling on several hundred customers every few weeks, or visiting 20 or so a week, or even fewer depending on the nature of the business. A salesperson selling a technical product to a large user — such as industrial paints to a car manufacturer — may be fully occupied in caring for the needs of that one customer.

Entry Qualifications

You aren't likely to need any formal qualifications except in areas of technical selling, where you may require a related degree. What you will need is a questioning and analytical mind to discuss and identify customer needs and to relate these to your products, as well as the social maturity to deal with people of all ages and at all levels of seniority.

You must be articulate so that you can present and defend a cogent argument clearly and persuasively. It's also important to be a good listener. You must be able to write lucidly so you can correspond with your customers, provide reports to management, and supply unambiguous briefings to your marketing, production, and service departments. In field sales your work is largely unsupervised. You therefore need to be self-reliant and a good organizer of your own work and travel schedules.

Training

Companies differ enormously in the quality of training they provide. Make sure you join a company with a structured training program which is not limited to basic knowledge of the product and a few days shadowing an existing salesperson.

Career Development

In field sales you typically move from salesperson to field sales manager or area sales manager. (In telephone selling the equivalent may be a telephone trainer.) Then you move on to deputy sales manager, sales manager, and sales director. The qualities needed in sales management are different from those needed in selling. You will probably be responsible for managing a team of salespeople, and may not do any direct selling yourself. Some people prefer the independence of remaining in the field. They may develop a portfolio of major customers, and can sometimes earn more than anybody else in the company.

✍ Further Information

Contact:

**Canadian Professional Sales
Association**
#310, 145 Wellington St.
Toronto, ON, M5J 1H8

**Canadian Association of
Wholesale Sales
Representatives**
#336, 370 King St. W.
P.O. Box 2, Toronto, ON, M5V 1J9

Travel Industry

The travel industry has a glamorous image, but offers few opportunities for graduates. In Canada, about 21,000 people work as travel counsellors. The industry is a $42 billion a year business with $31 billion of that spent on domestic travel by

Canadians. But despite that, most counsellors are college graduates and poorly paid. Despite the low pay, competition for travel counsellor jobs is intense. University graduates would likely have to take a travel counsellor course.

One fairly new area to consider is that of corporate travel professionals, who arrange the travel itineries for corporate managers and executives. As a travel counsellor, you must have extensive knowledge of the advantages and disadvantages of a variety of accommodations and transportation services. You must also have excellent abilities with computerized reservation and ticketing systems. Most counsellors must be certified through the Canadian Institute of Travel Counsellors and the Alliance of Canadian Travel Associations. You are eligible for certification after three years of work experience and completion of the mandatory courses and examinations.

✎ Further information

Contact:

**Alliance of Canadian Travel
Associations,**
#201, 729 Bank St.
Ottawa, ON, K1V 7Z5

**Canadian Institute of
Travel Counsellors**
#209, 177 Eglinton Ave. E.
Toronto, ON, M4P 1G8

Computer and Software Industry

The Canadian computer industry is fairly volatile, earning $10-20 billion per year and employing 150,000-200,000 software workers per year. One-third of these workers are employed by the software industry, the rest in banks, insurance companies, real estate firms, government, and the retail trade.

For some years only specialists could understand and run computer technology and programs; end-users had to employ specialists to run computer systems for them. For most organizations today, however, computers are a normal part of their business. Today's operator may be anyone — student, consulting engineer, nurse, author, business manager, scientist, shopkeeper, or teacher.

Graduates with a master's or bachelor's degree in computer science will likely find positions. In 1994, nine out of ten graduates found full-time employment. However, Colin Campbell, in his book, *Where the Jobs Are*, notes that creative software solutions require detailed knowledge of the area to which the software is directed. The implication for those in the field is continuous retraining. Jobs will be available in areas such as administration, finance, law, client services, sales, and training. There will also be a need for creative individuals who can make information and multimedia technology friendlier. Graduates of programs in mathematics, commerce, and business administration are most likely to be hired as systems analysts.

✍ Further Information

Contact:

**Canadian Business
Software Association**
#202, 160 Frederick St.
Toronto, ON, M5A 4H9

**Association for Systems
Management**
24586 Bagley Rd.
Cleveland, OH, 44138, U.S.A.

**Information Technology
Association of Canada**
#402, 2800 Skymark Ave.
Mississauga, ON, L4W 5A6

**Association of Professional
Computer Consultants**
PO Box 991, Station K
Toronto, ON, M4P 2V3

**The Canadian Information
Processing Society**
#205, 430 King St. W.
Toronto, ON, M5W 1L5

Library or Information Work

We live in a society which creates huge masses of information. In addition to the thousands of books, magazines, journals, and newspapers published each day, week, month, and year, there are theses produced by academic researchers, policy documents and records produced by every government department and agency, papers produced by businesses, and much more. As well as paper-based material, there are also films, videos, photographs, microfiche, audiotapes, computer records, and the Internet.

This material must be organized and managed so that data can be retrieved when needed. Some records have only a short useful life and can be scrapped quickly. Many must be kept for years for legal, administrative, and other purposes. Some are of historical significance and must be retained in permanent archives.

Libraries store much of these materials and records, and librarians manage them. Librarians in public libraries are responsible for the selection, purchase, cataloguing, and arrangement of books, periodicals, videos, compact discs, information packs, and other materials. Some run special services such as mobile libraries, children's activities, and business sections. Librarians also answer queries from the public.

Academic librarians serve both staff and students. In collaboration with their academic colleagues, they select materials to support the study and research taking place in the institution. Much time is spent showing students how to make the most of the facilities available (including the latest technology such as computerized catalogues). Many academic librarians specialize in a particular subject area.

Librarians and information specialists also work in the libraries of research organizations, companies, professional institutions, and other bodies. They usually manage specialist collections in a particular industry or field of science or technology. They may manage libraries in large companies. They will be required to help people locate the information they need for their work. They could be responsible for on-line data services.

Entry Qualifications

Both an undergraduate degree and a master's degree in Library Science are necessary to become a librarian.

Further Information

Contact:

Canadian Association for Graduate Education in Library, Archival, and Information Studies
School of Library and Information Studies
Dalhousie University
Halifax, NS, B3H 4H8

Canadian Association of Research Libraries
Morisset Hall
University of Ottawa
#602, 65 University St.
Ottawa, ON, K1N 9A5

Canadian Library Association
#602, 200 Elgin St.
Ottawa, ON, K2P 1L5

Self-Employment

Many of us, at one time or another, want to run our own business and be our own boss. The number of self-employed people in Canada is over two million, and growing. It's expected that an increasing part of the workforce will become self-employed in the years ahead. However, many of these people won't be running their own businesses in the usual sense, but doing contract work for employers.

It is true that some newly qualified graduates have started their own businesses and prospered, but they're in a minority. A high proportion of new businesses — even when they are started by experienced managers — fail.

66

There is a new spirit that's revitalizing the way we work in this country. It has nothing to do with mysticism or spiritual rebirth. It has to do with what we want out of work, what we choose to do with our lives, and how, when, and where we choose to do it.

Dorothy Leeds, author[14]

It isn't enough to have a first-class idea for a new or better product or service. You must also know how to market it. If you get your marketing wrong, you will almost certainly fail. You will also find that there's far more administrative work than you might at first imagine — much of it to satisfy Revenue Canada and local permit regulations. People setting up new businesses often underestimate the amount of money they need to survive the first few months and may fail because of this misconception.

It is better to learn some basic marketing, administrative, financial, and other skills before you set up your business. For your first few years, at least, you're likely to be working almost all your waking hours, including weekends. This isn't the time to learn the basic skills you will need. So, if it is your firm ambition to start your own business, you should get a few years of work experience and learn as much as possible while earning some capital. The single most useful area to learn is marketing, but working in any commercial area is valuable. While you're in work you should try and learn how the business operates as a whole and how the various functions interlink. You should make a particular point of learning how the business:

- identifies the needs of its customers and potential customers;

- tailors its products, and its level of service, to customer needs;

- provides prompt deliveries without holding too much finished stock;

- maintains a high and consistent standard of quality and service;

- handles customer complaints;

- communicates with its customers and potential customers;

- uses marketing, financial, and other information to make decisions;

- motivates and develops the skills of its employees;

- gets good service from its suppliers;

- ensures that its customers pay promptly.

Because any new business starts on a small scale, you may think it best to gain experience in a small company. However, these rarely offer formal training or the quality of experience you need. You will learn more from a structured training program with a big employer. The business principles are the same whether you are in a large or small firm.

You must be just as well-prepared if you plan to work as a freelancer of any sort, offering your talents or services as an individual rather than setting up a firm. You must be sure that you have sufficient expertise in the line of work you intend to follow. If at all possible, it's a good idea to test the water by doing some freelance work before you leave employment, to see if you can start to develop a portfolio of potential clients.

Starting a business is always a risk, but the potential rewards are high. By preparing yourself well, you can cut the risk of failure substantially. In addition to the commercial awareness and abilities that you have developed in employment, there are a number of personal qualities which are essential. You will need to be a good communicator (including a good listener), well-organized (especially in the way you handle paperwork), and able to manage your time effectively. You must have good negotiating skills, and both physical and mental stamina. Just about every business goes through difficult periods, especially in its early days. You will need a combination of singe-minded determination and unquenchable enthusiasm to see you through.

✍ Further Information

Contact:

Canadian Federation of Independent Business
#401, 4141 Yonge St.
North York, ON, M2P 2A6

Federation for the Advancement of Canadian Entrepreneurship
49 Wellington St. E.
Toronto, ON, M5E 1C9

National Entrepreneurship Development Institute
#30, 3601 rue Saint-Jacques
Montreal, PQ, H4C 3N4

Your local Human Resource Development Canada office for the following:

- **Human Resources Canada.** (1995). *Venturing Out: Starting a Successful Business.* Ottawa: Supply and Services Canada

- **Self-Employment Assistance Program**

- **Human Resources Canada.** (1995). *Minding Your Own Business.* Ottawa: Supply and Services Canada

- **Business Development Centres** (provide loans and technical advice)

Check the blue pages in the telephone book for:

- **Canada Business Services Centres**

- **Federal Business Development Bank**

The Royal Bank of Canada issues a *Source Book* for potential entrepreneurs.

Association of Collegiate Entrepreneurs
— Home page: http://www.hookup.net/~acecan

Canadian Youth Business Foundation
— Home page: http://www.cybf.ca

SOURCES OF ADVICE AND INFORMATION

You may find yourself facing a bewildering choice of educational and career options, and making a decision that is right for you may be challenging. Fortunately, there is a lot of help available. The more information and advice you can get, the better your chances of making a good decision.

The next chapter looks at the many people who can offer you advice. Don't lose sight of the fact that the quality of advice can vary. Never rely on only a single source.

The Appendix provides a list of further resources which should be helpful. It's organized under subject headings.

EIGHTEEN

SOURCES OF ADVICE

...If you prepare yourself at every point [of your life] as well as you can, with whatever means you may have, however meager they may seem, you will be able to grasp opportunity for broader experience when it appears. Without preparation you cannot do it.

Eleanor Roosevelt, former First Lady of the United States

You're probably already receiving a lot of advice about your future from friends, family and friends of the family, and teachers. You should consider the advice, even if you may decide to reject it later. It's always worth listening.

Advice is seldom welcome; and those who need it the most always want it the least.

Earl of Chesterfield

You should also actively seek advice yourself — from your guidance counsellor, from career counsellors at your local career centre, and from counsellors at your local Human Resource Development Canada office. Obviously, it's helpful to know how much trust you can put in each source. This chapter looks at some possible sources of advice and information, and how each of them may be useful.

Talk to the People You Know

Most of us find it easiest to relate to people of our own age. Discussing likes and dislikes with friends, and exchanging information and ideas, can help to clarify your thinking. Friends can also help you examine aspects of your character that may make you well-suited to some types of work. On the other hand, they are unlikely to have any more experience of university life or of the world of work than you have. Nor are their ideas on specific careers likely to be any more reliable than your own.

Parents and other relatives and family friends can give you lots of sound advice based on their practical experience. However, you and they need to understand that both the world of education and the world of work have changed a lot since they were your age. Their experiences will not apply to you directly.

When your parents were your age, only one in ten people went into higher education; now one in three do so. The status of university graduates has also changed since they left university. Employers have different expectations of graduates and no longer see them as an elite. Most of those graduating with a first degree have the status that a bright secondary school graduate enjoyed 25 years ago.

Parents and others can give useful factual information about the career they are in. Ask them what they actually do day to day, how they do it, and what skills they are using. What do they most like and dislike about their work? What training did they receive? How good are the opportunities for advancement?

Making Up Your Own Mind

Don't forget that someone's opinion can be coloured by particularly good or bad experiences at work. You also need to be aware that people of all ages have lots of misconceptions about other people's jobs. Unless they have specialist knowledge, members of your family are unlikely to be a reliable source of factual information on careers outside their own experience.

You and your parents should understand that careers which are attractive to them may hold no interest for you, and *vice versa*. If a parent has found great satisfaction in a particular career, it's understandable if they try to persuade you to follow in their footsteps. On the other hand, some parents who were unable to follow their own ambitions want to give their children the chance to do what they never could. In either case, you are unlikely to share the same career ambitions as your parents. Children aren't clones of their parents but unique individuals with their own set of abilities and preferences.

Work-shadowing

If any relatives or friends work in areas of interest to you, ask if there is any possibility of "job-shadowing" them for a typical day or week during your holidays. Your parents may also have contacts in career areas which interest you. They may be able to arrange for you to talk to them, visit their workplace, or even "shadow" them at work through a typical day or few days. This experience can be invaluable.

Teachers

Your teachers can guide you on your educational choices. This doesn't mean they will be familiar with all the degree courses which may interest you — the choices are too great and change too frequently. What they *can* do is indicate the subject areas in which you may be more likely to excel or struggle. Teachers can help you to focus your choices by identifying your strengths and weaknesses.

On the other hand, most of your teachers are no better placed than anyone else to give you reliable information about careers outside teaching. At times, you actually need to be cautious of how teachers relate your school work to your career ambitions. Teachers are not always fully aware of what a particular career entails or what skills are required.

Cooperative Education Teachers

Some teachers work as cooperative education teachers or are involved in job-shadowing responsibilities. These teachers may be more familiar with opportunities in the career area in which they specialize. You should talk with them both for information and the opportunity to take a cooperative education placement or an organized job-shadowing assignment.

Guidance Counsellors

Guidance counsellors in most schools have specific responsibility for career education, career information, and portfolio development. Find a counsellor in your school with whom you're comfortable discussing your future. The counsellor will help you to develop an education and career plan which you can revise, with the counsellor's help, on a yearly basis. Counsellors are also involved in setting up career days or career and education fairs. Make sure that you take advantage of these opportunities. As well, many counsellors now offer workshops and career courses designed to help develop the transferable skills necessary for you to make a successful transition to the working world.

Career Centres

Many school boards have established career centres to serve both students and residents of the community. These centres are staffed by highly qualified career counsellors. In addition to the information and workshops that may complement what you find in your school, many centres offer a battery of standardized tests that can help you with your career choice. Most centres have a range of services that include the following:

⊃ individual career counselling

⊃ a library of career information, both print and computerized

⊃ employer recruitment brochures

⊃   standardized testing

⊃   workshops on transferable skills like decision-making, goal-setting and planning, and résumé writing

⊃   career talks and career fairs

⊃   postings of employment vacancies

In some provinces, career centres have been established by government or community groups. Check with your school counsellor for the locations of centres in your area.

University campuses also have career centres. Again, take advantage of their programs and services.

Private Career Counselling

There are a variety of independent career consultants and groups to which you can turn, although most will charge you a fee for their services. Perhaps the two best-known services are the Jewish Vocational Service and the YMCA Career Planning and Development centres. All individuals and community groups like the YMCA will offer career counselling, testing, workshops, and assistance in locating employment opportunities. Again, you can check with your school counsellor for the career counselling services operating in your area, or contact your local information service.

Conclusion

Whatever decision you make regarding your career, you can dramatically increase your chances of finding a graduate-level job by making it at least one full year before you leave university. But what choice to make? By now, you should realize that few doors are closed to arts graduates, and that there is a lot of help available for you.

The educational and career choices you make now will have a considerable impact on the life you will enjoy in the years ahead. Seek advice. Ask for help if you need it. Reflect on your personal goals and aspirations. And choose. Then stride out on the path — your path — that emerges with each clear, bold step you take.

I look back on my life like a good day's work; it was done and I am satisfied with it. I was happy and contented, I knew nothing better, and made the best out of what life offered. And life is what we make it, always has been, always will be.

Anna Mary ("Grandma") Moses, painter

APPENDIX: ADDITIONAL INFORMATION RESOURCES

Education

Directory of Canadian Universities, 1995-96. Ottawa: AUCC Publications.

Frum, L. (1990). *Linda Frum's Guide to Canadian Universities*. Toronto: Key Porter Books Ltd.

Gibson, D. (1996). *Gibson's Student Guide to Ontario Universities*. Willowdale, ON: Gibson & Associates, Ltd.
   Gibson's Student Guide to Universities in Quebec and Atlantic Canada
   Gibson's Student Guide to Western Canadian Universities

Guidance Centre. *Spectrum 97* series. Toronto: University of Toronto Press.

O'Byrne, E. (ed). (1994). *U-choose. A Guide to Canadian Universities*. Don Mills, ON: Moving Publishers Ltd.

Careers

Beck, N. (1995). *Shifting Gears. Thriving in the New Economy*. Toronto: Harper Collins Publishers Ltd.

Bridges, W. (1994). *JobShift. How to Prosper in a Workplace without Jobs*. Reading, Mass: Addison Wesley Publishing Co.

Canadian Association of Career Educators and Employers, *Career Options*. An annual publication.

Campbell, C. (1994). *Where the Jobs Are. Career Survival for Canadians in the New Global Economy*. Toronto: Macfarlane Walter & Ross.

Careers Connections Series. Toronto:
Trifolium Books Inc. (1994)
   Great Careers for People Interested in the Performing Arts
   Great Careers for People Interested in Sports and Fitness
   Great Careers for People Who Like Working with People

Great Careers for People Who Want to be Entrepreneurs
Great Careers for People Interested in Film, Video, and
Photography

Choices Series (1992). Brookfield, Conneticut: The Millbrook
Press.

Feather, F. (1996). *Canada's Best Careers Guide.* Toronto:
Warwick Publishers.

Human Resources Development Canada. (1996).
Job Futures. (Volume 1, Occupational outlook. Volume 2,
Career outlooks for graduates.) Ottawa: Supply and Services
Canada

James, J.D. (1996). *Starting a Successful Business in
Canada* (13th edition). Self-Counsel Business Series. North
Vancouver: Self-Counsel Press.

Lang, Jim (1994). *Make Your Own Breaks! Become an
Entrepreneur & Create Your Own Future.* Toronto:
Trifolium Books Inc.

Internet Addresses

Canadian Association of Career Educators and Employers
http://www.cacee.com/workweb

CanWorkNet
http://hrdc.ingenia.com/canworknet

CareerMosaic
http://www.careermosaic.com

SchoolNet
http://schoolnet.carleton.ca/schoolnet/hmpage.html

JobGuide
http://www.wpi.edu/~mfriley/jobguide.html

Canadian National Graduate Registry
http://schoolnet.carleton.ca:80/NGR

Working and Living Overseas
http://www.magi.com/~issi/

Career Edge Internship Plan for Graduates
http://www.careeredge.org

Source Notes

[1] Fournier, G., and Pelletier, R. (1996). Beliefs of unemployed young adults regarding educational and career contexts: An exploratory analysis of vocational locus of control. *Guidance and Counselling*, 11(2).

[2] Campbell, C. (1994). *Where the Jobs Are. Career Survival for Canadians in the New Global Economy.* Toronto: Macfarlane Walter & Ross.

[3] Ovenall-Carter, J. (1996). Emerging options. *The Globe and Mail Report on Business*. October, 1996.

[4] Thompson, M.C. (1995). Just-in-time recruiting: A new way for employers and job seekers to find each other. *Career Options. The Graduate Recruitment Annual.* 1995-96. Canadian Association of Career Educators and Employers.

[5] Van Norman, M. (1995). What you need to know about the new workplace. *Career Options. The Graduate Recruitment Annual, 1995-96*, Canadian Association of Career Educators and Employers.

[6] Crozir, F., and Grassicle, P. (1996). I love my B.A.: The employment experience of successful bachelor of arts graduates. *Guidance and Counselling*, 11(2).

[7] Human Resources Development Canada (1996). *Job Futures.* Ottawa, Ministry of Supply and Services.

[8] *Putting the Pieces Together: Toward a Coherent Transition System for Canada's Labour Force.* (1994). Report of the Task Force on Transition into Employment to the Canadian Labour Force Development Board.

[9] Hurd, K. (1994). Stephen Covey. A matter of principle. *Acumen — Global Insight*, 1(7).

[10] Ontario Teachers' Federation. (1989). *Teaching. Is It for You?* Careers pamphlet.

[11] *What Can I Do with a Degree in....?* (1992). Career Centre, Erindale College, University of Toronto.

[12] Frank, J. (1996). Canada's Cultural Labour Force. *Canadian Social Trends*, Summer, 1996.

[13] *Four Things an Executive Should Know* (1963). In R. Harkness, J.E. Atkinson of the Star.

[14] Quoted in Campbell, C. (1994). *Where the Jobs Are.*

INDEX

actuarial work, 160-162
advertising, 70-72, 163-165
    account executive, 163-164
    copywriting, 70-72
    media department, 164-165
advice, 177-183
aptitudes, 14
archeology, 2, 73-77
art and design, 2, 91-97
art history, 2, 80
artist, 91-92
arts administration, 108
banking, 153-156
    Bank of Canada, 154-156
    branch management, 154-156
career centres, 181
classics, 2
commercials, 104
communication, 2
computer/software industry,
    170-171
cooperative education teachers, 181
correctional services, 134-135
    correctional service officers,
        134-135
    probation officers, 135
courses, 15
dance, 2, 98-99, 104-106
    ballet training, 105
    choreography, 106
    fitness coaching, 106
    modern dance training, 105
    other options, 105
    performance, 105
    teaching dance, 106
design, 92-97
directing, 107
drama, 2, 98-99, 102-104
economics, 3, 110-111
employers, 8, 44
employment, 20, 48-177
English, 2, 58-72
fashion arts, 2, 95
film, 94, 104
financial services, 149-162

accountancy, 149-153
    chartered, 151-153
    financial, 150, 152
    management, 150-152
general insurance, 161-162
geography, 3, 110
grades, 14-15
guidance counsellors, 181
history, 3, 78-82
    archivists, 79
    art gallery, 78
    conservators, 79
    curators, 80
    museum educator, 80
    museum, 78-82
humanities, 1
insurance, 156-159
    claims examiners, 157
    insurance adjusters, 157
    insurance agents/brokers,
        158-159
    underwriters, 157
Internet, 15
journalism, 58, 63-67
    broadcasting, 64
    news agencies, 64
    the national press, 64-65
language skills, 12
languages, 3, 83-90
library/information work, 171-173
life insurance, 161-162
linguistics, 3, 83-90
literary translation, 86-87
management, 136-148
    accounting and finance, 140
    buying, 139
    human resource, 140-141
    management services, 140
    marketing, 138
    product development, 137-138
    production management,
        138-139
    sales, 138
    warehousing and distribution,
        139

media studies, 2
modern languages, 3, 83-90
music, 3, 98-102
   and the media, 102
   classical, 100-101
   performing, 100
   popular, 101
   studying, 99-100
   therapy, 101
native studies, 3, 112
performing arts, 2
personal interests, 13, 14
philosophy, 3
police, 131-134
political science, 110
private career counselling, 182
producing, 107
prospects, 11
psychology, 3, 110, 111-113
public relations, 58, 67-69
public service, 116-125
   provincial/territory government, 112-123
   municipal, 124-125
publishing, 58-62
   editors, 59-61
   marketing, 62
   contracts and rights, 62
radio, 103
retailing, 165-166
salaries, 30
sales, 166-169
self-employment, 173-176
skills, 37-38
   adaptability, 43
   business awareness, 41
   communication, 37-39
   computer literacy, 40
   leadership, 44
   numeracy, 39
   personal self-management, 42
   problem solving, 39
   teamwork, 43
   time management, 42
social director, 107-108
social sciences, 3, 110
social work, 111-113
sociology, 3, 110, 112-113

speech pathologists/therapists,
   89-90
stage management, 106-107
stockbroking/investment dealing,
   159-160
study, 34
teachers, 180
teaching ESL, 84-85
   interpreting, 85-86
   translating, 86-88
teaching, 48-57
   elementary, 50
   secondary schools, 52-54
   colleges, 54-55
   universities, 55-57
technical and commercial
   translation, 87-88
television, 103
theatre, 103
three-dimensional design, 94-97
   craft work, 94
   fashion design, 95
   interior design, 94
   product design, 95
training, 24, 32
transferable skills, 25, 34-45
translating, 58
travel industry, 169-170
trends, 20-31
two-dimensional design, 93-97
   advertising, 93
   book publishing, 93
   image consultancy, 94
   industry and commerce, 94
   periodical publishing, 93
   textile manufacturing, 94
   TV, film and video, 94
underemployment, 25
unemployment, 25-26
uniformed services, 126-135
   armed forces, 127-131
   coast guard, 131
women's studies, 3, 112
work, 34
work-shadowing, 180
writing, 58